The Catholic Church and
the Politics of Abortion

The Catholic Church and the Politics of Abortion

A View from the States

EDITED BY

Timothy A. Byrnes
and Mary C. Segers

Westview Press

BOULDER • SAN FRANCISCO • OXFORD

This Westview softcover edition is printed on acid-free paper and bound in library-quality, coated covers that carry the highest rating of the National Association of State Textbook Administrators, in consultation with the Association of American Publishers and the Book Manufacturers' Institute.

Copyright © 1992 by Westview Press, Inc.

Published in 1992 in the United States of America by Westview Press, Inc., 5500 Central Avenue, Boulder, Colorado 80301-2847, and in the United Kingdom by Westview Press, 36 Lonsdale Road, Summertown, Oxford OX2 7EW

Library of Congress Cataloging-in-Publication Data
The Catholic Church and the politics of abortion : a view from the
  states / edited by Timothy A. Byrnes and Mary C. Segers.
    p.   cm.
  Includes index.
  ISBN 0-8133-8415-X
  1. Abortion—Religious aspects—Catholic Church.   2. Abortion—
United States—States.   I. Byrnes, Timothy A., 1958–   .
II. Segers, Mary C.
HQ767.3.C36   1991
363.4'6'0973—dc20
                                                                91-34430
                                                                CIP

Printed and bound in the United States of America

The paper used in this publication meets the requirements
of the American National Standard for Permanence of Paper
for Printed Library Materials Z39.48-1984.

10   9   8   7   6   5   4   3   2   1

For our families: Dolores, Gavin, and Brigid Byrnes,
Margaret W. Segers, and Jerry, Suzanne,
and Jean-Paul Segers Travers

Contents

Acknowledgments

We had a great deal of help in producing this book. Lyman Kellstedt of the American Political Science Association's Special Section on Religion and Politics allowed us to try out our ideas on a panel at the association's 1990 meeting in San Francisco. Paul Weber and John Francis Burke offered helpful suggestions at that session. Amy Eisenberg and Deborah Rich at Westview Press were helpful and supportive throughout. A. David Lynch of the City College of New York and Murray Karstadt of Rutgers University turned eleven chapters on five different word processing programs into a single manuscript. Needless to say, we could not have done it without them. Vicky Donner, supported by the City College Scholars Program, also assisted in readying the manuscript for publication. Dolores M. Byrnes prepared the index. Mary Segers acknowledges Dean Donald G. Stein and the Graduate School at Rutgers in Newark for the partial support provided by a 1990–91 graduate research award. Lastly, we both offer our gratitude to the contributors to this volume. All of the chapters of this book, with a single exception, were written explicitly for inclusion in this book; none have been published previously. We could not have asked for more enthusiastic responses to our requests to contribute nor greater responsiveness to the time constraints we set. The goodwill of the contributors allowed this book to be the collaborative effort we originally hoped it would be. That said, the views expressed by each individual author are those of that author alone.

Timothy A. Byrnes
Mary C. Segers

Introduction

Timothy A. Byrnes and Mary C. Segers

This book is a study in religion and politics. It analyzes the efforts of a major American religious institution—the Catholic Church—to shape public policy on one of the most controversial political issues of our time—abortion. Scholarly interest in the relationship between religion and politics has increased tremendously over the last decade. While much of the ground-breaking work in this area was broadly-based and quite general in scope,[1] a growing number of scholars have recently been building on that foundation by focusing on specific churches or religious movements and their roles in the American political process.[2] In this volume, we concentrate on Catholic political activity at a particular point in time and in a particular geographical context. Our focus is on the official Catholic response to the Supreme Court's recent retreat from *Roe v. Wade*. In its 1989 decision in *Webster v. Reproductive Health Services, Inc.*, the court indicated that it was willing to entertain and accept more aggressive regulation of abortion by individual states. The essays in this book represent the first published attempt to gauge the effects of *Webster* on abortion politics in the states, and to examine the efforts of a powerful religious group to influence abortion policy at the state level.

We have chosen the Catholic Church for this study of the relationship between religion and public policy because of the church's high public visibility on this issue and because of its strength and power in American public life. The Roman Catholic Church constitutes the largest single religious denomination in the United States, numbering 55 million Catholics or 23 percent of the population. Moreover, contemporary American Catholics do not fit the working-class ethnic stereotype of the past. According to a 1987 CBS/*New York Times* survey, Catholics tend to be both younger and better-off than non-Catholics. In terms of income and education, more than one-third of American Catholics report family incomes exceeding $35,000 per year, and 27 percent of Catholics have attended college, only two points lower than Protestants.

Politically, Catholics have achieved the highest positions of power in the United States. Since 1960 and the election of John F. Kennedy as the nation's first Catholic president, many other Catholics have run for president and vice-president, among them Eugene McCarthy, Edward Kennedy, Sargent Shriver,

1

Robert F. Kennedy, Thomas Eagleton, Geraldine Ferraro, Bruce Babbitt, and Joseph Biden. The U.S. Congress is 25 percent Catholic; Speaker of the House Thomas Foley is Catholic, as is Senate Majority Leader George Mitchell. Two Supreme Court justices, Antonin Scalia and Anthony Kennedy, are Catholic, and Clarence Thomas, President Bush's choice to replace Thurgood Marshall, is a proud product of Catholic education.

This powerful religious denomination has been and continues to be one of the most active elements in the *national* pro-life movement. But more importantly for our purposes, few American institutions can match the Catholic Church in organizational strength at the *state* level. Twenty-eight states have Catholic conferences that lobby state lawmakers on a wide range of public policy issues. And since the Supreme Court handed down its decision in *Webster,* these conferences have been active and in some cases very effective.

In this introductory chapter, we will lay the groundwork for discussion of the Catholic Church's role in the contemporary politics of abortion. We will begin with a brief description of the Catholic Church's teachings on abortion, and move on to a sketch of the history of restrictive abortion legislation in the United States. We will then describe the content of *Roe v. Wade,* the court's 1973 decision effectively legalizing abortion, and outline the strategies adopted by forces seeking to have that decision negated. We will also examine the court's ruling in *Webster v. Reproductive Health Services,* and suggest some of the challenges and opportunities that ruling presented to the Catholic Church and the rest of the pro-life movement. This chapter will end with an explanation of the criteria we used in commissioning the state-level case studies that make up the bulk of this book.

Catholic Teaching on Abortion

Contemporary Catholic moral theology holds that abortion, as an example of unjustifiable killing, is always an intrinsic moral evil. Historically, the church has always opposed abortion—but it has done so for a variety of reasons. Early Christians denounced abortion and infanticide as examples of the excesses and immorality of the pagan culture of Imperial Rome. They held that abortion, contraception, masturbation, homosexuality, and castration all interfered with the procreative purpose of human sexuality. Abortion was also considered a violent action inconsistent with the Christian ethic of love; and it was seen as a refusal to accept the sovereignty of God, who alone is the Lord of life. However, although early Christian rhetoric denounced abortion as equivalent to murder, the legal and moral treatment of the act was never consistent with the rhetoric. Indeed, from the third century onward, Christian thought was divided as to whether early abortion—the abortion of an "unformed" embryo—was in fact murder.

Following Aristotle, early church teaching held that a male fetus became "formed" or "animated"—that is, infused with a soul—at forty days after conception, while a female fetus became animated at a gestational age of eighty days. This distinction between "formed" and "unformed" fetuses was eventually incorporated into church law and remained intact until the nineteenth century. In reality, this meant that although Catholic Christianity condemned abortion as unjustifiable violence in violation of Gospel norms of love, in practice Catholic moral theology and canon law did not treat what we would now call first trimester abortions as murder.

In the nineteenth century, however, the discovery of fertilization and advances in embryology gradually influenced church theologians to think of fetal development as a continuum of human life from conception onward. And in 1869, Pope Pius IX promulgated the papal enactment *Apostolicae Sedis,* which abandoned the limitation under which excommunication was imposed only for those abortions of "ensouled" or "animated" fetuses. From that point on, the church has taken conception as the decisive moment in establishing an individual life worthy of respect as a human being.

It is worth noting, however, that the church has not pronounced definitively that the fetus is a human being from the moment of conception. Rather, the church holds that since we cannot say with certainty when human life actually begins, we should err on the side of never killing what could well be an actual human being. Christopher Mooney describes the church's reasoning as follows:

> The argument [is] that since there is no way, scientific or otherwise, to ascertain at what point exactly the human fetus becomes a human person (or, in more traditional religious language, when the human soul becomes present in the human body), abortion at any point after conception may in fact be taking the life of an innocent human person; but to risk actually doing such a thing can never be morally justified for any reason in any circumstances; therefore in practice the human fetus must always be treated as if it were in fact a human person at every moment of its existence.[3]

Catholic teaching derives its position on abortion, as well as its positions on racism, capital punishment, and the just war theory, from natural law, a tradition of moral reasoning traceable to Augustine, Cicero, and Roman Stoicism. As a result, the American Catholic bishops maintain that they are not imposing a sectarian theological teaching upon non-Catholic Americans but are appealing to a common western tradition of moral reasoning about proper public policy. They therefore resist any suggestion that Catholic efforts to influence public policy on abortion violate the separation of church and state, and they staunchly defend the church's right and duty to contribute to public debate and to help shape public opinion on important policy issues. At the same time, they recognize that their political appeals must consist of rational persuasion rather than appeals to papal or biblical authority. As Bishop James W. Malone, President of the National Conference of Catholic Bishops (NCCB), noted after the 1984 presidential election:

> In the public arena of a pluralistic democracy, religious leaders face the same tests of rational argument as any other individuals or institutions. Our impact on the public will be directly proportionate to the persuasiveness of our positions. We seek no special status and we should not be accorded one.[4]

When the bishops and other Catholic leaders speak on abortion, of course, they are addressing a highly controversial issue with a complex history. Since a basic understanding of that history is necessary for placing the Catholic Church's contemporary activities in their proper context, we now turn to a description of the development of abortion law in the United States.

A Brief History of Abortion Legislation
in the United States

Like other matters of marriage and family law, abortion was originally reserved, under the American federal system, to the jurisdiction of state governments. In 1800, no state-level statutes governed abortion in America. What minimal legal regulation that did exist was derived from the English common law notion that abortion performed before quickening was at worst a misdemeanor. Thus, in early nineteenth century America, first trimester abortions, and perhaps a good number of second trimester abortions as well, were legally permissible.

However, by 1900 every state in the Union had enacted a law prohibiting the use of drugs or instruments to procure abortion at any stage of pregnancy, except to save the woman's life. How these state laws got on the books is a fascinating story. Several authors have explained how our strict nineteenth century abortion laws were largely the result of lobbying by the newly organized medical profession.[5] In order to legitimate and consolidate their power, doctors were eager to halt the competition in abortion services from medical irregulars. To that end, the physicians and the newly-formed American Medical Association organized an effective media and lobbying campaign to outlaw abortion. They were successful, in part, because their desire to limit competition from midwives and other healthcare providers coincided with a social concern on the part of Protestant Americans about the population threat presented by large numbers of mostly Catholic immigrants streaming into the country from Southern and Eastern Europe. While native-born, Protestant, middle and upper class women were resorting to abortion to limit family size, immigrant, Catholic, working class women were having large families. Doctors were able to use the transformation in the demographics of abortion to awaken nativist fears among the Protestant upper and middle classes. Physicians did not shrink from expressing eugenic concerns when advocating restrictions on abortion.

For our purposes, it is interesting to note that religion did not figure prominently in the effort to outlaw abortion in nineteenth century America. The Roman Catholic Church was notably absent from the debate on the subject, and the organized Protestant churches had little to say on the subject until after the Civil War. By the second half of the twentieth century, of course, circumstances had changed dramatically, and the Catholic Church had become a major opponent of legal abortion. The church's aggressive involvement in the contemporary politics of abortion may reflect the enhanced political, social, and economic status of Catholics in the United States. No longer the immigrant church of the nineteenth century, American Catholics have come of age and sought to contribute their views to public debate and to public policy formation on a variety of issues ranging from nuclear war and economic justice to racism, and of course, abortion.

At the turn of the century, however, the church's assumption of a leading political role on abortion was still decades away. Yet, by 1900 every state had placed strict restrictions on abortion, and abortion went underground or, to use the classic phrase, into the "back alleys" of illegal practice. In reality, a double standard developed concerning access to abortion. For privileged women, abortions were performed by sympathetic private physicians who found they could interpret legal exceptions for therapeutic abortions as broadly or narrowly as conscience demanded. However, most abortions, and a particularly high percentage of abortions performed on poor women and on women in rural areas, were performed illegally, with grave risks to maternal health. Gradually, those physicians, public health specialists, social workers, demographers, and law-enforcement officials who saw firsthand the consequences of illegal abortions began to call for liberalization of the nation's restrictive abortion laws.

The Abortion Reform Movement

The abortion reform movement, begun in the 1930s, gained considerable momentum in 1959 when the American Law Institute (ALI), an influential body of legal academics and practicing lawyers, suggested a revision in its widely copied Model Penal Code. The proposed revision called for the legalization of abortion in cases where (a) the pregnancy would gravely impair the physical or mental health of the mother, (b) the child was likely to be born with grave physical or mental defects, or (c) the pregnancy was the result of rape or incest. During the 1960s, under the influence of ALI's code, Colorado, California, North Carolina, Georgia, Hawaii, and a number of other states began to reform their restrictive abortion statutes. In fact, by 1970, twelve states had considerably liberalized access to legal abortion.

Problems soon surfaced, however, with respect to these new laws that were often enacted primarily to protect doctors from prosecution. The laws generally prevented non-residents from coming into the state to procure abortions, and even for state residents, access to legal abortion was usually tightly controlled by physicians and hospital review committees. In addition, legal abortions tended to be very costly under these laws, leading poor women to continue to resort to "back-alley" abortions, which cost on average only one-third as much as a legal abortion. In short, the reform laws of the 1960s came under fire because they did not eliminate illegal, unsafe abortion in the United States; the abortion reform movement began to call for complete repeal of criminal prohibitions of abortion.

In 1967, the Clergy Consultation Service on Abortion, a major abortion referral network, was formed in New York City and rapidly spread nationwide. In 1968, a Presidential Advisory Council on the Status of Women called for the repeal of all abortion laws. In 1969, the National Association for the Repeal of Abortion Laws (NARAL) was formed (in 1973 its name was changed to the National Abortion Rights Action League). And in 1970, Hawaii became the first state in the nation to repeal its criminal abortion law, legalizing abortions performed before the twentieth week of pregnancy. New York, Alaska, and Washington followed suit that same year.

By 1973, in other words, a patchwork quilt had developed of various state-level statutes and regulations having to do with abortion. A few states offered so-called "abortion on demand," while others continued to prohibit almost all abortions. And because states retained jurisdiction over abortion, political activity related to that issue remained focused on the state level as well. Pro-choice groups lobbied state legislatures in favor of more liberal access to abortion, and the nascent right-to-life movement resisted. All of this changed in January 1973, however, when Justice Harry Blackmun, writing for a 7-2 majority of the Supreme Court in *Roe v. Wade,* declared that "the right of privacy [founded in the Fourteenth Amendment's concept of personal liberty and restrictions on state action] is broad enough to encompass a woman's decision whether or not to terminate her pregnancy."

Roe v. Wade and the Nationalization of American Abortion Law

Roe v. Wade concerned a Texas statute, substantially unchanged since 1857, that made it a crime to "procure an abortion" except for the purpose of saving the life of the mother. After hearing arguments on the case on two separate occasions, the court found this statute inconsistent with the Fourteenth Amendment of the U.S. Constitution and, in effect, declared a constitutional right to abortion. According to Blackmun's majority opinion, however, this right was not absolute; it had to be balanced against the state's legitimate interest in protecting maternal health and in preserving the potential human life of the fetus. Blackmun set out a trimester framework as a mechanism through which to balance these various interests. During the first third, or trimester, of pregnancy, government may not interfere with a woman's decision to terminate her pregnancy in any way except to insist that the abortion be performed by a licenced physician. During the second trimester, government has the power to regulate abortions only in ways designed to preserve and protect the woman's health. But during the third trimester, after the point of viability has been reached at which the fetus is capable of surviving independently of the woman's body, government may regulate or even prohibit abortion in order to protect fetal life. The only limitation on the states' authority in the third trimester is that they may not prohibit abortions performed to protect the life or health of the woman.

The court's decision in *Roe* did not come completely out of the blue. In the early 1970s, several cases concerning abortion had been working their way through federal appellate courts. And public opinion in the 1960s had shifted in favor of legalized abortion. Nevertheless, the court's ruling in *Roe* overturned forty-six of fifty state laws; the Supreme Court, in effect, wrote a new *national* abortion law. The court completely stripped the states of jurisdiction over abortion during the first trimester, and severely limited the states' authority during the second and third. As a result, abortion suddenly became, in the vast majority of cases, legal throughout the United States. And just as suddenly, opponents of legal abortion, including the Catholic Church, shifted their attention and energy to the courts, the Constitution, and the national political process.

The Politics of Abortion Since *Roe v. Wade*

By all accounts, the leadership of the American Catholic Church was stunned by *Roe v. Wade*. Cardinal John Krol, President of the NCCB, and Cardinal Terence Cooke, Chairman of the bishops' committee on pro-life affairs, accused the court of opening the doors to the "greatest slaughter of innocent life in the history of mankind." The church immediately began to mobilize antiabortion activities at the national level and through its local, parish networks. Dioceses were called upon to help fund the antiabortion effort within the church. Mail campaigns were organized to flood the Supreme Court and Congress with letters of protest. And a national campaign was begun in support of a human life constitutional amendment to overrule *Roe*. The church, of course, has remained deeply involved over the past two decades in the effort to restrict access to abortion in the United States, and many of its antiabortion activities will be discussed at length in subsequent chapters. For now, suffice it to say that all of those activities have been part of a larger pro-life effort that arose in opposition to legal abortion.

That right-to-life movement, outraged, mobilized, and energized by *Roe v. Wade*, adopted three political strategies in the 1970s and 1980s.

- It lobbied Congress and state legislatures in favor of an antiabortion constitutional amendment.
- It lobbied, again in Congress and state legislatures, for the elimination of any and all public funding of abortion services or abortion counseling.
- And it supported presidential candidates who opposed abortion and who promised to appoint Supreme Court justices likely either to overturn *Roe* explicitly or chip away at *Roe* by allowing greater and greater restriction of abortion by the individual states.

The first of these strategies has been unsuccessful. Neither an amendment outlawing abortion nor one simply returning initiative on abortion to the states has been reported out of Congress. And an effort to have the states themselves call a constitutional convention at which such an amendment (and who knows what else) could be considered has been turned aside. The other two strategies, however, have been much more fruitful. Opponents of abortion have succeeded in virtually eliminating the relationship between the federal tax coffers and abortion. The Hyde Amendment, passed by Congress in 1976 and upheld by the Supreme Court in 1980 in *Harris v. McRae,* ended use of Federal Medicaid funds for abortion services. And the Health and Human Services Department's reinterpretation in 1988 of Title X of the Public Health Services Act prevented family planning clinics that receive federal funds from disseminating any information or counseling related to abortion. It was this so-called gag rule that was upheld by the Supreme Court in 1991 in *Rust v. Sullivan.*

More significant and portentous than these developments, however, has been the appointment of five Supreme Court justices by Presidents Reagan and Bush, two vocal opponents of legal abortion. Before *Roe v. Wade,* presidents were marginal figures in abortion law, and the issue played a very limited role in presidential politics. After *Roe,* presidents became central figures in the abortion debate as the focus of that debate shifted to the Supreme Court and the U.S. Constitution. By 1991, as a direct result of the judicial appointments by Presidents Reagan and Bush, the right to abortion established by Justice Blackmun and his colleagues in 1973 had grown tenuous indeed.

All five justices who have retired in the Reagan-Bush era—Stewart, Burger, Powell, Brennan, and Marshall— were members of the original seven member majority in *Roe v. Wade,* while the two dissenters, Justices White and Rehnquist, remain on the court. As of this writing, several new members of the court have not yet expressed their own view on abortion's constitutional status. But it appears certain that they are in each case less enthusiastic supporters of abortion rights than were the justices they replaced.

But even if *Roe v. Wade* is not reversed, opponents of abortion rights can already claim several important judicial victories, the most significant of which was the court's decision in July 1989 in *Webster v. Reproductive Health Services, Inc.* In that case, Chief Justice Rehnquist, writing for a three-member plurality, found constitutional a Missouri law that prohibited the use of public facilities or employees for abortion services, prohibited public funding of abortion counseling, and required doctors to determine whether any fetus of *twenty* or more weeks gestation was viable, that is could potentially survive outside the womb.

The key finding in *Webster,* in terms of the politics of abortion in the United States, was the acceptance of viability testing, or put another way, the recognition of the state's interest in potential human life, at *twenty* weeks. This was a break with the trimester formula established in *Roe* and sent a clear signal to other states that the court was willing to consider restrictions of abortion that did not, strictly speaking, adhere to the governing judicial precedent. Indeed, Chief Justice Rehnquist stripped that precedent of much of its legitimacy when he declared that the "rigid *Roe* framework is hardly consistent with the notion of a Constitution cased in general principles, as ours is. . . . The key elements of the *Roe* framework—trimesters and viability—are not found in the Constitution or in any place else one would expect to find a constitutional principle."

Through its decision in *Webster,* the Supreme Court did not formally reverse *Roe,* but from the perspective of the antiabortion movement it did the next best thing. It invited states to reject *Roe* as a limitation on their statutory authority, and it emboldened states to pass laws that violated elements of *Roe's* "rigid framework." It was this invitation that prompted Justice Blackmun in dissent to charge that the court's judgment "foment[ed] disregard for the law and for our standing decisions." The signs of an explicit reversal, Blackmun warned, are "evident and very ominous."

The reaction to *Webster* was not as explosive as that to *Roe,* but the effect on the politics of abortion was nearly as fundamental. Initiative on abortion moved rapidly to the states, and legislatures from Guam to Louisiana and from Utah to Pennsylvania picked up Rehnquist's invitation and passed laws that either skirted *Roe's* framework or flouted it altogether. In addition to this legislative activity, the return of authority over abortion to the states resulted in renewed political debate across the country, as well as in tremendous pressure on state-level politicians to declare their own personal position on reproductive rights. It is no longer possible for governors or legislators to hide behind a constitutional right to abortion. That right still exists for the moment, but it exists in a tenuous state in which its extent and its limitations are very unclear. After nearly two decades, abortion has returned with force to the states, and in the process it has profoundly affected state officials, and offered complex new challenges to activists on both sides of the issue.

Moving Forward from *Webster*

This book, as we stated at the very beginning, concerns the Catholic Church's reaction to these challenges. It is, more exactly, a series of case studies that documents the reactions of various Catholic forces to the new and very uncertain politics of abortion. These case studies are examinations of the actions of one of the most central participants in a very important political debate. The Catholic Church's role in the politics of abortion is the subject of a great deal of discussion at the moment, scholarly and otherwise. We, and our contributors, wrote this book in order to inform that discussion. We felt it important to examine in detail what the church does, and to assess the political meaning of the church's activities.

In addition to furthering understanding of how religion influences public policy, however, this book also uncovers ways in which public policy and politics influence religion, or at least, the activities of American religious institutions. The strategies and actions discussed in this book were not the result of shifts in the Catholic Church's teaching on abortion or in the church's commitment to the issue. Rather, they were the result of political change that occurred far outside the church itself. Presidential elections, judicial appointments, state-level test cases, and Supreme Court decisions all combined to bring forth new approaches to abortion on the part of the Catholic Church. Politics mattered, in other words, when it came to shaping the nature and direction of this particular relationship between religion and politics.

One element of the growing literature on religion and politics has focused specifically on religious bodies as interest groups. Allen Hertzke, for example, in *Representing God in Washington,* examined the lobbying activities in Washington D.C. of a wide array of religious forces.[6] Our work on the Catholic Church and abortion emphasizes that churches represent God, if you will, not only in Washington but in Hartford, Trenton, Baton Rouge, Tallahasee, Albany, Springfield, and Harrisburg as well. Put simply, state-level issues and state-level politics require state-level lobbying on the part of religious spokesmen. Therefore, any religious body hoping to play a role in the politics of abortion in the 1990s must be well-prepared to work in the various state capitals. Federalism is still alive and well in the United States, and the Supreme Court, under the leadership of Chief Justice Rehnquist, is apparently determined to expand further the independence and jurisdiction of the individual states. Not only abortion, but affirmative action, civil rights, criminal justice, and a host of other issues will be fought out in the coming decade in state legislatures and governors' mansions. Students of religion and politics must be prepared to focus their attention on the sites where clergymen and politicians, churches and governments, will interact most meaningfully.

In terms of the Catholic Church, we have come away from our work on this book convinced that students of American Catholicism have to this point paid insufficient attention to the various state Catholic conferences around the country. These conferences represent the bishops of a given state in the political arena, and they vary substantially in terms of their cohesiveness and institutional viability. On the whole, these conferences are a crucial element in the Catholic Church's participation in the American political process. Regarding abortion specifically, we discovered that these conferences exhibit a substantial diversity of *political action* within the essential unity of opposition to abortion. State conferences, and the very significant differences among them, offer fertile ground for further study and analysis.

Because of the changes we have been discussing, public policy on abortion also invites further study. Very little state-by-state analysis has been done in recent years on the law and politics of abortion. As we argued above, such analysis was rendered largely irrelevant by *Roe v. Wade* and the Supreme Court's establishment of a fundamental constitutional right to abortion. Today, of course, such analysis is an indispensable tool for fuller understanding of the political and legal status of abortion in the United States. Indeed, state-level case studies, like those included in this book, will soon be a major element in the scholarly literature on abortion.

This book makes a contribution to that literature, but it is not, nor was it meant to be, comprehensive in scope. The case studies examine only a *sample* of states, albeit a sample we chose carefully on the basis of three criteria. To be included in this book, a state had to house a substantial Catholic population. We wanted to restrict ourselves to states where the church is at least potentially an influential actor in the local political process. A state like Utah, therefore, although it recently passed a very restrictive abortion law, was not included on our list. Mormons, rather than Catholics, are the major religious players in Utah.

Second, we chose states where the politics of abortion were particularly interesting for one reason or another, where something significant had taken place since the court handed down its decision in *Webster.* We included states like Pennsylvania and Louisiana because of the legislation that was enacted there. We chose others, New Jersey and Florida are two examples, because they were the sites of particularly sharp political battles involving abortion. Two states, New York and Illinois, were included because of the influential national Catholic spokesmen who reside there.

The third criterion for the inclusion of a state in this book was the availability of an appropriate person to perform the analysis and write the chapter under the onerous deadline we set. A number of states satisfied the first two criteria readily but, unfortunately, failed the third. In California, for example, Bishop Leo Maher of San Diego refused Holy Communion to a candidate for the State Senate because of that candidate's support for legal abortion. In Guam, a territory, of course, rather than a state, Archbishop Anthony Apuron raised the possibility of excommunicating any Catholic lawmaker who failed to support the territory's very restrictive abortion law. An exhaustive treatment of our subject would include these and other cases, and we wish we had been able to do so. But we believe our criteria led us to a significant sample of states that manifests substantial variance in both the political status of abortion and the antiabortion strategies adopted by leaders of the local Catholic Church.

The Supreme Court's new receptivity to restrictions on abortion has done more than reenergize the politics of abortion at the state level, of course. It has also challenged *national* organizations interested in abortion to reorient their own approaches to the political struggles associated with that issue. For that reason, the book begins with a chapter on the National Conference of Catholic Bishops and its reactions to the new politics of abortion. And it ends with chapters on the right-to-life movement and Catholics for a Free Choice. All three, to no one's surprise, have been deeply affected by the return of political and legislative initiative on abortion to the states.

We sent this book to the publisher in June 1991. Events did not stand still while the book was being written, and we do not expect them to stand still after it is published. The state legislature of Louisiana, for example, passed over the governor's veto the nation's most restrictive abortion law in late June 1991, after Christine Day had completed her chapter. Pennsylvania's Abortion Control Act, the subject of Thomas O'Hara's case study, was as of early Summer 1991 working its way through the judicial system, apparently on its way to the Supreme Court. At the same time, state courts in New York were suggesting that New York's *state* constitution contained within it the right to obtain an abortion. And perhaps most portentously, Justice Thurgood Marshall retired, and President Bush nominated Clarence Thomas as his replacement, just as we were readying the final manuscript for publication. Events such as these, of course, were just what motivated us to write this book in the first place. Abortion is the subject of tremendous controversy at the moment, and this book offers an account of the Catholic Church's role in that controversy through Summer 1991.

But the case studies included in this book are more than simply snapshots of particular historical moments. The church is sure to remain deeply involved in American politics, and these analyses of the church as a political actor offer insights into that involvement which transcend the current status of abortion rights. Moreover, these case studies can be read as early indicators of what will take place around the country if, as now seems almost certain, the Supreme Court formally reverses its ruling in *Roe v. Wade*. In the event the court declared that the right to privacy *no longer* included a woman's decision whether or not to terminate her pregnancy, the states would be faced with four basic choices.

- They could *outlaw* most abortions.
- They could *restrict* access to abortion through mandatory delays, viability testing, elimination of public funding, and other related measures.
- They could *protect* access to abortion through legislation.
- Or they could *guarantee* the right to abortion through state constitutional interpretation.

All four of these options have already been adopted in response to *Webster* by states included in this book.

- Louisiana has declared all abortions illegal except those performed to save the life of the mother or to terminate pregnancies resulting from incest or rape that has been reported promptly to the police.
- Pennsylvania has restricted access to abortion by mandating counseling, a twenty-four hour waiting period, spousal notification, and other barriers to abortion.
- Connecticut, through a statute that means different things to different people, has explicitly legalized all abortions performed before the point of fetal viability.
- New York, New Jersey, and Florida have all discovered, apparently at least, a right to abortion in their state constitutions that would be unaffected by changes in federal constitutional doctrine handed down by the Supreme Court.

The struggles associated with these choices are sure to be repeated in other states in the years to come. Should the court overturn *Roe v. Wade,* or even continue to narrow the rights enunciated in that landmark decision, the framework established here through examination of the Catholic Church's activities could serve as a useful starting point for general inquiries into state-level public policy.

We set out to write a book on the Catholic Church and the politics of abortion, but we are not surprised that we ended up with a book that sheds light on the future of American public policy on abortion as well. The Catholic Church is, and will continue to be, a central actor in the abortion debate in the United States. As the political struggles on that issue move back to the states, our analysis of the church's involvement in those struggles must shift accordingly. And as it does, our examinations of the Catholic Church as a political actor will yield conclusions as relevant to the study of politics and public policy as to the study of the church itself.

Notes

1. See, as examples, A. James Reichley, *Religion in American Public Life* (Washington, D.C.: The Brookings Institution, 1985) and Kenneth D. Wald, *Religion and Politics in the United States* (New York: St. Martin's Press, 1987).

2. See, as examples, Timothy A. Byrnes, *Catholic Bishops in American Politics* (Princeton: Princeton University Press, 1991), Mary C. Segers, ed., *Church Polity and American Politics: Issues in Contemporary Catholicism* (New York: Garland Publishing, Inc., 1990), Matthew C. Moen, *The Christian Right and Congress* (Tuscaloosa: University of Alabama Press, 1989), and Steve Bruce, *The Rise and Fall of the New Christian Right: Conservative Protestant Politics in America 1978-1988* (Oxford: Clarendon Press, 1990).

3. Christopher F. Mooney, *Public Virtue: Law and the Social Character of Religion* (Notre Dame: University of Notre Dame Press, 1986), p. 154.

4. *New York Times,* 13 November 1984, p. A22. For the full text, see *Origins,* 29 November 1984, pp.384–390.

5. See Marian Faux, *Roe v. Wade: The Untold Story of the Landmark Supreme Court Decision that Made Abortion Legal* (New York: MacMillan, 1988), Kristin Luker, *Abortion and the Politics of Motherhood* (Berkeley: University of California Press, 1984), James C. Mohr, *Abortion in America: The Origins and Evolution of National Policy* (New York: Oxford University Press, 1978), and Lawrence H. Tribe, *Abortion: The Clash of Absolutes* (New York: W.W. Norton, 1990).

6. Allen D. Hertzke, *Representing God in Washington: The Role of Religious Lobbies in the American Polity* (Knoxville: The University of Tennessee Press, 1988).

1

The Politics of Abortion: The Catholic Bishops

Timothy A. Byrnes

The Supreme Court of the United States transformed the politics of abortion in July 1989 through its decision in *Webster v. Reproductive Health Services, Inc.* By upholding several provisions of Missouri's restrictive abortion law, the court signaled its retreat from *Roe v. Wade,* invited other state legislatures to further limit access to abortion, and reinvigorated a political struggle over a very emotional issue.

The American Catholic bishops, long opposed to abortion and firmly committed to a constitutional amendment banning it, are active participants in this reinvigorated struggle. With the court's decision in *Webster,* limiting access to abortion has become a real political possibility for the first time since 1973. As a result, the bishops' faint and distant hope for a constitutional amendment has given way to immediate expectations of restrictive legislation at the state level. Those expectations, in turn, have led to a flurry of activity on the part of the National Conference of Catholic Bishops (NCCB) and its individual members.

In this chapter I will describe these activities and analyze them from the perspective of two central questions:

1. How has the Supreme Court's decision in *Webster v. Reproductive Health Services, Inc.* affected the Catholic bishops' approach to abortion as a legal and political issue?
2. How have the new political circumstances swirling around abortion in the wake of *Webster* affected the debate among the bishops concerning the formulation and articulation of their public agenda?

The Bishops and Abortion

As a general rule, the Catholic hierarchy's opposition to abortion, itself consistent, must be tailored to changing political circumstances if it is to be effective, or even credible. In particular, the bishops have to focus their antiabortion efforts on the appropriate level of politics. In the 1960s and early 1970s the bishops of various states denounced the liberalization of those states' abortion laws and mobilized the church's resources in opposition to legal abortion. The National Conference of Catholic Bishops coordinated many of these activities, and the bishops issued a number of collective statements emphasizing Catholic teaching on abortion. But as long as the issue remained on the state level of politics, the primary responsibility for opposing abortion remained in the hands of individual bishops or small groups of bishops from a particular state. It was not until the Supreme Court's decision in *Roe v. Wade* placed abortion on the *national* political agenda in 1973 that the NCCB became the central actor in the Catholic hierarchy's opposition to abortion. The NCCB's leaders forcefully denounced the decision and called for a constitutional amendment to nullify it. The bishops collectively supported and funded a number of national antiabortion organizations. And in the *Pastoral Plan for Pro-Life Activities,* released in 1975, the conference called for "well planned and coordinated political action" for the purpose of electing antiabortion candidates and passing an antiabortion constitutional amendment.[1]

This effort, to be sure, included an important local element. A constitutional amendment would require the support of congressmen, senators, and state legislators, all of whom are responsive to local constituencies of one kind or another. Nevertheless, the bishops' opposition to abortion was decidedly more national in focus after *Roe v. Wade* than it had been before. The issue of abortion was nationalized in 1973, and the bishops' antiabortion activities— their public statements, lobbying, and voter mobilization efforts—had to shift accordingly. In fact, this shift in focus led the bishops directly to active participation in the national political process in the 1970s and 1980s.

In July 1989 the Supreme Court reversed this process and tangibly reintroduced abortion to state and local politics. The issue moved from the national, judicial arena to the more local, political arena. And pro-choice and pro-life activists shifted their attention, in part at least, from votes on the Supreme Court to votes in various state legislatures. For their part, the bishops enthusiastically welcomed the court's retreat from *Roe v. Wade,* and called for legislative efforts to test further the court's evolving doctrine on a woman's right to terminate her pregnancy. But given that new circumstances required new approaches, the bishops also sharpened their focus on pro-choice Catholic politicians and rededicated their institutional and financial resources to the pro-life cause.

The Bishops and Catholic Politicians

In November 1989 the bishops released *Resolution on Abortion,* calling abortion "the fundamental human rights issue for all men and women of good will."[2] In this resolution the bishops summarized their own long and short range goals regarding that issue. Those goals were:

1. constitutional protection of the right to life of unborn children to the maximum degree possible

2. federal and state laws and administrative policies that restrict support for and practice of abortion
3. Continual refinement and ultimate reversal of Supreme Court and other court decisions that deny the unalienable right to life
4. Supportive legislation to provide morally acceptable alternatives to abortion, and social policy initiatives which provide support to pregnant women for prenatal care and extended support for low-income women and their children[3]

These objectives were well established, appropriately tailored to the circumstances at hand, and really not particularly controversial coming from the National Conference of Catholic Bishops. However, the bishops also urged "public officials, especially Catholics, to advance these goals in recognition of their moral responsibility to protect the weak and defenseless among us."[4] In addition, they declared in unequivocal terms that "no Catholic can responsibly take a 'pro-choice' stand when the 'choice' in question involves the taking of innocent human life."[5] This last passage was a bluntly stated message to Catholic politicians that their religious leaders expected them to oppose abortion in political as well as moral terms.

This expectation was not a new one, of course. It was established church teaching that a Catholic can never "vote for" or "take part in a propaganda campaign in favor of" a law that would "admit in principle the licitness of abortion."[6] And in 1984, Cardinal John O'Connor had insisted to Geraldine Ferraro, and by implication all American Catholics, that the church's position on abortion was "monolithic."[7] Nevertheless, the American bishops' forceful restatement of this teaching in 1989 resonated loudly in the new political context created by the Supreme Court's decision. In the past, many Catholic politicians had hidden behind the court's rulings and argued that while they opposed abortion personally, their political options were limited because they had sworn to uphold the constitution as interpreted by the Supreme Court. Whether such a position was based on nuance or duplicity is irrelevant for the purposes of this chapter because after July 1989 it was no longer a viable position for a politician, Catholic or not, to take. *Webster* meant that substantial legal restrictions on abortion were possible again; votes would be taken, records would be established. And in that context, the bishops declared that any vote by any Catholic politician in favor of maintaining abortion rights was by definition irresponsible and in fact un-Catholic.

Given the fact that these politicians and legislative battles would be found at the state and local levels of government, it fell to individual bishops to apply the NCCB's general dictum to specific political circumstances. A number of bishops did so in very public and controversial ways.

- Bishop Leo Maher of San Diego, California denied Holy Communion to Lucy Killea, a Catholic Democrat running for a seat in the State Senate, because, in his words, she had placed herself in "complete contradiction to the moral teaching of the Catholic Church" through her "media

advertisements and statements advocating the 'pro-choice' abortion position in the public forum."[8]
- Bishop Austin Vaughan of New York publicly warned Governor Mario Cuomo, another Catholic Democrat, that he was in "serious risk of going to hell" for his support of abortion rights and of public financing of abortions for poor women.[9]
- Bishops Elden Curtiss and Anthony Milone of Montana admonished all "Catholics who hold public office in [their] state to refrain from public statements which contradict . . . basic principles of Catholic morality."[10]
- Cardinal O'Connor, the chairman of the bishops' Committee on Pro-Life Activities said that "where Catholics are perceived not only as treating church teaching on abortion with contempt, but helping to multiply abortions by advocating legislation supporting abortion or by making public funds available for abortion, bishops may decide that for the common good such Catholics must be warned that they are at risk of excommunication. If such actions persist, bishops may consider excommunication the only option."[11]
- Bishop Rene H. Gracida of Corpus Christi, Texas actually excommunicated Catholic directors of abortion clinics, describing those directors' activities as "a sin against God and humanity and against the law of the Roman Catholic Church."[12]

These statements and others like them underscored the determination on the part of many bishops to apply a kind of internal discipline to the new legislative and legal battles over abortion. To be sure, not every bishop agreed with specific applications of that discipline, and I will return to the bishops' disagreements in this regard later in this chapter. Nevertheless, the conference's collective statement, even absent any particular reemphasis by an individual bishop, was unmistakable in its implications for a Catholic politician from either party who wanted either to support abortion rights or finesse his or her way around the issue. There is no way such a politician can deny that anything short of active support for more restrictive abortion law is starkly inconsistent with the clearly articulated teachings of the church's leadership. In the words of Bishop Maher, "a pro-choice Catholic is an oxymoron."

A Public Relations Campaign

Something happened on the way to more restrictive abortion law, however. Denied its cherished and accustomed protection of the U.S. Supreme Court, the pro-choice movement discovered substantial political resources. *Webster v. Reproductive Health Services* rendered certain types of more restrictive abortion law constitutional. But during the elections and legislative struggles of 1989 and 1990 it became apparent that support for restrictive laws, constitutional though they might be, was in many parts of the country politically dangerous. Politicians from both parties began to position themselves accordingly, and the Catholic bishops faced another challenge. Now that the pro-life movement was clearly on the defensive politically, what could the Catholic hierarchy do to help?

The bishops answered this question in April 1990 when their Committee for Pro-Life Activities announced the NCCB's intention to spend several million dollars over the next three to five years on a public relations campaign to popularize opposition to abortion.[13] Convinced that the pro-choice movement had presented its case more effectively, and that the media was biased against the pro-life cause, the bishops opted to mount their own information offensive. "We believe that the most critical issue in the United States is the problem of abortion," said Cardinal O'Connor, the chairman of the bishops' Pro-Life Committee, "and if we believe that then we should try to use the best possible means to communicate."[14]

In time, the bishops contracted the Wirthlin polling group to gauge public opinion on abortion, the Hill and Knowlton public relations firm to execute the campaign, and the Knights of Columbus to pay for it.[15] Just as they had in the 1960s and early 1970s, the bishops offered their unparalleled resources to the pro-life cause in its hour of need. Over the next several years, the bishops will use a variety of public relations outlets to convey their message that the important aspect of the issue of abortion is not *who* does the choosing but rather *what* is actually being chosen.

The Supreme Court's decision in *Webster* has affected the bishops' approach to abortion as a political issue, then, in the sense that it has substantially altered the political context in which the bishops act. Catholic politicians were required by church law to oppose abortion before *Webster*. But *Webster* has forced these politicians to face much more squarely the potential contradictions between their religious responsibilities and their political interests. The job of pointing out these contradictions to particular politicians in particular political circumstances has been taken up by individual bishops and state conferences of bishops rather than the National Conference of Catholic Bishops as a whole.

Likewise, the bishops were committed to, and supportive of, the pro-life movement long before *Webster*. But *Webster* has redrawn the politics of abortion and, in the estimation of the bishops at least, placed a premium on the kind of resources the American Catholic Church can bring to the question.

The court's decision in *Webster* also has affected the internal politics and discussions of the bishops' conference, and I will turn to those matters shortly. But before I do, I want to address the question of whether or not the bishops' responses to the new legal and political status of abortion will have their desired effect. In short, how successful are the bishops' antiabortion activities likely to be in the coming years?

Will the Bishops Succeed?

The key to answering this question is defining "success." In terms of the public relations effort, the bishops surely will be successful if success is defined as publicizing their view that abortion is the killing of an unborn child, and that such killing should not be tolerated in a just and humane society. As I said, the bishops feel their position has not received sufficient attention from the media. The public relations campaign, in so far as it bypasses the media and communicates directly with the American public, will go a long way toward redressing the imbalance that the bishops perceive.

However, translating more effective and more persistent *presentation* of the church's position on abortion into more *support* for that position is a delicate and questionable proposition at best. It is impossible to know before the fact, of course, but it is entirely possible that any pro-life sentiment the bishops mobilize through their communications campaign will be counteracted by the inescapably sectarian gloss that the campaign will apply to the bishops' cause. Cardinal O'Connor and others have said the bishops will base their antiabortion arguments on natural law rather than on Catholic teaching. But the campaign will be carried out under the auspices of the Catholic hierarchy and it will be paid for by the Knights of Columbus, a Catholic organization. For over two decades the bishops and their allies in the pro-life movement have been arguing that abortion is not a "Catholic issue." That argument will be harder to make in the future because of the bishops' new public relations strategy.

There are several ways one can define success in terms of the bishops' focus on Catholic politicians. First of all, the NCCB's declaration that "no Catholic can responsibly take a pro-choice stand" and the individual bishops' various interpretations of what that means in practice *could* convince pro-choice Catholic politicians to change their minds. Based on the public reactions of those politicians, so far, however, that outcome is very unlikely. Most pro-choice Catholic officeholders seem to agree with Representative Nancy Pelosi of California who said "there is no desire to fight with the cardinals or archbishops. But it has to be clear that we are elected officials, and we uphold the law, and we support public positions separate and apart from our Catholic faith."[16]

I am not aware of a single politician who has changed his or her position on abortion because of pressure applied by a Catholic bishop. In fact, any politician who did so would surely face a barrage of criticism for "taking orders" from an ecclesiastical authority. Catholic officeholders, in short, have serious constitutional, temperamental, and political reasons for refusing to fulfill what the bishops say are their responsibilities as Catholics. The bishops' reiteration of these responsibilities might disturb or sadden pro-choice Catholic leaders. But as Mario Cuomo said in response to Cardinal O'Connor's reminder that pro-choice Catholics may face excommunication from the church for their views, "it is not going to change anything."[17]

Even absent a change of heart or position by individuals, the bishops' pressure could still be deemed successful if it facilitated in some way the election of pro-life candidates. In actual practice, however, the bishops' actions may have exactly the opposite effect. Bishop Maher's criticism of, and denial of Holy Communion to, Lucy Killea, for example, apparently helped Ms. Killea, a Democrat, win an election in a heavily Republican district. The bishop's action turned the national spotlight on Killea's candidacy, elicited campaign contributions and other forms of support from pro-choice groups and activists from across the country, and arguably led some voters to support

Ms. Killea as a way of protesting the Catholic clergy's interference in the political process.

In terms of actually restricting abortion in California, in other words, Bishop Maher's efforts were sharply counterproductive. Ms. Killea, elected with his indirect help, took her seat in the State Senate and tipped that previously deadlocked body in favor of continued access to abortion. It is unwise to generalize from this one case, of course. But several members of the Catholic hierarchy have expressed concern that the application of church sanctions to pro-choice candidates will hinder rather than further the pro-life cause. "I don't think [penalizing Catholic supporters of abortion rights] would help us one bit to change America's thinking," said Archbishop John May as he ended his term as president of the NCCB. "It might even have an adverse effect."[18]

The chances of success for penalties or other types of pressure applied by Catholic bishops on Catholic politicians cannot be gauged without reference to much broader political developments. In fact, the very meaning, in political terms, of the bishops' opposition to abortion, regardless of the form that opposition takes, is dependent on circumstances that are not of the bishops' making. Since 1976, the bishops and other pro-life activists have operated within a context in which the two major political parties have differed sharply on the matter of abortion. Today, this context is in the process of very real and significant change. The Republicans, who first used abortion to drive a wedge in the Democratic electoral coalition, are now finding out that the issue cuts across their own coalition as well. Pro-choice segments of the Republican party were apparently willing to tolerate their party's opposition to abortion only so long as abortion was constitutionally protected. In light of *Webster,* and the court's reintroduction of abortion to the legislative arena, that tolerance is giving way to tension and the kind of political and cultural disputes that during the 1970s and 1980s were associated with the Democratic party.

In short, the partisan cleavage on abortion is already less clear than it was just a short time ago. What this means for the Catholic bishops is that their position on abortion and their pressure on Catholic politicians will lose some of its partisan edge and therefore some of its political relevance. As a rule, wherever two pro-choice candidates face each other, abortion and with it the Catholic bishops will recede into the political background.

This is not to argue, of course, that these conditions will prevail across the political spectrum. Nothing could be further from the truth, and in many campaigns abortion will be an important, emotional, and maybe even decisive issue. In these cases, local bishops may well play prominent public roles, particularly if one of the candidates is a Catholic. At this point, I would not predict what effect those bishops might have on a given contest. But I would say that, from the perspective of the pro-life cause, Bishop Maher's experience in California is not a very hopeful precedent. I would also say that political circumstances, particularly the Republicans' reaction to the pro-choice rumblings in their ranks, will play a very powerful part in determining the political relevance of the bishops' approach to pro-choice Catholics.

These comments and judgments are necessarily speculative, because we simply do not know what is going to happen to the politics of abortion in the coming years. In May 1991, for example, the Supreme Court upheld in *Rust v. Sullivan* regulations preventing caregivers in federally funded family planning clinics from discussing abortion with their patients. The court may even formally overturn *Roe v. Wade* before long. But regardless of where these events leave the bishops in terms of partisan politics and public policy, we do know that the Supreme Court's action in *Webster* has already affected the discussion among the bishops over the presentation of their collective agenda. The current status of this very important discussion is the subject of the remainder of this chapter.

A Sharp but Limited Debate

Students of the American Catholic hierarchy have a tendency to overstate the cohesiveness of the National Conference of Catholic Bishops. We use the phrase "the bishops" to describe a large group of men with varied temperaments, varied approaches, and on many questions, varied opinions. I have probably overused the phrase myself in my discussion of "the bishops'" reaction to *Webster v. Reproductive Health Services*. In fact, the various bishops' responses to the evolving legal and political status of abortion have reflected two distinct camps or schools of thought that have developed within the National Conference of Catholic Bishops over the last fifteen or twenty years.

One of these camps sees abortion as the overriding issue of our day and believes it is therefore appropriate to give abortion first priority on the Catholic Church's moral agenda. In political terms, this approach leads bishops to focus exclusively on candidates' stands on abortion and to encourage Catholic voters to do likewise. Cardinal Humberto Medeiros adopted this approach in 1980 when he reminded Catholics of the Archdiocese of Boston that "those who make abortion possible by law—such as legislators and those who promote, defend and elect these same legislators—cannot separate themselves totally from the guilt which accompanies this horrendous crime and deadly sin." Catholics, Medeiros said, should "vote to save our children, born and unborn."[19] Cardinal O'Connor of New York spoke from this same perspective in 1984 when he asked "how a Catholic in conscience could vote for an individual explicitly expressing himself or herself as favoring abortion."[20]

Bishops who belong to the other camp or who subscribe to the other school of thought do not question the church's unequivocal teaching on abortion, nor do they deny that issue's political importance. However, they prefer to advance the church's condemnation of abortion as a specific application of its more general reverence for human life in all its forms. As Cardinal Joseph Bernardin put it in formally articulating this broader approach, "the pro-life position of the church must be developed in terms of a comprehensive and consistent ethic of life."[21] Bishops who advocate this consistent ethic of life want the NCCB to oppose abortion in the political realm, but they want that opposition firmly linked to the bishops' positions on other life issues such as capital punishment, euthanasia, militarism, and social programs for the poor.

I have argued elsewhere that this dispute among the bishops and its complex relationship to the partisan competition between the Republicans and Democrats has been *the* key to the Catholic hierarchy's participation in the American political process during the 1970s and 1980s.[22] Here I will argue that this dispute has been affected in two ways by the Supreme Court's decision in *Webster v. Reproductive Health Services.*

First, the resurgence of abortion as a highly charged political issue has sharpened the bishops' discussion of their own political priorities. Bishops committed to the notion that abortion is the critical issue of the day have been heartened by the prospect of more restrictive public policy in this area, and they have spoken out forcefully on the political implications of these circumstances. Bishop James McHugh of Camden, for example, offered the following advice to Catholics planning to vote in New Jersey's gubernatorial election in 1989.

> We must give primary consideration to the sanctity and value of human life in our choice of political leaders. Therefore, in determining whom to vote for, we should be careful and highly selective. . . . Anyone who attempts to separate his or her personal moral convictions from the shaping of public policy is unreliable and unworthy of trust. Accordingly, I ask you to give life a chance and to place party loyalty in a secondary position in this election. Look at each and every candidate in light of his or her position on protecting the life of the unborn and the need to correct the present system of abortion on demand that exists in this country.[23]

As strong as Bishop McHugh's statement was, Bishop Myers of Peoria, Illinois was even more specific in terms of what "giving life a chance" should mean to Catholic voters.

> As voters, Catholics are under an obligation to avoid implicating themselves in abortion. There can be no assurance that voters will invariably have a qualified pro-life candidate to choose. In such a case, abstention is a permissible political response. . . . A Catholic may support the candidacy of someone who would permit unjust killing only when the real alternatives are candidates who would permit even more unjust killing.[24]

Bishops like McHugh and Myers see abortion as a political litmus test for all Catholics, voters and politicians. But other bishops, holding the same Catholic teachings as binding and facing similar political circumstances, argue that abortion and related political choices should be approached from the broader perspective of a consistent ethic of life. Bishop Walter Sullivan is a particularly enthusiastic proponent of this view.

> I find it hard to comprehend how an elected official can claim to be pro-life when he or she consistently votes against Aid to Dependent Children, health insurance for the poor, prenatal care and day care. Single issue orthodoxy is not persuasive when help and encouragement are denied women facing difficult life decisions.

. . . We as pro-lifers must be busier changing the hearts and minds of people rather than just wanting to change laws.[25]

The bishops of Wisconsin, speaking collectively, demonstrated it was possible to retain the consistent ethic even in light of the NCCB's characterization of abortion as the fundamental human rights issue of the day.

Because the right to life is the most basic of all rights, abortion retains a special priority among life issues, and no life ethic that fails to defend the right to life of the unborn can be called consistent. Nevertheless, while all life issues are not equal in importance, neither can concern for any one permit us to disregard the others. . . . People of good will can differ, both in their public policy priorities and the means of achieving them, but they ought not assume that only their priorities or methods are Christian or mandated by the teachings of the church.[26]

These statements are just a few representative examples of the many that have been made by American bishops over the last few years. Bishop after bishop has cited the court's new openness to restrictions on abortion and either reiterated abortion's overriding political importance or argued that abortion, regardless of how important, still should be approached within the context of Catholic reverence for life at all stages, born and unborn. As I indicated earlier, these two positions or approaches are not new. It is the political circumstances to which these approaches are related that are new, and those circumstances have raised the relevant questions in new ways and sharpened the political ramifications of the two schools of thought within the bishops' conference. The bishops' debate is not merely a theoretical or philosophical one. Today more than ever, it is a political one, involving different agendas, different advice to voters, and different attitudes concerning penalties and sanctions for pro-choice Catholics.

At the same time that political circumstances have sharpened the bishops' debate over their moral and political agenda, however, those same circumstances have also clarified the strictly limited nature of the bishops' differences. It is important to recognize and emphasize that the debate among the bishops was never about the content of Catholic teaching. Rather, it was about the way Catholic principles and convictions should be presented and advanced in a context in which no viable secular political force agreed with the bishops on all the major issues of the day. As we have just seen, this debate is still lively and meaningful. Underlying this debate, however, is a consensus that abortion is always immoral and that opposition to abortion is required of all Catholics. In light of *Webster,* and the NCCB's reaction to it, this consensus is clearer and more powerful than ever.

I can best document this unity through reference to statements recently made by Cardinal John O'Connor of New York and Cardinal Joseph Bernardin of Chicago. These two major figures in the American church are widely considered the leading spokesmen for the two competing approaches within the National Conference of Catholic Bishops. Yet O'Connor's "Abortion:

Questions and Answers" and Bernardin's "The Consistent Ethic Since Webster" share a great deal of common ground.[27]

Of course, the two cardinals differ on the relative *emphasis* that should be accorded various issues or groups of issues. O'Connor deemed abortion "the most important issue of our day," and brushed aside what he called the "single issue question" by arguing that "other issues, important as they are, are secondary to this direct taking of human life."[28] Bernardin, on the other hand, explicitly linked Catholic opposition to abortion to the church's position on other life issues, and warned of the "danger that we could make the mistake of some of the pro-abortion groups and narrow our public concern to a single issue, ignoring other threats to human life."[29] Regardless of these differences in emphasis, however, the two statements were remarkably similar in their support for more restrictive abortion legislation and their claims that all Catholic public officials must give active support to such legislation.

Cardinal O'Connor's views on abortion and the relationship between Catholic teaching and the law are very well known. He believes that all abortions are gravely immoral and that Catholics, bound by this teaching, have a responsibility to oppose access to abortion whenever possible. He restated these views in "Abortion: Questions and Answers." But Cardinal Bernardin, the author of the consistent ethic of life, stated exactly the same views in equally unequivocal terms. In "The Consistent Ethic Since Webster," Bernardin termed the right to life "the fundamental human right,"and he called for a reversal of *Roe* and [for] a legal order which protects the unborn." He also equated "pro-choice" with "pro-abortion" and pointed out that such a position, regardless of what one calls it "collides directly" with the "church's objective moral teaching" that all "directly intended abortions are . . . immoral."[30]

It is not at all surprising, of course, that Cardinal Bernardin holds these views. He is, after all, a Catholic bishop, and for many years he was the chairman of the bishops' Committee on Pro-Life Activities. But given the political choices currently facing Catholic politicians it is illuminating that Bernardin also believes that "to hold the moral position of the Catholic Church—that all directly intended abortion is morally wrong—and not to relate that moral position to civil law would be a grave abdication of moral responsibility."[31] Explicitly referring to the matter of Catholic politicians, Bernardin said he is "firmly committed to the position that public officials who recognize the evil of abortion have a responsibility to limit its extent, to work for its prevention, and to protect unborn life."[32]

On this point, he and Cardinal O'Connor are in complete agreement. Addressing the same matter of Catholic politicians, O'Connor doubted "if a public official is being morally consistent if he or she personally believes abortion is killing but simultaneously believes his or her office requires supporting it, funding it, or refusing to even work for legislation opposed to it. While it is true that there are varying political strategies for changing any law which allows the unborn to be killed, in my view it cannot be seriously debated that the law must be changed."[33]

It is true that Bernardin and O'Connor differ on the important matter of the role that sanctions should play in the bishops' approach to politicians who take a pro-choice position on abortion. O'Connor, in his statement, raised the prospect of excommunication for these politicians while Bernardin argued "that the church can be most effective in the public debate on abortion through moral persuasion, not punitive measures."[34] It is also true that at least one bishop, Rembert Weakland of Milwaukee, wants to allow "politicians as much latitude as reason permits even as we expect them to be consistent, compassionate, and respectful of the dignity of life in all its aspects and developments."[35]

Nevertheless, Bernardin, the leading spokesman for the consistent ethic of life, and O'Connor, who once said "if the unborn in a mother's womb is unsafe it becomes ludicrous for the bishops to address the threat of nuclear war or the great problems of the homeless or the suffering of the aged," agree that the church's position on abortion is, indeed, "monolithic" *and* that Catholic politicians have the unavoidable responsibility of seeking to apply that position to the civil law.[36]

I want to stress that I have no doubt this agreement is a longstanding one. I am not arguing that the bishops' consensus on abortion or on the binding nature of the church's teaching on that subject was created by the court's decision in *Webster v. Reproductive Health Services, Inc.* What I am arguing is that the court's decision has created a political context in which that consensus has become clearer to Catholic citizens, Catholic politicians, and anyone else who is interested in the bishops' participation in the political process. Bernardin's consistent ethic, or seamless garment, has always included unwavering opposition to abortion. But in the past, that seamless garment was used as a kind of protective cloak by Catholic politicians who tried to compensate for their support of abortion rights by stressing their commitment to church teaching on other life issues. *Webster* has stripped this cloak away by confronting these politicians with concrete political choices concerning abortion, and by highlighting a firm and public consensus among the Catholic hierarchy that "no Catholic can responsibly take a 'pro-choice' stand when the 'choice' in question involves the taking of innocent human life."

As I argued in the first part of this chapter, it is not at all clear to me that the bishops' consensus and reenergized opposition to abortion will have a significant effect on abortion law or on the positions and fortunes of Catholic politicians. But in terms of the internal cohesiveness of a national episcopal conference long divided over the articulation and presentation of its moral agenda, *Webster* and the bishops' responses to it have at one and the same time sharpened that division *and* clarified its limits.

Notes

1. "Pastoral Plan for Pro-Life Activities," in Hugh J. Nolan, ed., *Pastoral Letters of the United States Catholic Bishops, Volume IV, 1975-1983* (Washington, D.C.: National Conference of Catholic Bishops, 1983), p. 87.

2. *Origins*, 16 November 1989, p. 395.

3. Ibid., p. 396.

4. Ibid.

5. Ibid., p. 395.

6. This statement is from a "Vatican Declaration on Abortion." See *Origins,* 12 December 1974, p. 390.

7. See, in particular, *New York Times,* 9 September 1984, p. A1, and 11 September 1984, p. A1.

8. Bishop Maher's letter to Ms. Killea was reproduced in *Origins,* 14 December 1989, p. 457.

9. *New York Times,* 24 January 1990, p. B1.

10. *Origins,* 14 December 1989, p. 458.

11. *Origins,* 28 June 1990, p. 105.

12. *New York Times* 30 June 1990, p. A7.

13. *New York Times,* 6 April 1990, p. A1.

14. *National Catholic Reporter,* 20 April 1990, p. 5.

15. *New York Times,* 13 May 1990, p. A18.

16. *New York Times,* 25 June 1990, p. A1.

17. *New York Times,* 15 June 1990, p. B2.

18. *New York Times,* 20 November 1989, p. A16.

19. Cardinal Medeiros' actions were recounted in Andrew H. Merton, *Enemies of Choice: The Right to Life Movement and its Threat to Abortion* (Boston: Beacon Press, 1981), p. 115.

20. *New York Times,* 25 June 1984, p. D13.

21. *Origins,* 29 December 1983, p. 491.

22. See Timothy A. Byrnes, *Catholic Bishops in American Politics* (Princeton: Princeton University Press, 1991).

23. *Origins,* 14 December 1989, p. 461.

24. *Origins,* 31 May 1990, p. 43.

25. *Origins,* 21 June 1990, pp. 87–88.

26. *Origins,* 14 December 1989, pp. 463–464.

27. See *Origins,* 12 April 1990, pp. 741–748 and 28 June 1990, pp. 97–115.

28. *Origins,* 28 June 1990, pp. 107–108.

29. *Origins,* 12 April 1990, p. 745.

30. Ibid., pp. 746–747.

31. Ibid., p. 746.

32. Ibid., p. 747.

33. *Origins,* 28 June 1990, pp. 105–106.

34. For O'Connor's discussion of excommunication see ibid., p. 105. For Bernardin's comments see *Origins,* 12 April 1990, p. 747.

35. *Origins,* 31 May 1990, p. 39.

36. For O'Connor's statement see the *Village Voice,* 25 December 1984, p. 16.

2

Abortion Politics Post-Webster: The New Jersey Bishops

Mary C. Segers

In July 1989, the U.S. Supreme Court inaugurated a new era in abortion politics in the United States. In upholding a Missouri statute restricting abortion *(Webster v. Reproductive Health Services)*, the Court signaled a shift in the debate from national to state politics, from courtrooms to legislatures, and from judicial appointments to election campaigns. Since New Jersey was one of only two states which held statewide elections in 1989, national attention focused on the Garden State as a case study, a test of how state elections and state politics would be influenced by the changing conditions of the abortion debate post-*Webster*.

Several factors make New Jersey an interesting choice for our study of the Catholic bishops' campaign to restrict abortion in the fifty states. First, although small in size, New Jersey is the ninth largest state in population and is a virtual "microcosm of the United States, with urban, suburban and rural areas, significant blue-collar ethnic areas as well as sizable black and Hispanic populations."[1] Not surprisingly, political analysts usually watch New Jersey as a "swing state" in presidential elections and regard it as a barometer of the mood of the national electorate. Secondly, Roman Catholic presence in New Jersey is strong. Catholics are the largest single religious group in the state: 41 percent (3,160,054) out of a population of 7.5 million. In addition, about half of the voters are Catholic. Third, although New Jersey is a heavily Catholic state, opinion polls consistently show the state to be largely pro-choice. It is also one of a handful of states continuing Medicaid funding of abortion—this as the result of a 1982 State Supreme Court decision.[2] It is intriguing that a state with such a significant Catholic presence is strongly pro-choice with respect to law and public policy.

A fourth factor in our selection of New Jersey for this study of abortion politics at the state level is that the Garden State has been the scene of considerable activity on this issue in the two years since the Supreme Court's *Webster* ruling. Abortion was an important issue in the 1989 gubernatorial and state assembly elections. Moreover, the state's Catholic bishops have used a variety of strategies and tactics to influence electoral and public policy outcomes, and have pressured candidates and voters in both the 1989 statewide and 1990 federal election campaigns. Fifth and finally, New Jersey is of interest in the post-*Webster* period because both the substance and the rhetoric of the Jersey bishops' arguments to restrict abortion are prototypical of the policy approach taken in the early 1990s by the National Conference of Catholic Bishops.

It is impossible to discuss adequately the efforts of New Jersey's Catholic bishops to influence that state's abortion policy without briefly describing the political context of the Garden State. Accordingly, the first section of this essay presents general information on the political culture of New Jersey, the Catholic presence in the state, and poll data on public attitudes towards abortion. The second section analyzes the significance of the abortion issue in the 1989 gubernatorial and legislative elections and examines the bishops' efforts to educate public opinion and mobilize Catholics during the election campaign.

In the third section, I examine events since the 1989 election. These include the 1990 federal elections, the activity of non-Catholic religious groups in the state, and renewed efforts by Catholic bishops to discipline pro-choice Catholic politicians and to shape public discourse on abortion. Finally, the fourth section evaluates the efforts of New Jersey's bishops to influence abortion politics and policy in terms of both political effectiveness and ecclesiology. I argue that many actions taken by the church in New Jersey were typical of the approach taken by the NCCB in the national arena. At the same time, the church in New Jersey showed remarkable restraint compared with bishops and other official church representatives in other parts of the United States.

The Political Culture of New Jersey

New Jersey is the ninth largest state in population and the most densely populated state in the nation. There are 567 municipalities in the state and no county land remains unincorporated. Despite the fact that the state is sandwiched between the large metropolitan areas of New York and Philadelphia, Jerseyans have a strong penchant for home rule and local control. Jersey voters are also independent-minded: its two U.S. senators are Democrats, but it went Republican in the last three presidential elections and had a popular liberal Republican, Thomas Kean, as governor throughout the 1980s.

Roman Catholic presence in New Jersey is strong; like other states in the Northeast, New Jersey is heavily Catholic in population. There are six episcopal dioceses in the state with a combined population of 3,160,054 Catholics or 41 percent of the state's population of 7.5 million. Archbishop Theodore E. McCarrick heads the Newark archdiocese, the state's largest (and the eighth largest diocese in the country). The other diocesan bishops are John C. Reiss of Trenton, James T. McHugh of Camden (who is also a member of the Committee for Pro-Life Activities of the National Conference of Catholic Bishops), Frank J. Rodimer of Patterson, Edward T. Hughes of Metuchen, and Michael J. Dudick of the Byzantine Catholic Diocese of Passaic. These bishops, together with their auxiliaries, form the New Jersey Catholic Conference (NJCC), a state office and staff organization which monitors the New Jersey state legislature in Trenton and attempts to influence public policy at the state level. In the nation as a whole, there are 28 such state Catholic conferences, organizations supported by each diocese in that state, with offices that operate with guidelines from the U.S. Catholic Conference in Washington, D.C.[3]

The New Jersey Catholic Conference, like most state conferences, deals generally with education, pro-life issues, and issues of social justice. According to William Bolan, Jr., Executive Director of the NJCC, priority is given to healthcare, education, employment, and justice for the poor. The Conference works legislatively on abortion, right-to-die legislation, and artificial insemination. The Conference also works to increase homeless-shelter funds, as well as job retraining for the unemployed and tuition-tax credits for parents of parochial school children.[4]

Although the chief bishop or "ordinary" in his diocese may act individually on any issue, New Jersey's Catholic bishops have often acted in concert on a number of significant issues. In the 1980s, for example, they favored state-mandated sex education programs in the schools, opposed surrogacy in the celebrated 1987 "Baby M" case as the commercialization of children and the exploitation and dehumanization of women, and supported Operation Rescue by criticizing harsh penalties for Rescue members who broke the law.

Besides the bishops and the NJCC, several other Catholic groups are active politically on the abortion issue. An established pro-life infrastructure composed of diocesan pro-life commissions, Knights of Columbus councils, and organizations such as the National Conference of Catholic Women works diligently to restrict access to abortion. Through coalitions and overlapping memberships, these groups have ties to conservative evangelical groups such as Concerned Women of America and to organizations such as the New Jersey Right to Life Committee. For example, the pro-life director for the diocese of Metuchen, Rita Martin, is a former president of the New Jersey Right to Life Committee, and current legislative director of Citizens Concerned for Life of New Jersey; she is also a member of the Citizens Bioethics Committee which has been instrumental in fashioning a right-to-die statute for the state legislature.

Despite its large Catholic population, opinion polls show the state to be largely pro-choice. The Eagleton-*Star-Ledger* Poll, conducted by Rutgers University's Eagleton Institute of Politics and the Newark *Star-Ledger,* the state's largest newspaper, surveyed the attitudes of state residents about abortion both before and after the *Webster* decision in 1989. When asked by pollsters (Do you agree or disagree that the decision to have an abortion is a private matter that should be left to the woman to decide without government interference?) in March 1989 and again in September, a large majority of New Jerseyans (80 percent and 77 percent) agreed that the abortion decision should be left to the woman. An Eagleton-*Star-Ledger* poll also showed that a large majority of Catholics (73 percent) and of Protestants (78 percent) agreed that the abortion decision is a private matter.[5]

Other polls confirmed the results of the Eagleton-*Star-Ledger* survey. A poll of approximately 1,000 voters taken by *The Record,* a large-circulation newspaper in northern New Jersey, found Jerseyans to be substantially more pro-choice than the nation at large.[6] While national polls show that between the polar extremes of pro-abortion and antiabortion, there is a large group of Americans who oppose abortion on demand and who favor some but not all restrictions on abortion, both *The Record* and the Eagleton-*Star-Ledger* polls show that Jerseyans diverge from national opinion in significant respects. According to the Eagleton-*Star-Ledger* survey, close to a majority, 48 percent, said women should have the right to abortion in all circumstances; another 44 percent said abortion should be allowed in certain circumstances only; only 5 percent said abortion should not be allowed in any circumstances. The contrasting national figures are respectively 25 percent, 53 percent, and 19 percent.[7] Janice Ballou, director of the Eagleton-*Star-Ledger* Poll, emphasized how much New Jerseyans differed from the nation on this point: "Compared to national polls that show less than 3-in-10 Americans support legal abortion in any circumstances, this state has close to a majority who favor this position."[8]

The fact that a heavily Catholic state such as New Jersey is also largely pro-choice is of some interest. According to the polls, Catholics are virtually indistinguishable from Protestants in supporting legal abortion during the first trimester in cases of rape and incest, fetal deformity, and when a woman's physical health is endangered. A majority of Catholics also approves of legal abortion in the first three months if the woman is under 18 (52 percent; Protestants 61 percent); and if the woman feels she cannot afford a child (52 percent; Protestants 55 percent). However, Catholics differ from other New Jerseyans in the case of a woman's desire not to have a baby. Whereas a majority (53 percent) of all voters approves of legal abortion in this case, Catholics are evenly divided between those who oppose and those who approve (47 percent; Protestants 61 percent). The Eagleton poll also found some differences in intensity of conviction between Catholics and Protestants, and this is undoubtedly a reflection of the ambivalence Catholics often feel about the issue.[9]

Why is New Jersey substantially more pro-choice than the nation at large? Several factors might explain why New Jerseyans are likely to land on the pro-choice side when it comes to abortion policy. The state has many highly educated suburban voters and union members likely to be somewhat liberal on some issues; it also has a high percentage of Jewish voters (9 percent of *The Record* sample was Jewish). Even more than other Americans, Jerseyans are ambivalent about the role of government. A significant number favor less government intervention in economic matters and personal lifestyle issues, but more government assistance to solve crime, drug, and environmental problems. It is no accident that the Libertarian party is relatively strong in the state and regularly fields candidates in statewide elections. Perhaps the citizens of this most densely populated state in the nation are especially sensitive to issues of privacy—the kind of zonal privacy that the Supreme Court cited in *Roe v. Wade* to shield a woman's sexual and reproductive life from public intervention and scrutiny. Operation Rescue, which has been active in the state, may have sensitized voters to the burdens to women that would follow upon restrictive legislation. These elements in the political culture of the Garden State help to explain the preponderance of "liberal" attitudes towards abortion policy.

Politically, it should be noted, the abortion issue is not a partisan issue but crosses party lines. There is no pro-life plank in the platform of the New Jersey Republican Party (unlike the platform of the National Republican Party), and prominent Republican state legislators are firmly pro-choice. Similarly, some Democratic leaders and legislators are pro-life. However, neither politicians nor party leaders had to concern themselves with abortion policy during the 1980s because both Republican Governor Thomas Kean and his predecessor, Democratic Governor Brendan Byrne, supported legal abortion. Against the prospect of a governor's veto, no antiabortion legislation was introduced in the state legislature. Thus by 1989, New Jersey had a large number of state senators and assemblymen who never really had to take a position on the abortion issue. This changed suddenly in July 1989. The *Webster* decision made abortion a major issue in the 1989 New Jersey elections, and candidates could no longer avoid taking a stand.

The 1989 New Jersey Election

It is difficult to convey fully the impact in New Jersey of news of the Supreme Court's ruling in *Webster* that states would be permitted to restrict abortion. One journalist commented that every woman in the Garden State read the morning newspaper the day after the Supreme Court announced its decision. Since New Jersey and Virginia were in the midst of gubernatorial election campaigns, national media attention focused immediately on these two states to gauge the impact of *Webster* in state electoral politics.

In the November 1989 election, Democratic Congressman Jim Florio defeated Republican Congressman Jim Courter for the governor's seat. The Democrats also gained control of the state assembly, winning forty-four seats to the Republicans' thirty-six. Since the Democrats already controlled the senate, which was not up for election in 1989, the gubernatorial and assembly elections put them in control of state government.

How important was the abortion question in this election? Automobile insurance rates—by 1989 New Jersey had the highest in the nation—mattered most (32 percent) to the 1,653 voters who participated in a *New York Times-*CBS exit poll; abortion was second, along with the environment (22 percent).[10] The *Times-*CBS poll also showed a close relation between how people felt about abortion and how they voted. The front runner Jim Florio, a Roman Catholic, campaigned throughout as a pro-choice candidate; he declared immediately after *Webster* that, as governor, he would veto any legislation to restrict abortion. Jim Courter had long opposed abortion: he signed a Congressional amicus brief in the *Webster* case asking the Court to reverse *Roe v. Wade.* After *Webster*, he voted in August, 1989, against Medicaid funding of abortions in Washington, D.C. During the campaign, however, Courter, aware of opinion polls showing the pro-choice tendencies of New Jerseyans, tried to soften his stand by saying that, as governor, he would not propose restrictive legislation. According to the exit poll, of those who support easy access to abortion, 68 percent voted for Florio; of those who want to tighten the rules, 54 percent; and of those who want to ban abortion, 47 percent. Overall, Florio took 62 percent to Courter's 38 percent.

In the course of the New Jersey election campaign, several facts became evident. First, there was a strong resurgence of a broad-based pro-choice movement which seemed to have caught the right to life movement unprepared. New Jersey pro-choicers seemed able to draw on a broad range of people concerned that *Roe* might be reversed, mobilizing across class, race, gender, and party lines. They organized Choice-New Jersey, a coalition of thirty-five groups, which coordinated statewide efforts to inform voters of the candidates' positions on abortion policy. Choice-Pac focused on the assembly races and raised $200,000 in four months in order to run voter-identification projects in selected districts ($183,00 was raised in-state). State branches of the National Organization for Women (NOW) and the National Abortion Rights Action League (NARAL) focused on the race for governor. Other women worked in Democratic party committees as well as in organizations such as the Women's Agenda, New Jersey Right to Choose, and the state chapter of the Religious Coalition for Abortion Rights (RCAR). In the course of the 1989 campaign, it became clear that a protest reaction against *Webster* swept the state and brought about a resurgence of pro-choice activism.[11]

A second point demonstrated by the New Jersey 1989 election campaign was the strong political appeal of the pro-choice position framed as preserving a woman's right to decide. This approach was exemplified in the newsletter of the Women's Agenda, one of many women's rights organizations in the state. Working from a 1981 League of Women Voters' statewide survey, Roberta Francis, former director for women's issues of the League and current Director of the New Jersey State Division on Women, drew a sharp distinction between the legality and morality of abortion. The public policy issue was defined as choice, and nothing else. Arguing that it was possible to be antiabortion and pro-choice, the Women's Agenda focused the basic issue on whether the government or a woman should decide to continue or terminate a pregnancy. By framing the issue in this way and labeling their opponents antichoice (not pro-life), the pro-choicers made the right to decide the moderate, mainstream position in the campaign.

It is generally agreed that the issue of abortion was significant in New Jersey in 1989. Debra Dodson, a political scientist with the Eagleton Institute's Center for American Women and Politics, has concluded that the abortion issue affected the 1989 New Jersey election in three ways. It mobilized activists and volunteers (mostly on the pro-choice side); it shaped the way the candidates ran their campaigns; and finally it influenced the vote itself. In her analysis, Florio's pro-choice position helped add several points to his victory margin while Courter's ever-changing position on abortion policy diverted attention from his stand on other issues and made it difficult for him to close the gap with Florio.[12] Dodson's careful analysis was reinforced by the comments of

Courter's campaign manager, Ken Connolly, who conceded that the campaign was dominated by the abortion issue to the detriment of his candidate.[13]

The Role of the Bishops in the 1989 Election

How did the New Jersey bishops react to the *Webster* decision and to the return of abortion politics to the state level? Immediately after the Supreme Court ruling, and throughout the 1989 election campaign, the bishops took steps to influence the political debate about abortion policy. Their actions consisted, first, of a series of statements and appearances designed to remind citizens, especially Catholic voters, of what the bishops called their moral obligation to support pro-life candidates. Second, the bishops undertook an unusual effort to use Sunday masses to conduct a political mobilization.

The state's senior bishop, Archbishop Theodore E. McCarrick of Newark, reacted immediately to the *Webster* decision with a brief statement announcing the Catholic bishops' support for "all steps, whether by legislation or amendments to our state constitution, to protect the lives of the unborn in the State of New Jersey."[14] Ten days later, McCarrick issued a strong pro-life message to all Catholics, rebutting major pro-choice arguments and hailing a new definition of Catholics as the "pro-life people." While he avoided specific mention of the New Jersey elections, he sought to restate clearly Catholic teaching on the humanity of the unborn in anticipation of the "political maneuvering," "speeches" and "media coverage that will sometimes editorialize in the place of giving factual accounts."[15]

Other New Jersey bishops joined McCarrick's efforts to influence public opinion. In the fall, Bishop Edward T. Hughes of Metuchen addressed the annual "Red Mass" for the state's Catholic attorneys reminding them of their obligation to take whatever steps necessary to protect fetal life. On September 24th, Bishops James McHugh of Camden and Auxiliary Bishop David Arias of Newark addressed a "Rally for Life" in Trenton organized by the Knights of Columbus and the New Jersey Right to Life Committee.[16]

As public opinion surveys repeatedly indicated broad support for a woman's right to decide, Archbishop McCarrick began to accommodate his message to these political realities. Acknowledging publicly "that the majority of people of New Jersey do not favor legislation that would make every abortion impossible," he claimed nonetheless that polls showed that "The people are not in favor of terminating the life of a baby just because its parents wanted a boy and not a girl, or because they wanted to buy a better automobile, or because a vacation was coming up that childbirth would make inconvenient. In other words, most men and women do not favor unlimited abortion on demand." McCarrick indicated that even if abortions were permitted to save the life of a mother, or after rape or incest, these categories constituted only 5 percent of all abortions. Thus pro-lifers had the task and duty of saving the lives of the remaining "95 percent innocent unborn children."[17] In articulating this "middle ground" or compromise position, McCarrick anticipated what would become a standard approach of the National Conference of Catholic Bishops to abortion policy in the 1990s: make some concessions to accommodate the so-called "hard cases" of abortion while appealing to the public for a legal ban of most abortions.

In a final effort nine days before the election, McCarrick directed that a letter declaring that Catholics are responsible to vote for candidates who uphold Catholic moral values be read at all Sunday masses in the Newark archdiocese. In the letter, he stated:

> In the next few years many judgments will be made in government that will directly impact on human life. We are about to select a number of persons who will make these judgments. It is not consistent for us to think one way and vote another. Each of us is responsible before God to integrate our beliefs with our behavior. . . . In our prayers and in our actions, in public and in private, in the political process and in our personal lives, by our vote and by our courageous witness to others, we must actively defend what is morally right. We must defend the innocent life of that little baby in its mother's womb.[18]

Aware that, in the context of an election campaign, this letter might be seen as an effort to tell Catholics how to vote, McCarrick had one of his auxiliaries, Bishop John Smith, issue several caveats to pastors and parish priests. Smith told priests that the letter "should be read in its entirety without editorial or additional interpretive comments," adding that it had "been carefully written to reflect the moral teaching of the church and to avoid legal pitfalls." Smith also cautioned priests that "endorsement of any political party or candidate from the pulpit is a violation of both civil law and ecclesiastical discipline."[19]

McCarrick's message was reiterated in a formal statement released by the New Jersey Catholic Bishops and the New Jersey Catholic Conference one week before the election. The bishops reminded legislators and political candidates "that each person is a unified moral agent, and therefore they cannot claim that they personally recognize the immorality of abortion while at the same time they support or act to facilitate abortion by others." The hierarchy called "upon every Catholic, and upon all who believe with us in the sanctity of human life, to accept the moral responsibility of taking clear, effective, direct action to defend human life by their vote."[20]

A second tactic employed by New Jersey's Catholic bishops during the 1989 election campaign was the use of Sunday church services as an occasion for political mobilization. On Respect Life Sunday (October 1, 1989), Catholics in the Archdiocese of Newark and the Dioceses of Trenton and Metuchen were asked during Mass to sign pledge cards authorizing the pro-life commissions to use the resulting list of names (called a "Life Roll") in lobbying for pro-life legislation. Parishioners were asked to indicate whether they would write or visit their elected representatives, join a pro-life prayer group, or help in some other way. This appeal was made during the time usually reserved for the homily. The appeal to sign was preceded by a statement from the archbishop which said:

> Legislators who are personally opposed to abortion but who do nothing to back up that position are looking for votes among the living without counting the cost

of the innocent dead. The love of Jesus celebrated in this Eucharist impels us to form our consciences and to act upon them in the voting booth. We have a duty to vote and a duty before God to uphold our moral position with our vote.[21]

How did Catholics respond to this unusual effort to use the pulpit for purposes of political mobilization? An informal survey among friends and colleagues garnered the following. Some parishes did not distribute the cards. Some Catholics objected verbally and in writing that Project Life Roll came dangerously close to church endorsement of Republican candidates. In one parish, a priest preached a sermon on God's compassionate love and said he could never judge the decision of a woman who had had an abortion; at the end of that Mass, the pastor announced that pro-life parishioners had cards at the back of the church if anyone was interested. In still another parish, the priest read the archbishop's statement, gave a homily urging parishioners to enroll, then sat silently for ten minutes waiting for people to sign up.

According to Rita Martin, pro-life director for the Metuchen diocese, all together 225,000 New Jersey Catholics (roughly 7 percent) signed up for Project Life Roll. The computerized list made from the cards will be used to lobby legislators and to demonstrate Catholic support for pro-life legislation. People who signed Life Roll cards will be asked to contact their legislators when pertinent legislation is pending.[22]

Despite the attempts of the New Jersey bishops to influence electoral outcomes and public opinion, these efforts were to little avail. A strongly pro-choice candidate won the gubernatorial election and the state assembly shifted in the direction of pro-choice. To be sure, the abortion issue was not the only issue in the election nor was it the chief factor accounting for the Florio victory. Issues such as automobile insurance and environmental protection also figured prominently. But the abortion issue was significant; in a major post-election study, Dodson and Burnbauer found that it affected campaign dynamics, campaign rhetoric, and voting decisions.[23]

How effective were the efforts of the Catholic bishops in delivering the Catholic vote to the pro-life candidate in the New Jersey governor's race? What impact did their speeches, letters, and Project Life Roll have in influencing Catholic voters? Again, according to the *New York Times*-CBS exit poll, 44 percent of Florio voters were Catholic while 25 percent were Protestant. Of Courter voters in their sample, 34 percent were Protestant while 46 percent were Catholic. When these percentages are translated into numbers of voters, it appears that approximately 604,850 Catholics voted for Florio while 384,473 Catholics voted for Courter.[24] In other words, of 989,323 estimated Catholic voters (projecting from the *Times*-CBS sample), 61 percent went for Florio while 39 percent went for Courter. Three out of five New Jersey Catholics voted for the pro-choice gubernatorial candidate in the 1989 New Jersey election. Note that the breakdown among Catholics appeared to reflect the breakdown among voters generally. Thus, despite their church's strong anti-abortion position, New Jersey Catholic voters were virtually indistinguishable from non-Catholic New Jerseyans in their 1989 vote.

Were the bishops' efforts more successful in persuading Catholics to vote for pro-life Assembly members? This too seems unlikely, given the shift of the assembly from a pro-life majority in 1988-89 to a pro-choice majority in 1990-91. However, it is extremely difficult to draw any conclusions here. Available data do not support assertions that the state legislative elections were a referendum on abortion, or on any other issue, for that matter. According to Dodson and Burnbauer, only 4 percent of voters statewide said abortion was a decisive issue in their choice of Assembly representatives. In general, Dodson and Burnbauer found that voters seem to reject issue-voting in state legislative contests. Other factors—incumbency, political party, and name recognition—appear to be more salient in voter choices.[25]

To summarize this account of the activities of the New Jersey bishops during the 1989 election campaign, we may say the following. The bishops mounted an intensive effort, using grassroots mobilization and media access (access to religious and secular media) to persuade Catholics and non-Catholics to elect legislators who would restrict abortion. Moreover, in carrying out this concerted effort, the bishops did not violate constitutional norms of church-state separation, and they were within their rights, as citizens and as religious leaders, in addressing the moral dimensions of public issues during the election campaign. They were careful to adhere strictly to the letter of the law concerning electoral activity by tax-exempt religious institutions. Indeed, the actions of New Jersey bishops were moderate, reasonable, restrained, and cautious—when compared with measures taken subsequently by bishops in other states—for example, denial of communion to a pro-choice assemblywoman in California, threats of excommunication to Catholic lawmakers who morally oppose but publicly support legalized abortion, and actual excommunication of clinic administrators. However, despite the bishops' intensified efforts to shape public opinion, their campaign did not dissuade 61 percent of New Jersey Catholics from voting for a pro-choice Catholic governor, nor did their efforts counter the movement of the new Assembly in a pro-choice direction.

The New Jersey Bishops and Abortion Politics in the 1990s

The activities of the New Jersey bishops intensified in 1990 as the American Catholic hierarchy grew more concerned about Catholic voters and officials who claimed to oppose abortion on moral grounds while favoring its continued legalization. At its biennial meeting in November 1989, the NCCB stated that "No Catholic can responsibly take a 'pro-choice' stand when the 'choice' in question involves the taking of human life."[26] In the aftermath of the *Webster* decision, this statement seems to have spurred individual bishops across the country to intervene more directly in politics generally and in political campaigns in particular. In New Jersey, church sanctions against pro-choice Catholic politicians took the form mostly of speaker bans at church functions.

To commemorate the seventeenth anniversary of *Roe v. Wade* in January 1990, the New Jersey bishops issued "Choose Life: An Expanded Statement of Principle." This lengthy document criticized feminist arguments for women's moral autonomy and rejected arguments of public officials who personally oppose but publicly support legalized abortion. The bishops argued that "To recognize that an act is immoral obliges one in conscience to take appropriate action to prevent it." They did not specify which actions or policies were appropriate to prevent abortion but simply assumed that restrictive measures were the most suitable policy options. However, they did "call upon legislators to provide substantial funding to support the life-saving, life-affirming programs of families, churches and agencies on behalf of those (pregnant women, the elderly, the infirm) in difficult situations."[27]

In May 1990, Camden Bishop James McHugh, disturbed at the number of Catholic politicians switching from a pro-life to a pro-choice political position, declared that pro-choice Catholics in public office should be barred from speaking at church-sponsored events and serving in any church ministry or office. He also said the Knights of Columbus should consider excluding Catholic pro-choice politicians from the organization. (The Knights of Columbus is a Catholic fraternal organization which numbers many Catholic politicians among its members, including Senator Edward Kennedy and Governor Jim Florio).

McHugh subsequently issued a policy directive to the priests of his own Camden diocese stating that pro-choice Catholics in public life should not be considered for such positions as deacon, lector, or Eucharistic minister. Nor should such Catholics be invited to speak at graduation ceremonies, lectures or other public events where the invited speaker is granted "positive recognition or approval."[28]

Predictably, Bishop McHugh's new policy provoked controversy since it appeared to be an attack on Governor Florio. A spokesman for the bishop denied that the diocese of Camden was "out on a witch hunt for prochoice politicians." However, when pressed by reporters, McHugh explained that Governor Florio and his high-level appointees would fall within the restrictions of the policy. "If Gov. Florio still claims to be a Catholic, then yes, he would fall into these categories and he would be somebody who would not be welcome to speak. In our diocese, he would not be given any honorary position. There's no question he has taken a strong pro-choice position."[29]

In response, a spokesman for the Governor said Florio is Roman Catholic but considers his religious beliefs to be private. "He has said in the past that his religious beliefs are a personal matter, and not a matter for discussion." The Governor's spokesman said Florio subscribes to the constitutional separation of church and state, and also believes that a woman has a right to choose whether or not to terminate a pregnancy.

While Bishop McHugh denied that his original remarks were aimed at Governor Florio, the Governor apparently did not think so, for two days later he resigned from the Knights of Columbus "in order that the Knights would not be embarrassed or placed in a difficult position."[30] While Florio explained his action as taken to spare the Knights embarrassment, it could also be perceived as an instant response to the bishop's threat—that is, Florio's immediate resignation preempted his bishop and the Knights from expelling him.

In taking on New Jersey's Governor, Bishop McHugh staked out a position as the most forceful member of the New Jersey hierarchy on this issue. Bishop McHugh, it should be noted, has a long history of involvement in abortion politics; in 1966 while serving as the director of the Family Life Bureau of the United States Catholic Conference, he invited a small number of abortion opponents to serve as advisors to a "National Right to Life Committee" (legally incorporated after *Roe* and now the dominant anti-abortion organization).[31] He currently serves as a member of the NCCB Committee for Pro-Life Activities. Since McHugh issued his speaker ban, two other New Jersey bishops have followed suit: Bishop John Reiss of the Trenton diocese and Bishop Edward Hughes of Metuchen. However, Archbishop McCarrick has not instituted such a policy in Newark, and Bishop Frank Rodimer of Paterson decided not to censure or ban Catholic pro-choice lawmakers, preferring persuasion to coercion.[32]

Recent Developments in Abortion Politics in New Jersey

Since January 1990, Governor Florio's administration has been at the helm in Trenton and the 1990-1991 state legislature has been preoccupied with major policy initiatives. In his first six months in office, Governor Florio overhauled the state's automobile insurance system, pushed through legislation banning assault weapons, slashed budget expenditures, doubled the income tax for those earning more than $100,000 gross income, increased the sales tax from 6 to 7 percent while expanding its coverage, boosted taxes on alcohol and cigarettes, and radically changed the way public schools are financed by giving millions to poor and middle-class school districts at the expense of more affluent ones. Reeling under the impact of Florio's tax policies, Jersey citizens instigated a major tax revolt in the Garden State which, like other states in the Northeast, suffers from declining state revenues and fiscal problems in the nationwide recession which began in late 1990.

In the midst of these major changes, abortion politics has receded somewhat into the background. Nevertheless, while the abortion issue no longer commands center-stage, the political struggle over abortion has continued—principally in these areas: the November 1990 Congressional elections, the introduction of new policy proposals in the state legislature, and Protestant and Jewish opposition to the initiatives of the Catholic bishops.

In the 1990 Congressional elections, the abortion issue was clearly overshadowed by the tax revolt against Gov. Florio. Opposition to Florio tax policies was so strong that it almost cost Democratic Senator Bill Bradley his U.S. Senate seat. Running against a relatively unknown Republican challenger, Christine Whitman, Bradley barely managed to survive the anti-tax, anti-Democratic onslaught. Since both Bradley and Whitman were pro-choice, abortion was not an issue in their Senate race.

Abortion was an issue in a few Congressional contests, especially in New Jersey's fourth Congressional district where Representative Christopher Smith, co-chair of the Congressional Pro-Life Caucus and a Catholic, was challenged by Mark Setaro, a pro-choice Democrat and also a Catholic. Setaro campaigned in part on the abortion issue, arguing that a woman, not the government, must have the choice to decide whether or not to have an abortion. Since Setaro is a church-going Catholic, his stance came to the attention of Trenton Bishop John C. Reiss, who barred him from serving as a lay minister and lector at his home parish. In the November election, Smith, a Republican incumbent, won handily, benefitting from the advantages of incumbency and from the tax revolt against Florio and the Democrats.

The New Jersey Congressional delegation currently stands at ten pro-choice representatives and four pro-life representatives. Its two U.S. Senators, Bill Bradley and Frank Lautenberg, are pro-choice; both voted against the nomination of David Souter to the U.S. Supreme Court in September 1990. Thus, at the federal level, the state's Congressional representatives reflect the largely pro-choice character of public opinion in New Jersey.

As for legislative initiatives, several proposed bills have been introduced in the 1990–1991 state legislature. Pro-lifers have proposed two different parental notification statutes, one in the Assembly and the other in the Senate.[33] As of this writing, both languish in committee with little prospect of being reported out for a vote. Pro-choice Assemblyman Neil Cohen has introduced two bills relating to abortion rights. One would impose penalties for blockading access to a medical facility. The second would enable rape victims who become pregnant and choose to have an abortion to receive funds from the Violent Crimes Compensation Board to cover the cost of the procedure. Both bills are pending, with reasonably good chances of passage in the Democratically-controlled legislature.

Finally, the post-*Webster* activities of New Jersey's Catholic bishops have triggered a counter-response by the state's Protestant and Jewish clergy. In October 1990, the New Jersey Religious Coalition for Abortion Rights (RCAR) issued a lengthy statement as a theological rebuttal to the January statement of the Catholic bishops. The RCAR statement asserted that present law regarding abortion, as defined in *Roe v. Wade*, "in no way encroaches on the rights of a religious group to practice its faith." However, they argued that "a more restrictive law would violate the rights of numerous religious groups and denominations who affirm a woman's right to choose. To silence the voices of these believers will stifle religious freedom for all."[34]

The RCAR statement was noteworthy for the diversity of religious groups represented. Signers included Presbyterian, Episcopal, Methodist, Lutheran, United Church of Christ, and Unitarian-Universalist members and clergy, as well as Catholics for a Free Choice-South Jersey. Also signers were members of Conservative and Reform branches of Judaism, B'nai B'rith Women, Temple Sisterhoods, the American Jewish Committee, and the American Jewish Congress.

In its "religious affirmation in support of choice," RCAR chairmen said they "resented [the bishops'] insinuation that their position is the only moral, religious and traditional position on abortion." Claiming that the Catholic bishops' stance "certainly does not represent the views of all the religions in the state," the coalition emphasized that "the majority of New Jersey's religious denominations are solidly pro-choice."

The RCAR statement also protested "the anti-democratic spirit of the anti-choice movement," arguing that, "In a true democracy, the acceptable approach to such fundamental disagreement is tolerance of difference . . . especially when religious difference is at the root." RCAR signers noted further that "In a democracy, politicians are primarily accountable to a pluralistic constituency, not to their church," and they therefore asked "those who disagree with our own theology to nonetheless respect this boundary."

The RCAR statement contained a lengthy biblical, theological, and ethical analysis of abortion and the status of the fetus. It concluded with the suggestion that the entire religious community should be able to work together for a more just society that would result in fewer unwanted pregnancies and make the choice to bear children a more realistic option.

In response, Bishop McHugh of Camden rejected the RCAR statement as "theologically unconvincing, insulting, divisive, morally confused, and dis-honest." He deplored the RCAR attempt "to reduce the abortion decision to an untouchable private choice of women," and insisted that any respectable ethical analysis of abortion must take into account a variety of factors. Bishop McHugh accused RCAR signers of misrepresenting, even denigrating Catholic teaching and said that if the RCAR statement was representative of the thinking of other religious bodies, he considered "the possibility of interfaith dialogue in New Jersey seriously threatened." He concluded that RCAR's proposal was "not an invitation to dialogue, but a throwback to the anti-Catholic bigotry of the past."[35]

The New Jersey Bishops and Abortion Politics: Analysis and Evaluation

How might we evaluate the efforts of the New Jersey bishops to influence abortion policy? One approach is to analyze the bishops' efforts in terms of mass politics and elite politics. Traditionally, Catholic Church leaders in the United States have quietly engaged in elite politics; that is, they have used their power and influence, perceived or real, to lobby state legislators and other public officials to achieve desired ends. For historical reasons (namely, Protes-tant fears of papal dominance), they have maintained a low profile, refusing to endorse political candidates or otherwise to engage in partisan politics. What is remarkable about the American Church's crusade against legalized abortion is that the church has openly entered the arena of mass politics with a view to mobilizing and influencing public opinion, that is, the views of ordinary voters and of public officials, especially Catholic lawmakers. This process began, of course, with the official church's reaction to *Roe v. Wade* and is exemplified in the NCCB's 1975 Pastoral Plan for Pro-Life Activities. Moreover, the church has, on occasion, come close to abandoning its non-partisan posture—as in the 1984 election when several prominent bishops attacked Democratic vice-presidential candidate, Geraldine Ferraro, for her position on abortion policy.

In the post-*Webster* period, New Jersey was the first heavily Catholic state to hold elections and so it became a testing ground for the bishops' efforts to influence mass politics at the state level. In New Jersey in 1989 and 1990, a number of tactics were tried: use of parishes as bases of political mobilization in Project Life Roll; efforts to publicly pressure recalcitrant Catholic officehold-ers by banning them from speaking at church functions or serving as parish officials; and use of the media to communicate to ordinary citizens a message which was different in rhetoric and substance from previous Catholic proposals on abortion policy.

These efforts of the bishops to shape abortion policy can be evaluated from the standpoint of political effectiveness and from an internal, ecclesiological perspective. In terms of political effectiveness, we should note the obvious—that Catholics, like other Americans, have rights to participate in the political process, rights which extend to bishops and clergy as well as to ordinary churchgoers. So the question to ask about the political tactics of the bishops is not whether the bishops have a right to seek to influence the policy process (they do), but whether the tactics the bishops use are appropriate means to achieve their policy ends.

From both an ecclesiological perspective and a political standpoint, the effectiveness of Project Life Roll is questionable. In the context of a 1989 New Jersey gubernatorial campaign which presented a clear choice between a pro-life Protestant Republican and a pro-choice Catholic Democrat, Project Life Roll came dangerously close to partisan endorsement of a candidate. Moreover, in authorizing use of Sunday Mass to enroll Catholics in a citizens' pro-life lobby network, the New Jersey bishops abandoned a broad respect-life strategy in favor of a single-issue focus on abortion. In their pre-election statements, the Jersey bishops neglected to remind parishioners about the poor, the handicapped, unjust tax structures, the needs of the elderly, the plight of AIDS victims, the homeless, the increasing numbers of abused and impoverished children, pollution, violence towards women, the destruction of the environ-ment, and other serious problems. By their words and actions, they signaled a concern with one issue alone—protection of fetal life. This departure from a consistent life ethic was typical of the American bishops' post-*Webster* approach to abortion politics nationwide—at least in the first year following the 1989 decision.

Project Life Roll was also questionable from an ecclesiological perspective. The Catholic Mass is an inappropriate forum for conducting political mobili-zation campaigns. It could be argued that using sermon time to exhort a captive audience of congregants to sign political pledge cards is coercive of conscience and disrespectful to Catholic citizens who have a right and a duty to make their own judgments about sound public policy. Within the church bishops are moral teachers, but in a pluralist democracy members of the hierarchy do not necessarily have either the competence or the right to tell citizens how to vote or what policies to support.

Finally, Project Life Roll was imprudent because it politicized the Mass and because it suggested that there is a single policy position which all Catholics should adopt. There are no automatic answers in Christian theology and Catholic teaching to the vexing questions of public policy raised by the abortion issue. Abortion policy must balance the conflicting claims of different interests (believers, agnostics, atheists) as well as the competing values of freedom, order, equity, justice, and privacy. There is no single Catholic solution to this *policy* dilemma just as there is no single Jewish or no single Methodist answer.

The propriety and effectiveness of church sanctions against pro-choice Catholic lawmakers also seems questionable. Catholic public officials such as New Jersey Governor Jim Florio, New York Governor Mario Cuomo, California State Senator Lucy Killea, California Congresswoman Nancy Pelosi, Rhode Island Congresswoman Claudine Schneider, and New Jersey State Senator Henry McNamara[36] must represent Catholics and non-Catholics alike. In a religiously diverse democracy, they must make public policy for believers and non-believers. If the church's moral teaching against abortion is not persuasive to a majority of the citizenry, there is little warrant for using the coercive sanctions of public law to ban abortion.

Moreover, a secular audience in a democratic society is probably not going to be enlightened, much less persuaded, by the spectacle of church authorities resorting to ecclesiastical sanctions to keep Catholic lawmakers in line. In this sense, the bishops' sanctioning of public officials is counter-productive and self-defeating. The church insists that abortion is a moral not a religious issue, an action which all women and men can agree is wrong. However, by publicly threatening Catholic citizens and lawmakers with canonical penalties, the bishops only confirm that abortion is a sectarian issue, a Catholic problem, a matter of ecclesiology rather than of public policy.

Sanctioning Catholic officials in the post-*Webster* era has been less severe in New Jersey than in other states. Nevertheless, many Catholic lawmakers have expressed outrage at the mere mention of sanctions or ecclesiastical penalties. In a political race between a pro-life Catholic and a pro-choice Catholic (such as the 1990 Smith-Setaro contest in New Jersey's Fourth Congressional District), a bishop's application of ecclesiastical sanctions to the pro-choice Catholic politician is in effect partisanship in an election campaign—something that American Catholic bishops have traditionally avoided. It also appears to be issuing instructions to voters from the pulpit, an act not calculated to endear the clergy to Catholic voters or politicians.

Like their fellow citizens, American Catholics are committed to the principle of church-state separation and disapprove of clerical meddling in political campaigns. The bishops seem to have realized this. After the blitz of episcopal attention from June 1989 to June 1990 (the first year after *Webster,*) the Catholic hierarchy settled down and hired the public relations firm of Hill & Knowlton to advise them on how best to convey their message to the American public. In the 1990s, the NCCB's approach to abortion politics stresses an appeal to the middle ground, based on poll data which indicate that many Americans support legal abortion, yet oppose abortion on demand. This new strategy focuses on the large number of abortions performed in the United States and describes most of these as "abortion for convenience." The bishops characterize such abortions as selfishly motivated and do not understand or accept the feminist or civil libertarian conception of abortion as a question of a woman's right to decide. Moreover, they contend that a true feminist would not permit, condone, or practice abortion. Tactically, they have begun to publicize and support pro-life feminist groups, and to stress the church's obligations to assist involuntarily pregnant women by creating alternatives to abortion. Finally, the bishops' new strategy insists that one cannot be Catholic and pro-choice with respect to public policy. They urge Catholic officeholders to endorse restrictive policies and Catholic voters to support pro-life candidates.

In their statements and actions in 1989 and 1990, the Catholic bishops of New Jersey anticipated the substance, rhetoric, and tactics of the NCCB's post-*Webster* approach. During the 1989 election campaign, for example, Archbishop McCarrick acknowledged the political reality that most New Jerseyans would not support a complete ban on abortion. He therefore indicated a willingness to compromise—to accommodate the so-called "hard cases" of abortion (rape, incest, threat to woman's life) while appealing to the public for a legal ban on most abortions. Moreover, in their public pronouncements, the New Jersey bishops made little effort to understand the concrete realities of women's lives and they rejected outright feminist arguments for women's moral autonomy. The bishops insisted that the substance of one's decisions is at least as important as the procedural right to make such reproductive decisions.

The tactics used by the hierarchy in New Jersey also anticipated strategies later employed by other bishops in other states. These included heavy reliance upon secular and religious media, use of parishes and diocesan pro-life commissions as bases of political mobilization, and public pressure on Catholic officeholders and candidates to support restrictive policies. However, the actions of the Jersey bishops were moderate and restrained compared with measures taken subsequently by bishops in other states. In New Jersey, Bishop McHugh and two other bishops resorted to speaker bans and to denial of minor parish posts to pro-choice Catholic politicians. However, McHugh stopped short of calling for excommunication and denial of the sacraments to discipline Catholic supporters of legal abortion. Describing such penalties as "spiritual penalties which are primarily intended to deter people from obtaining or performing abortions," McHugh argued that the use of spiritual penalties is not the most appropriate approach when dealing with Catholics in public life. Perhaps the caution and restraint shown by the New Jersey bishops in the two years since *Webster* is something which other bishops in other states might emulate as they confront abortion politics in the 1990s.

Conclusion

What is the future of abortion politics in New Jersey? For the present, the Garden State appears to be firmly pro-choice despite a well-organized pro-life network which draws upon the Catholic Church and a variety of fundamentalist and conservative evangelical groups. As of spring 1991, the only pro-life legislation which has any chance of passage is a parental notification bill; however, two such bills are currently bottled up in committee with little chance of getting to the floor for a vote. Even if the state legislature were to pass such a statute, the threat of a veto by Governor Florio is very real. Although the entire state legislature is up for reelection in November 1991, the current expectation is that the legislature will remain largely supportive of the right to legal abortion.

What policy changes can we expect in New Jersey if the Supreme Court reverses *Roe v. Wade* and returns the abortion issue to the states? Like Connecticut and Maryland, New Jersey has a law on the books which is a formidable obstacle to the passage of restrictive abortion laws. In 1982 the New Jersey Supreme Court held that the state must fund Medicaid abortions to save the life or preserve the health of the mother. In *Right to Choose v. Byrne,* which invalidated a state statute prohibiting Medicaid funding of abortions except in life-threatening pregnancies, the state Supreme Court ruled the law unconstitutional because it denied equal protection to women who sought abortions for health reasons rather than for life-threatening ones. The *Right to Choose* court found the New Jersey constitution to be more expansive than the federal constitution in protecting fundamental rights, and the court therefore felt free to reach a decision contrary to that reached by the U.S. Supreme Court in *Harris v. McRae* (1980).[37]

Right to Choose v. Byrne is viewed as a strong constitutional guarantee of abortion rights in New Jersey. Because of this state supreme court ruling, any restriction on abortion would probably be ruled in violation of the state constitution. Even if *Roe v. Wade* were overturned, restrictions on abortion still would conflict with the state constitution. Thus pro-life activists contend that no substantial antiabortion legislation can be passed until the state constitution is amended. They have proposed an amendment which reads: "Nothing in this Constitution requires abortion to be funded, provided, or facilitated; nor forbids the legislature to regulate and restrict abortion or the funding thereof."[38] If this were passed by voters, the state legislature would be free either to restrict abortion or to affirm abortion rights.

As for pro-choice activists, they rely increasingly on *Right to Choose v. Byrne* for constitutional protection of abortion rights in New Jersey in the event *Roe v. Wade* is reversed. The equal protection reasoning of *Right to Choose* even provides grounds, in their view, for a possible court challenge should the state enact a parental notification law. Their reasoning is that a young woman has as much right to equal access to abortion as an adult woman. Beyond this, pro-choice advocates are considering whether a law similar to the 1990 Connecticut statute, which declared a woman's right to abortion up to fetal viability, could be enacted in New Jersey.

Much of this discussion of strategy for the future is speculative and conjectural. What seems clear is that New Jersey pro-life activists will continue efforts to restrict abortion in this state which at present has one of the most liberal abortion laws in the country. And if the Catholic bishops' activities from 1989 through 1991 are any indication, the institutional church will continue its efforts to shape abortion politics and policy through legislative lobbying and through political mobilization of Catholics.

Notes

1. Debra L. Dodson and Laura D. Burnbauer, *Election 1989: The Abortion Issue in New Jersey and Virginia* (New Brunswick, New Jersey: Eagleton Institute of Politics, Rutgers University, 1990), p. 7.

2. *Right to Choose v. Byrne* 450 A2d 925, 91 NJ 287 (1982).

3. Ian Jones, "Down Home, Bishops' Groups Ply Politics," *National Catholic Reporter,* September 16, 1988, pp. 11–12.

4. Jones, p. 12.

5. Eagleton Institute of Politics, Rutgers University, *The Eagleton-Star-Ledger Poll,* March and October 1989.

6. David Blomquist, Michael Rappeport, and Paul Lehmann, "Abortion After *Webster:* The Florio Victory in New Jersey," unpublished paper presented at 86th Annual Meeting of the American Political Science Association, San Francisco, September 1990.

7. *Boston Globe,* April 13, 1989, p. 23.

8. Interview with Janice Ballou, director of the Eagleton–Star-Ledger Poll, December 6, 1989.

9. *The Eagleton-Star-Ledger Poll,* March and October 1989.

10. *New York Times/Channel 2 News New Jersey Election Day Poll,* November 7, 1989. Channel 2 is the local affiliate (WCBS-TV) of CBS. Copy supplied to me by the Eagleton Institute of Politics.

11. For a description of New Jersey pro-life groups active in the 1989 election campaign, see Mary C. Segers "Semantics & Style in an Abortion Campaign: Defining the Issue in New Jersey," in *Commonweal,* January 12, 1990, p. 12.

12. See Debra L. Dodson & Laura D. Burnbauer, *Election 1989: The Abortion Issue in New Jersey and Virginia,* Executive Summary, p. 2; also Dodson & Burnbauer, *Election 1989,* pp. 37–108; also M.C. Segers, "Semantics & Style in an Abortion Campaign," *Commonweal,* January 12, 1990, p. 11. Personal interview with Debra Dodson constituted an additional source, October 1989.

13. *Star-Ledger,* November 10, 1989, p. 16. Kathleen Donovan, Chair of the New Jersey State Republican Party during the Courter campaign, confirmed the importance of the abortion issue in the 1989 election. Interview with Donovan, December 4, 1990.

14. Press Release, Office of Communications and Public Relations, Archdiocese of Newark, July 3, 1989.

15. Monica Maske, "McCarrick Issues a Strong Pro-Life Message," *Star-Ledger,* July 14, 1989, p. 1.

16. Steve Peter, "Pro-Life March on Trenton: Rally Draws Thousands," *Catholic Advocate,* (Newark archdiocesan newspaper) September 27, 1989, p. 1.

17. Archbishop Theodore E. McCarrick, "'Abortion on Demand' Opposed," *Catholic Advocate,* September 27, 1989, p. 20.

18. Letter of Archbishop Theodore E. McCarrick, printed in *Catholic Advocate,* November 1, 1989, pp. 1 and 4.

19. Anthony F. Shannon, "McCarrick Abortion Letter to be Read at all Weekend Masses," *Star-Ledger,* October 28, 1989, p. 5.

20. "Choose Life," Statement of Catholic Bishops of New Jersey, October 30, 1989. Copy supplied to me by William Bolan, Executive Director, New Jersey Catholic Conference.

21. Text reprinted in Parish Bulletin of St. Teresa of Avila Church, Summit, New Jersey, October 1, 1989.

22. Interview with Rita Martin, November 1989.

23. Dodson & Burnbauer, *Election 1989: The Abortion Issue in New Jersey and Virginia,* Executive Summary, p. 2.

24. According to figures supplied by the Office of Legislative Services, New Jersey Legislature, Governor Florio received 62 percent of the vote in the November 1989 elections, or 1,374,661 votes. Jim Courter received 38 percent of the vote, or 835,811 votes. I have arrived at estimates of Catholic voters by calculating on the basis of percentages from the *Times/CBS* poll (reported above in the text). These figures are, of course, approximations based on the exit poll.

25. Dodson & Burnbauer, *Election 1989: The Abortion Issue in New Jersey and Virginia,* Executive Summary, pp. 8–10. See also David Wald, "Abortion Issue Called a Key to Elections," *Star-Ledger,* July 17, 1990, p. 1.

26. *Origins* 19:18 (November 27, 1989), p. 189.

27. "Choose Life: An Expanded Statement of Principle," *Catholic Advocate,* January 17, 1990, p. 11.

28. Patricia Cappon, "Bishop Urges Sanctions Against Catholic Politicians Who Are Pro-Choice, *Star-Ledger,* May 19, 1990, p. 6. For the complete text of Bishop McHugh's speech of May 18, 1990, see "Abortion and the Officeholder," *Origins* 20:3 (May 31, 1990), pp. 40–42.

29. *Newsletter,* Right to Choose, June-July 1990, p. 2. Right to Choose is an advocacy organization in New Jersey.

30. *New York Times,* May 22, 1990, p. B2.

31. See James R. Kelly's discussion in chapter nine of the early years of the pro-life movement.

32. See Robert Schwaneberg, "A 'Gag' on Speaking: Trenton Bishop Bars Pro-Choice Politicians," *Star-Ledger,* July 31, 1990, p. 1. For Paterson Bishop Frank Rodimer's decision not to ban or censure Catholic pro-choice legislators, see Michele DiGirolamo, "Pro-Choice Officials Won't Be Punished," *Daily Record,* July 30, 1990, p. A1.

33. On June 27, 1990, State Senator Francis J. McManimon introduced S2853, a proposed parental notification statute requiring forty-eight hours notice to at least one parent of an unmarried pregnant minor before she may have an abortion. In February 1991, Assemblymembers John Rooney, Marion Crecco, and Chuck Hardwick introduced A4483, a bill requiring notification of both parents (if they live at the same address). See also *Star-Ledger,* June 29, 1990, p. 33.

34. The New Jersey Religious Coalition for Abortion Rights, *Religious Affirmation in Support of Choice,* October 22, 1990. Interview with Myra Terry and Kathleen Sharts of New Jersey RCAR, January 22, 1991.

35. *Catholic Advocate,* November 7, 1990, p. 19.

36. State Senator Henry McNamara, a Republican and a Catholic, wrote an open letter to his constituents in 1990, in which he endorsed the right of the individual to decide the abortion question and supported the New Jersey State Supreme Court decision permitting Medicaid funding for abortion. He also indicated support for policies which offer concrete alternatives to abortion and stated that "Parents should be given reasonable opportunity to counsel their daughters." Letter of State Senator Henry P. McNamara to Right to Choose, dated December 6, 1990. See also Peter Yerkes, "A Matter of Conscience," *The Record,* March 5, 1990.

37. *Right to Choose v. Byrne* 450 A2d 925, 91 NJ 287 (1982). See also *Harris v. McRae* 448 U.S. 297 (1980).

38. *Catholic Advocate,* March 14, 1990, p. 4. In March 1990, a legislative conference of Citizens Concerned for Life suggested that the first priority of pro-life groups should be an amendment to the state constitution to overturn the New Jersey Supreme Court decision in *Right to Choose v. Byrne.* See also *The Archbishop's Pro-Life Commission Newsletter,* fall 1990, p. 2, in which the Public Policy Committee of the Newark Archdiocese's Pro-Life Commission states that "A concerted effort will be made in the next 2 or 3 years to present an amendment to the N.J. Constitution. The N.J. Supreme Court has made far-reaching pro-abortion decisions that, in effect, prevent any meaningful restrictions on abortion. The only means to pass strong pro-life laws in New Jersey, even should *Roe v. Wade* be overturned by the U.S. Supreme Court, will be to amend the N.J. constitution."

3

The First Test of Webster's Effect: The Florida Church

Rebecca M. Salokar

The eyes of the country and the eyes of a lot of the world are on Florida. Whatever happens in Florida is going to be viewed as very significant. . . . If Florida does nothing, that puts a dampening effect on antiabortion rights legislators in other states. Florida is not known as a place where the Legislature is heavily pro-choice.

—Molly Yard, President, National Organization for Women

The landmark Supreme Court case, *Webster v. Reproductive Health Services,*[1] was but hours old when Bob Martinez, the Republican governor of Florida, sought to put his state at the forefront of the resuscitated national abortion battle. All indicators suggested that Florida was one of the easier targets for the antiabortion forces seeking to limit popular access to abortions through state legislation. Mobilization of pro-life forces ran at a fever pitch across the state with the Roman Catholic Church, both institutionally and through its individual members, playing a significant leadership role. Despite the efforts of the governor, the church, and its allies, the saga that played out from mid-1989 through the elections of 1990 produced no significant changes in Florida's abortion laws. Two years after *Webster,* the hope and optimism of the pro-life movement in Florida has faded.

In this chapter, I discuss the Florida abortion battle surrounding the special legislative session of 1989 and the statewide elections of 1990. Of particular importance is the role that the Catholic Church played in organizing and energizing the grassroots pro-life forces in Florida and the very public, albeit religious, campaign sponsored by the church hierarchy. Guided by the directives of the National Conference of Catholic Bishops (NCCB), the Florida experience suggests that political and ecumenical activity on the pro-life front shifted significantly from the national church leadership to the state, diocesan, and parish levels in the period immediately before and after the *Webster* decision.

Following a brief description of the Florida political landscape and a history of abortion in the state, I discuss the organization of the Catholic Church in

Florida and its pre-1989 pro-life activities. The heart of this chapter focuses on the church and its role in the 1989 special legislative session and the efforts of the pro-life forces to influence the elections of 1990. Finally, I review the current state of affairs with respect to the church and pro-life activities given the 1991 legislative session and planning for the 1992 elections.

Florida: A Sketch of Culture, Politics, and Abortion History

Florida is, in some sense, a state divided both culturally and economically. Historically, social scientists identified two divisions within the state: the northern and central, agricultural-based region and the southern and coastal, service-based region. Over the past fifteen years, however, the "I-4 Corridor," an east-west tract stretching from Daytona Beach through Orlando to Tampa has gained its own political and economic importance. Reflective of south Florida in its reliance on tourism, high density development, and rapid growth, the "corridor" has maintained many of the conservative political traditions of north Florida but with less predictability.

These regional differences were reflected in a 1989 poll conducted by the Institute for Public Opinion Research at Florida International University on the abortion and religion issue. When asked whether a woman should be able to obtain a legal abortion, 38 percent of the respondents statewide supported abortions for any reason, 42.5 percent for limited circumstances and 17.4 percent responded "not at all." Clear differences emerged between south Florida where 43.6 percent supported abortions in all cases and north Florida where only 34.4 percent supported unlimited access. The central and Treasure Coast or "I-4 Corridor" had the highest percentage of respondents who believed abortions were unacceptable in all circumstances (19.0 percent) and only 32.4 percent thought there should be unlimited access.[2] These same respondents in central Florida were the most positive about the importance that religion played in their lives, although north Floridians appear to be more active in church groups.[3]

Florida has been traditionally viewed as a fairly conservative state, dominated by Southern Democrats in the political spectrum. Recent changes in electoral behavior suggest that the Republican party is gaining a strong foothold, especially among the growing Hispanic population of south Florida and the northern, more traditionally "southern" population. Republican voter registrations have increased from 29 percent in 1980, to 39 percent in 1990 and the Republican party has gained 15 percent more seats in the state legislature in the past decade.[4] In the 1988 presidential election, Florida was the fifth most supportive state for George Bush, registering a 60.9 percent vote for the Republican candidate.

Given this southern conservatism and an increasing alliance with the Republican party, it is not surprising that Florida is one of the few states that has consistently sought to impose more restrictive abortion laws. Abortion was legalized by Florida statute in 1972 and abortion clinics soon came under licensing and reporting requirements. In 1979, the Florida legislature mandated that pregnant women consult their husbands prior to obtaining an abortion and that minors obtain parental or judicial consent in seeking an abortion. Although both facets of this legislation were rejected by the federal courts, parental consent legislation resurfaced in 1988 and played a critical role in the 1989 abortion battle.

As of December 1989, Chapter 390 of the Florida Statutes permitted abortions under the following conditions:

- Abortions could be performed at any time prior to birth. However, third trimester abortions must be certified by two physicians as necessary to save the mother's life or preserve her health (including emotional and mental health).
- Abortions must be performed by licensed physicians.
- Abortions must be performed in state-licensed clinics, hospitals or physicians' offices with the exception of emergencies and third trimester abortions which must be performed in a hospital.
- Written consent must be given by the woman or her guardian prior to an abortion.
- Clinics must be licensed by the Department of Health and Rehabilitative Services (HRS) and all providers must maintain accurate records and file reports on abortions performed.
- If an abortion is performed during viability, the doctor must "use skill, care, and diligence" to save the fetus.
- Experimentation on a live fetus is forbidden and fetal remains must be disposed of in accordance with HRS regulations.
- Medical personnel cannot be required to participate in an abortion if they disagree with the procedure as a matter of conscience.
- Abortion referral and counseling agencies must provide information on alternatives and a detailed explanation of the abortion procedure.
- In accordance with the federal Hyde Amendment, Florida Medicaid does not fund abortions except in life-threatening situations.

The Department of Health and Rehabilitative Services, the agency charged with collecting data on abortions in Florida, reported 62,539 abortions in 1988, or an abortion rate of 25.1 per 100 pregnancies.[5] This number, however, is probably depressed due to the weak reporting requirements and the lack of sanctions imposed on clinics failing to report. The Allen Guttmacher Institute estimates that 79,286 abortions were performed in Florida during that same year. The Guttmacher report also indicates that only 1 percent were performed after the twentieth week of pregnancy, while most (90 percent) were obtained during the first twelve weeks of gestation.[6]

The Church in Florida

In 1989, Florida was home to over twelve million people and growing daily. Catholics make up about 12.4 percent of the population or 1,539,058 persons.

The first Catholic diocese, St. Augustine, was founded in 1870 and served the entire state of Florida. It was not until 1958 that a second diocese was organized in Miami. With its rapid population growth, Miami became the sole Archdiocese in Florida within ten years. Now known as the Province of Miami, the state is divided into six dioceses and one archdiocese. In 1989, there were 420 parishes and forty-seven missions staffed by one archbishop, six bishops, two auxiliary bishops, 721 priests and 1431 religious women.[7]

The Florida Catholic Conference (FCC) serves as the eyes, ears, and voice of the Florida bishops in the state capital of Tallahassee as well as in Washington, D.C. Its role is "to encourage social justice and moral fortitude in secular society,"[8] while serving as the liaison between the church, its hierarchy, and government. Like the church in Florida, the FCC is a relatively young organization. It was founded in 1969, and Thomas A. Horkan has served as its sole executive director. Two associates provide support in the areas of education and social services.

The FCC not only appears before governmental bodies on behalf of the church, it also provides information to the parishes on a range of relevant social issues. For example, the FCC published a brochure in May of 1990, which specifies the various lobbying activities that parishes may participate in or initiate. Additionally, the FCC is a key participant in the annual Red Mass for state legislators and lawmakers and works closely with the Florida Council of Catholic Women (FCCW) to organize a grassroots lobbying network.[9] The FCCW and the FCC have routinely published surveys of candidates' positions on a range of social issues, including abortion, prior to state-wide elections.

In the early 1970s, when it appeared that abortion would be legalized in Florida and the United States, the existing dioceses each established their own version of a pro-life ministry. Commonly known as "Respect Life," these offices are responsible for a range of "life" issues including abortion, care for pregnant mothers, AIDS buddy programs, and care for the elderly and infirm. In following the National Conference of Catholic Bishops' Pastoral Plan for Pro-Life Activities (originally issued in 1975, reissued in 1985), the Respect Life offices promote education and public information, pastoral care for pregnant women and their children, and direct a public policy effort to insure favorable "life" legislation. Each year, October is designated as Respect Life month and a special emphasis on "life" issues is made in the parishes through sermons and activities.

As an organization, Respect Life is in the delicate position of performing ecumenical service while avoiding blatant political activities. Although it does not directly participate in political lobbying due to the tax-exempt status that the church enjoys, the Respect Life ministry plays a key role in encouraging Catholics to act individually or within their parish. Frequent activities include Walks for Life that are held every year on or near the *Roe v. Wade* anniversary by individual parishes. These serve as both fund raisers and to promote community visibility.[10]

In 1981, Monsignor John P. McNulty began conducting Respect Life Pilgrimages from St. Petersburg to a shrine at St. Augustine to pray for world peace and respect for life. What began as three pilgrimages a year has now developed into a monthly event. Known as "Msgr. Respect Life," it was Msgr. McNulty who advised the bishop of St. Petersburg in 1970, "you might want to consider starting a Respect Life program in each parish." The bishop's response was a simple, "Do it."[11]

On abortion issues, Respect Life works very closely with the Florida Right to Life (RTL) organization and its local chapters. This commonality of purpose is best exemplified in the Archdiocese of Miami where the Respect Life ministry holds concurrent meetings with the non-sectarian RTL.[12] Respect Life of Miami also participates in the South Florida Pro-Life Coalition, a network of regional pro-life organizations.

Learning to Mobilize, 1986–1988

The large mobilization of pro-life forces in 1989 and 1990 was not a spontaneous event, but rather the culmination of a growing attentiveness to the abortion issue in Florida. In the three years prior to the call for a special legislative session on abortion, a series of events provided the groundwork for increased political involvement by the Catholic Church. In this section, I discuss some of the critical experiences that served as precursors for the broad grassroots activity of 1989.

Pro-life forces perceived a major victory in 1986 when Bob Martinez, a Catholic, was elected to the governorship of the state of Florida. Previously a registered Democrat, Martinez switched parties in 1983, and became only the second Republican to serve as governor in the state since Reconstruction. His campaign positions included strong statements against abortion, in favor of parental consent for minors in acquiring abortions, and opposition to school based health clinics that provide abortion or contraceptive counseling, referral, or services.[13] Although a great many domestic and economic issues were to confront Governor Martinez during his four years of service, "life" issues seemed to head up his agenda from the start.

Just prior to Martinez's election, the Catholic bishops of Florida mobilized their dioceses and the FCC against a legislative plan to establish school-based health clinics. These clinics, in addition to providing a wide range of services, would have also offered information on sexually-transmitted diseases and contraception. In an April 1986 pastoral letter, the Florida bishops criticized the public school system for its failure to effectively educate students and curtail "the high incidence of teenage pregnancy, premarital sex and promiscuity, venereal disease, abortion, and the rising rate of sex-oriented crimes."[14] The FCC successfully engaged in direct lobbying efforts to block the funding of school-based health clinics and parishioners were encouraged to oppose the funding plans in letters to then-Governor Bob Graham and their legislators.

Earlier that year, Joan Andrews, a Catholic pro-life activist, was arrested at an antiabortion demonstration at a clinic in Pensacola. Charged and subsequently convicted of burglary, criminal mischief, and resisting arrest without violence, Ms. Andrews was sentenced to five years in state custody in September of 1986. The sentence far exceeded the Florida Sentencing Guidelines of 364 days in a county facility, making "St. Joan" a hero and a martyr for the pro-life movement in Florida.

Life Walks were held across the state during 1986 and 1987, sponsored in part by the Catholic Respect Life ministry in conjunction with the Right to Life organization and other pro-life groups. Catholic participation was evident in an April 1986 march where Bishop Thomas V. Daily of the Diocese of Palm Beach addressed the participants. Additionally, the *Florida Catholic,* a state-wide newspaper that served five dioceses, featured an article on Jean Doyle, the executive director of the Florida Right to Life organization and a Catholic. Right To Life was credited with sending 30,000 postcards to its members just prior to the November elections, supporting and identifying pro-life candidates.[15]

Three pro-life bills, including a parental consent requirement, were introduced in the state legislature in 1987, and were subsequently defeated in committee. The FCC brought its lobbying forces to Tallahassee and filled the hearing room with Catholic women in support of the bills. The defeat, however, was merely a precursor to the 1989 legislative session in which the same committee, chaired by the same legislator, would stymie the progress of other antiabortion legislation.

Pro-life activists mobilized a year in advance of Pope John Paul's visit to Miami in September of 1987, to ensure that the fourteen abortion clinics located in Dade County would not be operational during the Papal visit. A coalition effort, the Pro-Life Non-Violent Action Project, publicized its intentions and sought local support. Interestingly, the Archdiocese of Miami went out of its way to announce that it was not sponsoring this drive, but that out-of-state groups were the key participants.[16] Although abortion clinics remained open during the papal visit, several well-attended pro-life demonstrations curtailed business at a few clinics and merited media attention.

A school-based health clinic for a Miami high school was again funded by the legislature in mid-1987, in the amount of $600,000. Although birth control was only one of the twenty-four services to be offered, Governor Martinez used his line item veto to block the program. In a statement issued through his press secretary, Martinez announced, "We are philosophically opposed to clinics that also do sex counseling."[17]

Joan Andrews, the symbol for pro-life activists in Florida, remained in jail serving her five-year sentence throughout 1987, despite pressure by the church and pro-life groups on Governor Martinez and the cabinet to commute her sentence. Martinez clearly wanted to release Ms. Andrews, but it was not until October of 1988, that the governor garnered the necessary three cabinet votes to commute the sentence. Ms. Andrews served a total of two years in state prison for entering an abortion clinic and removing the electrical cord from an abortion suction machine in an unattended room. Incidentally, Ms. Andrews is still active in pro-life activities in Florida primarily through Operation Rescue.

On June 15th, 1988, Governor Martinez signed into law Florida's second attempt at requiring parental consent for an abortion for a minor. Tied to an abortion clinic licensing bill that was being renewed under sunset provisions, the parental consent amendment had originally been introduced as a separate bill by state Senator Marlene Woodson (R-Bradenton) with the backing of Florida Right to Life and the FCC. It was clear, however, that it would never have moved through the requisite committees due to their pro-choice membership. In linking the parental consent to the clinic licensing, parliamentary procedure virtually assured its passage.

Despite the legislative victory, the parental consent law did not take effect on October 1, 1988, as mandated. Three doctors and the owners of a women's clinic in Jacksonville filed suit in federal court on September 30th, claiming that the Florida statute was vague and lacked the administrative rules necessary for its implementation. The legislature had failed to specify the judicial jurisdiction to be employed in determining a minor's maturity and capability to make the abortion decision without parental consent. Rather, the legislature had delegated the specifics to the Florida Supreme Court. Granting an injunction, the federal district court agreed as to the vagueness, but subsequently lifted that injunction in February 1989, following the Florida Supreme Court's issuance of judicial guidelines to be used in lieu of parental consent. Although this ended the federal lawsuit, the parental consent bill was yet to meet its ultimate challenge in state courts.

Anticipating Success—Early 1989

The 1989 anniversary of the *Roe* decision prompted yet another statement by the Florida bishops on abortion. But the 1989 statement differed significantly as the bishops intentionally republished their last five annual statements, reiterating the intransitive nature of the position of the Catholic Church on abortion.[18] The bishops may have sensed a change in the times. On January 9, 1989, less than two weeks before the *Roe* anniversary and the release of the bishops' statement, the Supreme Court of the United States had noted probable jurisdiction in the *Webster* case. Clearly, the preamble to the Missouri legislation that stated that human life begins at conception would have attracted the bishops' attention.

Florida experienced a flurry of pro-life demonstrations in the early months of 1989. Rescues took place in Jacksonville in February and a series of "spring break" rescues were planned for the south Florida area in March and April. As Operation Rescue gained increased visibility in the state, members of the Catholic Church were increasingly swept up in the massive arrests. Of the 90 arrests in Jacksonville, two individuals were Catholic priests.[19] A Redemptorist priest from Venice, Florida, was also arrested during a June rescue in St. Petersburg; his colleague, another priest, remained on the picket line. On the following Sunday, Father Joseph Rowan discarded his Father's Day sermon and spoke of his experiences to the congregation.[20]

The anticipated "spring break" rescues in south Florida prompted a response from the Florida bishops. Unlike Archbishop Roger M. Mahony of Los Angeles who announced church support for the Operation Rescue organization, the

Florida bishops issued a written statement assuring the public that the Catholic Church was not formally a part of Operation Rescue. "We respect the consciences of those individuals who are involved in Operation Rescue. It should be made clear however that they are acting as individuals and do not represent the Church."[21] The bishops also clarified the activities which they condoned and supported in protesting abortions. One of these, a rosary vigil, was sponsored by Bishop Thomas V. Daily two days after the release of the bishops' statement.

In what proved to be an increasingly popular tactic by the church in Florida, the first rosary vigil in Palm Beach drew more than 300 participants. Information on the vigil had been disseminated by the diocese to parishes with instructions that the vigil be announced at all Sunday Masses and that priests urge attendance.[22] Following a prayer service at a nearby church, Bishop Daily led a motorcade to the Aware Womancare Clinic in Lake Worth. Following all legally-mandated requirements for the demonstration and auto procession, the motorcade even enjoyed a police escort to and from the clinic. While at the clinic, the bishop and his followers quietly prayed the rosary, refusing to speak to reporters or others. "Wherever there's an abortuary, we should pray—but always in the law, in consultation with your local pastor. Do it in Ft. Pierce, Stuart, West Palm Beach, anywhere, but do it within the law."[23]

As the anticipation built around the *Webster* case, rallies were held statewide. A week before the oral argument of the case, Rosemary Gallagher, the FCC legislative aide who manages social policy, spoke of the future of the pro-life movement in Florida. "The battle will only start when the Supreme Court decision is made. There will be many years of hard work here [at the state capital]."[24] Her prediction at the Tallahassee rally was more than accurate.

Anticipating the importance of abortion in the 1990 election, Mason Dixon Research conducted a poll in early May of both voters and legislators in the state. The headlines of May 10th, 1989, in the *Miami Herald*, "Floridians support the right to obtain abortions," and in the *Tallahassee Democrat*, "Abortion ban not favored in state," should have served as an early warning to Governor Martinez and other pro-life advocates. Although most voters (63 percent) and legislators (60 percent) agreed that abortion was morally wrong, the results were less clear on allowing women the right to a legal abortion (voters: 50 percent in favor, 43 percent opposed, 7 percent unsure; legislators: 51 percent in favor, 49 percent opposed). In contemplation of the *Webster* decision, the pollsters also asked whether the respondents favored returning to the pre-1973, state by state abortion laws and found strong opposition from both constituents (56 percent) and lawmakers (64 percent).[25]

Interestingly, the poll also suggested serious problems for the Republican Party in Florida should abortion become a campaign issue, "rending it into nearly equal-sized 'pro-life' and 'pro-choice' factions, and putting it at a disadvantage in election campaigns against a pro-choice Democrat."[26] In sum, the poll and the *Miami Herald* rightly predicted that pro-life advocates were not going to have an easy time using the legislature to impose more restrictions on legalized abortions. Little did the analysts realize that the judicial route in Florida was to be just as difficult.

On May 2, 1989, a pregnant and unmarried fifteen-year-old petitioned the Lake County Circuit Court for permission to obtain an abortion. In an unusual move, Judge Jerry Lockett appointed a pro-life attorney as guardian ad litem for the fetus in addition to naming counsel for the petitioner, identified in the record as T.W. The crux of the argument again revolved around the vague language of the judicial alternative to parental consent and on May 5th, Judge Lockett announced that due to the vague language, the judicial path to consent was unconstitutional. This forced the plaintiff to obtain consent from her parents, the only section of the statute left intact. On appeal, Florida's Fifth District Court of Appeal substantially upheld the trial court's finding, but declared the entire statute, including parental consent, void, clearing the way for T.W.'s abortion (May 12, 1989).

However, the guardian ad litem appointment by the trial court confounded the case. Through a variety of motions, the guardian managed to obtain a temporary stay from the Florida Supreme Court on May 13th. Three days later, the Florida Court lifted the stay and scheduled arguments on the statute for September. Within hours, the guardian ad litem appealed to the U.S. Supreme Court where Justice Anthony Kennedy also imposed a temporary stay pending a review of the record. This stay was lifted two days later. Finally, on May 22nd, the Florida Supreme Court cleared the way for young T.W. to obtain her abortion.

Despite the legal wrangling of May 1989, the parental consent law was not yet analyzed and tested by the Florida Supreme Court. Unfortunately for some, the court's scheduled hearings in September and its subsequent decision in this case would dampen the spirits of the pro-life organizations and boost the pro-choice movement at a critical point in Florida politics. Clearly, no one anticipated that the timing of the T.W. decision would be so important to the abortion issue in Florida.

As the decision date of the *Webster* case drew near, strategy sessions were held to lay the groundwork for future action. Respect Life officers from across the state met in Tallahassee with Bishop Daily, the head of the Pro-Life Committee for the Province of Miami, to map out strategies for the church. Respect Life ministries received numerous calls from "foot soldiers . . . volunteering to join."[27] These "foot soldiers" would be called upon in the wake of the *Webster* decision with the excitement of a new energy for the pro-life movement in Florida and in the nation.

Post-*Webster:* Setting the National Pace

The *Webster* decision was but hours old when both the pro-life and pro-choice camps began their strategizing and posturing. Rallies in south Florida were hastily orchestrated for the evening of July 3rd, by the National Organization for Women who met at the Federal Courthouse in Fort Lauderdale, and by pro-life groups who joined forces at a church in Miami.[28]

The church and state lawmakers were also immediate in their commentary and plans for the future of abortion in Florida. Bishop John Favalora of the

Diocese of St. Petersburg praised the ruling and said that it "calls for all of us to offer support to pregnant women and unborn children so that abortions will no longer have to be considered an option."[29] He also urged citizens to contact their lawmakers. "As responsible citizens, we must also exercise our civil right to inform local legislators of our pro-life stance and of our expectation that the Florida Legislature will uphold the right to life of the unborn for any forthcoming legislation."[30] Archbishop Edward McCarthy of Miami also emphasized the need for political action, encouraging lobbying activity by the FCC and the Respect Life ministry. "We'll try to raise [legislators'] consciousness and we'll be praying. That's a pretty powerful weapon."[31]

Newspaper stories across the state on July 4th not only announced the Supreme Court's decision, but addressed the probability of a special legislative session for Florida. One representative in the State House, Tom Banjanin (R-Pensacola), had even prepared a draft bill that included most of the key points of the Missouri statute. By July 14th, Rep. Banjanin had formally filed the proposed legislation that specifically stated, "the life of each human being begins at conception."[32]

Governor Martinez wasted no time in acting on the apparent grant of state power by *Webster.* On July 5th, he announced that he would call a special legislative session on abortion for the fall. Within days, the governor also met with pro-life legislators and members of pro-life organizations including the FCC's executive director, Thomas Horkan. Horkan noted that, "there is some concern . . . that the state not act too quickly and make mistakes" in drafting more restrictive abortion legislation.[33] But on July 25th, Martinez announced that the special session would commence on October 10th and last for four days. He promised that his administration would be forthcoming with proposed legislation for consideration at the session.

Legislators expressed early wariness at the prospect of a special session on abortion. The proposed dates were just a short year before the biannual elections and could pose grave risks for the elected representatives. The *Palm Beach Post* announced, "For state lawmakers, 'free ride' on abortion ends," and the *Orlando Sentinel* proclaimed, "Abortion—a life and death issue for politicians too."[34] John Stipanovich, Martinez's re-election campaign manager, was somewhat accurate in stating, "Everyone who has no meaningful conviction on this [abortion] is going to be paralyzed by fear or hovering near the edge of hysteria."[35] What he didn't realize was that even those with convictions would feel the political heat of having to take a publicly announced position, thereby alienating some portion of their constituency.

There was a sense of triumph and zeal in the statements of both pro-life and pro-choice leaders when discussing the tests that politicians were about to undergo with the abortion issue. The director of the Florida Abortion Rights Action League, Janice Compton-Carr, said, "Every candidate for every public office will have to answer to his or her position on abortion. They don't have a free ride anymore. . . . The court's decision is going to force legislators to make public decisions they've never had to make before and we'll be watching." For the antiabortion groups, lobbyist Carole Griffin of Tallahassee, threatened,

"Sure, we'll be targeting the ones we think we can beat if they're on the wrong side of this issue."[36]

Bishop Daily of Palm Beach led his second rosary vigil at a clinic in Port St. Lucie on July 19th. Encouraged by the news that the first clinic targeted by a rosary vigil had closed (allegedly due to threats and harassment), this second vigil was held at a "sister" clinic with hopes for similar results. Some 400 Catholics participated, again at the urging of the bishop and diocesan priests. Although the vigil had been planned in advance of the *Webster* decision, the increased attendance reflected the raised hopes of the Catholic constituency and the sense of urgency surrounding the upcoming legislative session.

The following day, Bishop Daily met with representatives of Catholic pro-life groups in Tallahassee to map out strategies for the special session. In addition to letter-writing campaigns, organizations were encouraged to implement the "Rosaries for Life" and other peaceful demonstrations. Coincidentally, the month of October had traditionally been "Respect Life" month in Florida and would require even more programmatic attentiveness as the special session drew near.

The months of July, August, and September were a flurry of unprecedented grassroots organizational efforts. Rev. Pat Mahoney of Rescue South Florida announced, "We are talking with pro-life leaders from throughout South Florida and we are getting together to form a political coalition."[37] In August, Florida Right to Life announced the formation of a state-wide network uniting pro-life forces. "The whimpers of dozens of individual anti-abortion groups could be turned into one roaring voice."[38] The pro-choice organizations also came together through "Voice for Choice," an umbrella organization including NOW, Planned Parenthood, the League of Women Voters, the ACLU, and the Florida Business and Professional Women's Association.

By late August, the lobbying activities of the Catholic Church were accelerating. Bishop Daily's third rosary vigil attracted 800 Catholic and non-Catholic participants to a clinic in Boca Raton. The bishops of Florida released a special statement on the legislative session, urging "every parish and every Catholic in Florida and all people of good will to join with us in raising our voices in defense of these innocents by speaking and writing to our legislators, our governor and other public officials."[39] Bishops also issued individual appeals to their parishes for increased Catholic participation. Bishop Favalora of St. Petersburg used a taped message that was played at all Masses in the diocese to encourage Catholics to "be the voices to speak on behalf of the voiceless unborn."[40] Similar statements were made by the state deputy of the Florida Knights of Columbus, a 30,000 member organization, and Bishops Daily of Palm Beach and Symons of Pensacola-Tallahassee.

The press wasted little time in employing the pollsters to evaluate once again the abortion issue in Florida and include the prospects for Governor Martinez's reelection. In late July, Mason-Dixon research once again confirmed that Florida was not the pro-life state touted among national analysts. Over 65 percent of those polled opposed the special legislative session on abortion, 44 percent felt that there should be no new laws, and 61 percent agreed with the statement that the abortion decision should be left entirely to a woman and her doctor.[41]

More damaging, however, were the findings on Martinez's popularity and the voting tendencies of Florida citizens. This same July poll indicated that a majority (53 percent) of the respondents gave Martinez negative marks on his performance in office. Furthermore, only 24 percent said they would re-elect the governor if the elections were held at the time of the poll. Previously unmeasured, however, were the findings that an incredible 30 percent of the electorate were single-issue pro-choice voters.[42] The Martinez camp was unwavering in spite of the dismal outlook. "We're going to do our best on this issue and then move on. If we are going to take some licks, we'll take them this October rather than next October," said Stipanovich.

A final aspect of the July poll involved the religious background of respondents. As expected, Jewish voters and those who were not associated with a particular religion were most strongly opposed to changing the laws on abortion. But curiously, Catholic and white evangelical respondents would not have provided a large base of support for increased abortion restrictions. "Only one in three of those voters said the laws should be tougher," significantly less than one would expect.[43]

Another survey was conducted by the *Tallahassee Democrat* in early August and found that fifty-seven members of the House were pro-choice, thirty-seven wanted more restrictive legislation, nine were undecided, and sixteen refused comment. In the Senate, eight lawmakers refused to respond and one was undecided, while seventeen would leave the law alone, and thirteen would tighten restrictions. The survey also found that at least two Catholic legislators were pro-choice. Another strong antiabortion legislator changed her position after a poll in her district indicated that 75 percent of her constituents were pro-choice. She joined at least five other staunch abortion opponents who would defect if pushed to a vote. Thus, even as early as the first two weeks of August, the outlook for the legislative session was bleak.[44]

Increased political activity was reflected in the capital as more than 1,000 lobbying registration forms were sent out in anticipation of the special session mostly to antiabortion groups. According to records of the Florida House, "the lobbying ranks on both sides of the issue have increased tenfold in the past month—from fewer than ten to 100."[45] Five new political action committees had filed with the state Division of Elections; four were choice groups, one was antiabortion. Mail was already flooding the lawmakers' offices. Since the July 3rd ruling, Martinez had received 12,442 letters dealing with abortion and the daily average was increasing as the session drew near. Legislators' mail included objects symbolizing each camp's philosophy: coat hangers from the choice movement and an inch-long plastic fetus from the life constituents. By the second week of August, hotel rooms in the capital area were booked for the special session.

The month before the special session was to hold some surprises for both the pro-choice and pro-life movements in Florida. In August, Ileana Ros-Lehtinen (R), formerly a state senator, ran successfully for the congressional seat left vacant by the death of Claude Pepper. Her pro-life stance on abortion was an element of the election against Gerald Richman, a Democrat. Although Sandra Faucher, director of the National Right to Life Committee Political Action Committee, claimed that abortion, "was a hot issue of the campaign, up til election day,"[46] most analysts would attribute Ros-Lehtinen's success to her Cuban-American heritage and constituency.

As mid-September approached, it seemed that the Martinez administration was more interested in kicking off the reelection campaign than in the legislation the governor promised to deliver for the session. In fact, advance legislative hearings were held in Tallahassee the week of September 15th, and the committees had yet to see any proposed legislation from the executive branch. That same day, Governor Bob Martinez was in Orlando initiating his reelection bid with a kickoff party.

The winds were shifting and it appeared that the legislative session would be a hopeless exercise in addition to a financial burden for the taxpayers of Florida who were footing the bill. Even the *Miami Herald,* the state's largest newspaper, called on Martinez to cancel the special session. In a September editorial, the Governor was sharply criticized:

> If Gov. Bob Martinez has a blueprint and a political strategy to go with his rough sketch for changes in Florida's abortion laws, he had better make them public fast. Otherwise, he rightly will be held responsible for a capitol circus that will make Florida—and its anti-abortion governor—look foolish. . . . Governor Martinez seems to have created a lose-lose situation for himself. If he cannot find a solution this week, he should cancel the special session and save Florida its expense, acrimony, and futility.

The advance legislative hearings before the House Health Care Committee provided the Catholic Church with a direct appeal to the legislators. Mr. Horkan, director of FCC, testified and had several young witnesses prepared to make statements. However, Rep. Elaine Gordon (D-North Miami), chair of the committee, refused to allow anyone under the age of eighteen to participate in testimony. "We are trying to keep this from being an opportunity for circus tactics," she said. Those that were refused access included an adopted thirteen-year-old and a four-year-old girl who was allegedly born at twenty-one weeks after conception. Due to the time-consuming nature of the hearings, many scheduled witnesses brought by the FCC were delayed until late in the day or not heard at all. Rosemary Gallagher, social concerns associate for the FCC, was irate, "Never in my eighteen years in doing this kind of work has a group I've worked with been treated so shabbily."[47]

On September 17th, the pro-life movement in Florida got an unexpected windfall. The *Miami Herald,* in its Sunday feature magazine, "Tropic," ran an exposé on an abortion clinic in south Dade County and the horror stories of unsafe medical practices, botched abortions and lawsuits. The stories were not sanitized; they were presented in a very personal, journalistic manner. It was apparent that the article was meant to shock the public and the politicians. In that, the story was successful and at a very precarious time in Florida politics.

It didn't take long for Florida's Department of Health and Rehabilitative Services (HRS) to inspect the clinic named in the *Herald* article and close it down. A second clinic was closed on September 27th for similar health reasons. The response from the pro-choice organizations was mixed. On the one hand, many saw the newly-directed attention to clinics as a political ploy by the governor and the pro-life movement. Others argued that women, pro-choice or not, were interested in assuring that all women could obtain medically safe abortions.

On the political front, a different discussion took place. While the governor and others began calling for legislation to increase the powers of HRS in order to close unsafe clinics, the opposition pointed to the emergency closings as evidence that the agency needed no further jurisdiction. HRS had closed clinics in Dade County; no new legislation was needed. But Martinez and the pro-life advocates saw this as an opportunity to call for further restrictions on abortion and advocated imposing hospital health standards on the abortion clinics, a rather dramatic and costly imposition.

Late September also brought a heightened level of diverse activities by the church. The *Florida Catholic* began a series entitled, "A Consistent Ethic of Life," "as a public service in preparation for the special legislative session on abortion."[48] Weekly copies of the newspaper containing the series were sent to each legislator, including a September 29th editorial that explained the church's position and lobbied the representatives to restrict abortion in Florida. The September 29th issue also featured a page entitled, "Write for Life," which listed the names of Florida senators and representatives with their official addresses. "Readers are encouraged to write their senators and representatives in support of legislation that would limit abortion."[49]

Bishop Thomas V. Daily of Palm Beach also used the *Florida Catholic* and his weekly articles to encourage Catholics to action. His September 15th editorial clarified the role of the church in political action.

> There is also the whole question of public policy and the involvement of individuals in the area of public programs and political action. While the Church does not engage in partisan politics or endorse candidates for public office, it certainly can be very much involved in encouraging its members in parishes, as parishioners, to become involved in the promotion of life, especially among the unborn, and especially now as we anticipate the special session of the Florida Legislature, Oct. 10–13.[50]

In the Diocese of St. Petersburg, a joint deanery meeting was held to address the issue of abortion. Attending were some sixty priests and deacons who heard from pro-life politicians and advocates.[51] In the state's capital, plans by the Diocese of Pensacola-Tallahassee included a range of activities for the days leading up to the session, including a special Holy Hour and Mass on the opening day of the session. Round-the-clock prayer vigils were scheduled for October 9th, as well as a day of fasting and prayer on October 8th. The major public event was to be a pro-life march and rally on the eve of the session in Tallahassee. Catholics from other dioceses were encouraged to attend and the local parishes worked to provide accommodations and overnight arrangements. Finally, the planners also asked that churches across the state ring their church bells at noon on October 10th, to show support for the unborn.

Msgr. McNulty of St. Petersburg led two bus loads of parishioners to Tallahassee on September 25th for a Rosary Vigil on the steps of the Capitol. There, two members of the group visited the offices of the governor, the Speaker of the House and Senate President, leaving silk roses and "messages of prayer." Carrying figurines of the Three Wise Men, Msgr. McNulty described his mission, "We just came up to pray that God would bless these men and women of the Legislature."[52]

Other activities included a pro-life rally sponsored by the West Coast Coalition and Right to Life organizations, held in St. Petersburg's Al Lang Stadium on September 30th. Committed pro-life legislators and political figures were often invited speakers at the many rallies and marches. In addition to this very visible show of strength, one parish even developed its own Respect Life video, "There is a Way," which was made available to parishes across the state.

It wasn't until September 26th that seven legislative bills were formally proposed for consideration at the special session. In addition to incorporating many of the Missouri restrictions upheld by *Webster,* the legislation included establishing a state adoption center, enhancing statistical reporting requirements for abortion and complications, imposing a seven-day waiting period and mandatory counseling prior to an abortion, and requiring notification to husbands in cases where he is the "father of the child." In response to the clinic closings, one bill offered provisions for bringing clinics under the ambulatory surgical center law, a more stringent standard of medical care and inspections.

As the session approached, however, the outlook for the pro-life campaign looked dimmer. It was clear that the key committees, dominated by pro-choice legislators, would have to keep all bills concerning abortion off the floors of the House and Senate. Should a bill reach the floor, it could serve as a tool or vehicle for the pro-life advocates who planned to amend it with more restrictive legislation. The hope by the pro-life camp was that one bill concerning clinic regulation may have a chance at survival. "There's a crack open to us and it may allow us to get to the floor some bill that would bring more regulation of clinics," said Rep. Jim Hill (R-Jupiter).[53]

The crushing blow to the pro-life cause in Florida came on October 5th, only five days before the session's opening. The Florida Supreme Court, having heard oral arguments on the T.W. case in September, published its decision striking down the parental consent legislation as unconstitutional. In *In re T.W., A Minor,*[54] six of the seven justices used the state's privacy amendment to protect a woman's abortion decision. By a narrower margin (4–3), the court ruled that the privacy right extended to minors due to the "unambiguous language of the amendment"[55] which extends to "every natural person."[56] Furthermore, the court also held that the appointment of a guardian ad litem for the fetus "was clearly improper."[57]

Despite the court's ruling and intensified calls to cancel the session, Governor Martinez did not back down. A last minute poll by the *Miami Herald* reflected no change in public attitudes toward abortion.[58] More than 60 percent of the respondents felt that the state should not interfere in a woman's decision to obtain an abortion. Furthermore, the survey found that, "Strength of religious sentiment, rather than religious preference itself, appears to be the strongest motivation for anti-abortion feelings." Rep. Jerry Rehm (R-Clearwater) seemed to express the sentiments of a large number of church-goers, "I don't think the statutes of the state are the place to put theology. I'm a convert to Roman Catholicism, but the Bible is the appropriate place for those teachings."

On the eve of the special session, some 8,000–9,000 people rallied at a "Celebration of Life" on the steps of the Capitol. Governor Martinez addressed the crowd, "I stand with you because for [so] long you have been the voice of the unheard. Those who have rights but no one to listen to them, they will be listened to in the state of Florida. . . . This is democracy at work."[59] One of the speakers, Dr. Mildred Jefferson, perhaps sensing the futility of the session, urged those in attendance to warn their legislators of the November 1990 elections. "If your legislator has failed to speak out against abortion, then let him know that when November 1990 comes around he will have to pay the price."[60]

The special session opened on the morning of October 10th and by day's end, it was clear that no legislation would survive. In fact, some legislators called for ending the session the following day rather than expend further tax dollars for two more unproductive days. "There's really no reason to stay much longer. We've proved that it's a waste of time," reported Senator Jack Gordon (D-Miami Beach), Senate majority leader.[61] The Senate Health and Rehabilitative Services committee rejected four bills the first day of the session by large margins (9–3 and 8–4 votes). The House committees only held hearings the first day of the session, waiting for action in the Senate before proceeding to call for committee votes.

Day Two of the special session was also its conclusion. Despite a last-ditch effort by pro-life legislators in the Senate to bring an abortion clinic bill to the floor, the session ended on October 11th. In some sense, however, all was not lost by the pro-life advocates. The parliamentary procedure employed to force the clinic bill out of committee in the Senate did allow for some floor debate and put Senators on the record with a vote on whether to allow floor consideration of a single bill. Another small victory was achieved in that the Senate agreed to appoint a Select Committee on Abortion Clinic Regulation that would report back to the Senate within a month. But this was the extent of the gains for the pro-life movement in Florida.

Editorials and stories in the *Florida Catholic* following the session ranged from outrage and disappointment to "look how far we have come" optimism. Mr. Horkan of the Florida Catholic Conference expressed optimism, saying that "the enemy has been flushed out, the issues have been defined and the pro-life forces have mobilized." The front page suggested that the battle was not over: "Pro-life advocates eye '90 elections, legislative session."[62] "We lost a skirmish, but we did not lose the war," explained Judy Glocker, vice president of Florida Right to Life.[63]

A Second Battle: 1990

The sun had not even set on the end of the special legislative session before plans for 1990 were proposed by the pro-life advocates. Ken Connor, president of Florida Right to Life, mapped out a three-pronged strategy for the next year. First, antiabortion forces would focus on the 1990 election, making it "a referendum on abortion."[64] Second, in response to the *T.W.* decision, a petition drive would be initiated to obtain the requisite 383,000 signatures needed to reconsider the personal privacy provision of the Florida Constitution. Finally, the author of the *T.W.* decision, Justice Leander Shaw (soon to be Chief Justice), would be targeted in November of 1990 through his retention election. Surprisingly, no specific plans were mentioned for the regular legislative session scheduled for April.

The new decade began with yet another statement by the Florida bishops on the *Roe* anniversary. In the eight paragraph statement, the bishops carefully spelled out the hope given by the *Webster* decision and the political institutions in Florida that "thwarted every effort to restore any semblance of dignity or protection for unborn children." But the bishops also offered encouragement. "Despite the difficulties, we must take heart. . . . The court decision and the legislative impasse must be overcome, and we pledge our support for that effort through the implementation of our Pastoral Plan for Pro-Life Activities."[65]

The new year also brought a continuation of several of the church's now established pro-life events. Rosary vigils continued outside abortion clinics across the state and Bishop John Snyder of St. Augustine, who had never participated in such a demonstration, joined the ranks of demonstrators.[66] The January March for Life was held, as it had been every year since the *Roe* decision. In February, a "We Are For Life" Youth Convention for Life, was organized to bring Catholic high school students together in the Palm Beach Diocese for a day-long meeting.[67]

Despite the losses the pro-life movement had suffered, Florida's bishops seemed more sure of themselves when addressing the secular and political policymakers. Evidence of this is seen by the actions of Bishop John Nevins of Venice who sent a telegram to Lane Kirkland, President of the AFL-CIO, during a February meeting of the organization's executive council held in Bal Harbour, Florida. The AFL-CIO had been considering adopting a policy which supported "choice," thus allowing the labor union to use the issue as an element of their political endorsements in the upcoming elections. Nevins wrote of his concern as "a pro-life citizen of this country as well as the bishop of the Catholic community in Venice," that the new policy considerations would promote "a great, great divisiveness within the labor movement at a time when unions should be encouraged and protected."[68]

As the regular April legislative session opened, it was clear that no abortion bills would be formally proposed for full consideration. The Legislative Report

of the Florida Catholic Conference explained the lack of proposed legislation
by pointing to the special session and suggesting that a similar fall-back strategy
would be employed.

> Since the same committees would have jurisdiction over abortion bills in the
> regular session, no pro-life bills have been filed. If a bill is killed in a committee,
> its provisions cannot be amended onto other bills on the floor. For that reason,
> pro-life legislators have felt that the best opportunity for adopting any pro-life
> legislation this year is in floor amendments, not in the filing of bills.[69]

Ken Connor, president of Florida Right to Life, described the strategy as
"guerilla approach: Monitor, watch, look for the opening and strike."[70]

The legislative session did provide some minor successes for the pro-life
organizations. The state passed a bill that included the creation and funding
of an Adoption Information Center, designed to encourage adoptions throughout the state. This bill had originally been introduced during the special
session. Additionally, adoption subsidy payments were increased. In an indirect
victory, pro-life advocates managed to get two roll call votes in the House on
proposed abortion amendments (state funding of abortion and clinic reporting
requirements).[71] Although the bills failed, the amendments provided pro-life
organizations with more accurate "targeting" of legislators for the November
1990 elections.

A major pro-life rally was held in Tallahassee just weeks into the legislative
session. The theme urged citizens to "Remember in November, Vote Pro-
Life." Governor Martinez addressed the nearly 10,000 people, asking for their
electoral support and encouraging them to hold legislators accountable for the
failure of the special session. The FCC played a prominent role at the rally
although the demonstration was not a church-sponsored event.

The opening of the legislative session also brought a major surprise to state
politics. Since Martinez had declared his candidacy for reelection, the race had
been shaping up as Martinez against Democrat Bill Nelson, a congressional
representative. But on April 12th, Lawton Chiles, the retired long-time member
of the U.S. Senate, jumped into the race and changed every pollster's outlook
on the election. It was generally believed that Martinez would beat Nelson,
but Chiles was another question. The campaign was to be even more interesting
since Chiles had limited all contributions to his campaign treasury to $100
per individual.

As the 1990 campaigns were getting underway, the Archdiocese of Miami
attempted to address Catholic pro-choice candidates who would use their
position to "create media controversy with religious authorities." Although
the Archdiocese's statement was in response to a local candidate who supported
abortion in spite of his religious beliefs, the Archbishop was probably trying
to skirt the confrontations that New York had witnessed between Governor
Mario Cuomo and the church. In issuing guidelines, the Archdiocese stated,
" 'The Church can have no part in this.' It's not a matter of 'the Church getting
into politics but politics getting into the Church.' "[72] The guidelines also
suggested that Catholics and Christians, "can no longer regard their religion

as the controlling element of their private lives while leaving their public lives to be controlled by [a] secular idea."

In May, the Florida Catholic Conference issued its "Guidelines for Pastors and Parishes on Lobbying and Electioneering." The brochure specifically points to the abortion issue by recalling the Florida bishops' statement of January, "Abortion has become the fundamental human rights issue for all men and women of good will at this stage of our nation's history." Although followed by the caveat that abortion is not the only issue, it is clear that abortion is still the most prominent on the Florida church's agenda.

The brochure outlines specific activities that parishes may and may not engage in with respect to the upcoming elections. Interestingly, the guidelines start with encouragement "Parishes and other institutions may, *and in some cases should,* engage in issue-oriented activities and lobbying" (emphasis added). Permitted activities include non-partisan registration drives, get-out-the-vote campaigns, and the distribution of materials (including surveys and polls) that emphasize "educational objectives" in accordance with a list of stipulations. Prohibited activities include church endorsements and evaluations or negative campaigns for or against specific candidates or political parties. Because the church enjoys a tax-exempt status, pastors and religious leaders are, "urged to avoid endorsements or other political activity. . . . Although not prohibited, it may be difficult to separate their personal activity from their role as a representative of the Church."

Other than editorials and occasional articles in the two Catholic newspapers in the state that encouraged pro-life voting, the Florida church did not seem to be very energetic in targeting pro-choice legislators for the November elections. Even the campaign against Chief Justice Leander Shaw merited only a July editorial in the *Florida Catholic*.[73] Most of the attention seemingly was focused on the gubernatorial campaign.

Among the challengers Martinez faced in the September primaries, the most serious threat was from a Republican woman, state senator Marlene Woodson-Howard. The major difference in their campaign platforms was the abortion issue; Woodson-Howard was an abortion-rights advocate. Martinez won the election handily with 68.9 percent of the vote to Woodson-Howard's 19.8 percent.

Chiles also put down his primary challenger, Nelson, with 69 percent of the vote; Nelson garnered 31 percent. As an omen for the general election, Chiles had not only won, but he did it with a mere two million dollars to Nelson's expenditure of six million. With respect to abortion, both Nelson and Chiles had not been seen as firm advocates of "choice." In 1988, Nelson voted in favor of the Dornan amendment which barred the District of Columbia from using tax funds for abortions. In 1989, he changed his vote to allow the expenditure of such funds suggesting a political move to engender favor from choice advocates in the state.

Chiles had opposed abortion for over twenty years except in cases of incest, rape and the endangerment of the mother's life. The "Groggy Gringo" changed his position during the primary campaign when Nelson made a point of Chiles' rather conservative position during the debates. "To me, it's a personal issue. It's a human rights issue. I'm not comfortable with making it a political issue," said Chiles in an interview for the *New Republic.*[74] Although Martinez would try in his last minute campaign ads to make Chiles' appear as a "flip-flopper" on the abortion issue, Chiles successfully avoided entering the abortion fray, attending only one pro-choice event during his eight months on the campaign trail.

The November elections brought discouraging news to pro-life advocates in Florida. Although the gubernatorial race had been too close to predict in the final days of campaigning, Chiles defeated Martinez with 56 percent of the vote. Martinez had played all of his cards, including four visits by President Bush to the "swing" areas and campaign expenditures that doubled the Chiles' treasury ($10.6 million to $5.2 million). However, Martinez was unable to erase the failures of not one, but four special legislative sessions that he called as governor. Clearly, the abortion issue played a role in the campaign, but its significance is uncertain due to the many problems that Martinez and the State of Florida faced during his tenure.

The campaign to unseat Chief Justice Leander Shaw was unsuccessful, but sent a fair warning to pro-choice forces on the court. Shaw was forced to raise and spend more than $300,000 to retain his seat on the Florida Supreme Court, a seat that is generally retained with well over 90 percent of the vote. In 1990, however, Shaw not only faced the threats of antiabortion advocates over the *T.W.* decision, he had also attracted the ire of a grassroots organization unhappy with his votes to overturn criminal verdicts. Despite these two campaigns against him, Shaw retained his seat with a 59 percent favorable vote, significantly less than usual.

Most state house and senate campaigns avoided the abortion issue in 1990, and incumbency proved to be the determining factor in most elections. One campaign where abortion was an issue made for an exciting race. In south Dade County, activist Fran Bohnsack (D) challenged incumbent Bruce Hoffman (R), stressing his antichoice position. Although she lost, Bohnsack managed to make it close by garnering 48 percent of the vote.

Overall, pro-life advocates made little headway in the 1990 elections. Given the failed special legislative session of 1989, and the dismal election returns, one Respect Life coordinator could only sum up the political results of two years as, "Depressing. We lost some ground legislatively."[75] Despite the political losses, however, the coordinator pointed to her ministries to pregnant women and children as an ongoing task; "We always have women in need," she said.

As the 1991 regular legislative session approached, not one antiabortion bill had been introduced to the legislature. It was not until early March that Senator Rick Dantzler,(D-Okeechobee), proposed legislation requiring abortion clinics to have life-size replicas of fetuses shown to women seeking abortions, defining life as beginning at conception, and requiring physicians to notify patients of possible side effects of the procedure. This bill was filed so late that it was not even mentioned in the Florida Catholic Conference's legislative report to the dioceses. The bill has little chance of becoming law this year; there are other issues such as budget shortfalls that have dominated the legislative session to the exclusion of controversial subjects, including abortion.

Conclusion

The special session on abortion and the 1990 elections suggest that the Catholic Church's pro-life efforts have produced mixed results in the state of Florida. Although neither of these events resulted in more restrictive abortion regulations or the election of sympathetic politicians, incremental successes have been attained. Moreover, the Catholic Church has managed to develop an extensive and active network throughout the state that can mobilize quickly and join with secular organizations to mount a significant campaign in the area of abortion politics.

The *Webster* decision did much to energize an already growing, diocesan-based movement in Florida. Each of the dioceses had a functioning Respect Life ministry prior to the Supreme Court decision. The *Webster* decision and the call for a special session on abortion seemed to encourage even more attention to the third directive of the national Pastoral Plan for Pro-Life Activities: the establishment of a public policy effort for "life" legislation. Under the leadership of Bishop Thomas V. Daily of Palm Beach, the Respect Life ministries and parishes across the state were mobilized and encouraged to participate in public pro-life activities. The response was overwhelming as parishioners exhibited a "show-of-force" through demonstrations, letter-writing campaigns, and prayers.

However, the events leading up to the special session were political in nature and well beyond the control of the church. The *T.W.* decision and the abortion clinic closings played a significant role in setting the stage for a legislative session that was bound to fail. Polls indicated a divisiveness among the electorate on the abortion issue and politicians were extremely wary of alien-ating a significant portion of their constituency.

Despite the failure of the special session, the church continued its pro-life efforts in the year between the session and the elections, albeit at a reduced intensity. The church's power in the political process was evident in the retention election of Chief Justice Shaw, especially when it joined forces with other grassroots organizations. The church had worked hard to support Gov-ernor Martinez in his reelection bid, however, his electoral failure cannot be directly tied to the abortion issue. Martinez had failed in his public policy efforts in more areas than abortion, and he was held to account at the polls in 1990.

In some sense, the Catholic Church in Florida has returned to its "normal," pre-*Webster* level of political activity. Ministries to pregnant women and children continue in the state through the Respect Life offices and other church-sponsored service providers. Rosary vigils are still conducted through-out Florida at abortion clinics and Life Walks are held to mark the anniversary of the *Roe* decision in January. These efforts notwithstanding, the Catholic Church in Florida has stepped back into its less visible role within the political sphere, waiting for yet another opportunity to move to the forefront of the antiabortion movement.

Notes

1. 492 U.S. 490 (1989).
2. Arthur J. Heise, Hugh Gladwin and Douglas McLaughen, eds., *FIU/Florida Poll* (Miami: Florida International University Press, 1989), p. 202.
3. Ibid., pp. 166, 203.
4. Rhodes Cook, "GOP's Florida Growth: Fluke or Foreboding?" *Congressional Quarterly Weekly*, Vol. 48, (April 14, 1990), p. 1162.
5. Anne H. Shermyen, ed., *1990 Florida Statistical Abstract* (Gainesville: University Presses of Florida, 1990), p. 68.
6. *Palm Beach Post*, October 2, 1989.
7. *Florida Catholic*, November 3, 1989, p. 23
8. Ibid., p. 24.
9. Ibid.
10. Joan Crown, Associate Director of Respect Life for the Archdiocese of Miami (Phone interview: March 8, 1991).
11. *Florida Catholic*, February 15, 1991, p. 12.
12. Crown, supra n. 10.
13. *Florida Catholic*, August 22, 1986, p. 10.
14. Pastoral Letter issued by the bishops of the Province of Miami on April 25, 1986.
15. *Florida Catholic*, November 14, 1986, p. 20.
16. *Florida Catholic*, November 7, 1986, p. 4.
17. "A Challenge to School Clinics," *Newsweek*, August 10, 1987, p. 54.
18. *Florida Catholic*, January 20, 1989, p. 1.
19. *Florida Catholic*, February 17, 1989, p. 2.
20. *Florida Catholic*, June 30, 1989, p. 3.
21. *Voice*, April 28, 1989, p. 3.
22. *Florida Catholic*, April 14, 1989, p. 13.
23. *Florida Catholic*, April 28, 1989, p. 2.
24. *Florida Catholic*, April 21, 1989, p. 3.
25. *Tallahassee Democrat*, May 10, 1989.
26. *Miami Herald*, May 10, 1989.
27. *Voice*, July 21, 1989, p. 10.
28. *Voice*, July 7, 1989, p. 5.
29. *Tampa Tribune*, July 4, 1989.
30. *Voice*, July 7, 1989, p. 3.
31. Ibid.
32. *Tallahassee Democrat*, July 4, 1989.
33. *Florida Catholic*, July 14, 1989, p. 1.
34. *Orlando Sentinel*, July 9, 1989.
35. Ibid.
36. *Palm Beach Post*, July 9, 1989.
37. *Voice*, July 7, 1989, p. 5.
38. *Florida Catholic*, August 11, 1989, p. 1.

39. *Florida Catholic,* August 8, 1989, p. 6.

40. Ibid.

41. *Miami Herald,* July 27, 1989.

42. *Miami Herald,* July 28, 1989.

43. *Miami Herald,* July 27, 1989.

44. *Tallahassee Democrat,* August 13, 1989.

45. *Palm Beach Post,* August 13, 1989.

46. *Florida Catholic,* November 3, 1989, p. 7.

47. *Florida Catholic,* October 22, 1989, pp. 1–7.

48. *Florida Catholic,* September 22, 1989, p. 1 and September 29, 1989, p. 1.

49. *Florida Catholic,* September 29, 1989, p. 16.

50. *Florida Catholic,* September 15, 1989, p. 12.

51. *Florida Catholic,* September 29, 1989, p. 7.

52. Ibid.

53. *Florida Catholic,* October 6, 1989, p. 3.

54. 551 So.2d 1186 (1989).

55. Ibid., p. 1193.

56. *Florida Constitution,* Art. I, sec. 23.

57. 551 So.2d 1186, p. 1190.

58. *Miami Herald,* October 8, 1989.

59. *Florida Catholic,* October 13, 1989, p. 6.

60. Ibid.

61. *Miami Herald,* October 11, 1989, p. 1A.

62. *Florida Catholic,* October 20, 1989, p. 1.

63. Ibid., p. 7.

64. *Miami Herald,* October 12, 1989.

65. *Florida Catholic,* January 19, 1990, p. 24.

66. *Florida Catholic,* January 12, 1990, p. 2.

67. *Florida Catholic,* February 9, 1990, p. 13.

68. *Florida Catholic,* April 13, 1990, p. 1.

69. *Florida Catholic,* April 6, 1990, p. 2.

70. *Orlando Sentinel,* April 16, 1990.

71. *Florida Catholic,* June 8, 1990, p. 3.

72. *Florida Catholic,* April 20, 1990, p. 1.

73. *Florida Catholic,* July 6, 1990, p. 3.

74. Fred Barnes, "Groggy Gringo," *The New Republic,* November 12, 1990, pp. 17–19.

75. Crown, interview, supra n. 10.

4

The Consistent Life Ethic
in State Politics:
Joseph Cardinal Bernardin and
the Abortion Issue in Illinois

MaryAnne Borrelli

The author of the consistent ethic of life and an acknowledged leader of the Roman Catholic Church in the United States, Archbishop Joseph Cardinal Bernardin has a well-established reputation as an activist in life issues. Without discounting his influence, however, one must recognize that there has been a steady increase in the numbers subscribing to a pro-choice position in Illinois since the 1989 *Webster* decision. As pro-life and pro-choice organizations mobilize more and more voters, state legislators are recognizing abortion as an important electoral issue. Yet abortion is only one of the issues confronting Illinois politicians and, due to problems with the state budget and with redistricting plans, it may not receive particular attention in upcoming General Assembly sessions. A study of abortion politics in Illinois, therefore, obliges one to evaluate the impact of Roman Catholic church leadership upon the general population, to investigate how pro-life and pro-choice activists define their coalitions, and to see what priority a state legislature will assign abortion once it has become a dangerous campaign issue.

Bernardin and the Consistent Ethic of Life

Joseph Louis Cardinal Bernardin, Archbishop of Chicago, first achieved national stature in 1968 when he became the full-time General Secretary of the National Conference of Catholic Bishops (NCCB) and of its social action agency, the United States Catholic Conference (USCC). While in this post, he gained a reputation as a mediator, able to reconcile apparently irreconcilable factions; because of this ability, he was later invited to chair several of the NCCB's most influential committees.[1] He also chaired the committee that drafted the now-famous pastoral, "The Challenge of Peace: God's Promise and

Our Response."[2] Bernardin's most extraordinary and original contribution to understanding life issues, however, has been "the consistent ethic of life," sometimes known as "the seamless garment." This ethic, or theory, was intended to present the pro-life stance of the American Roman Catholic Church.

Bernardin articulated the consistent ethic of life in 1983, while chairing the committee that coordinated the pro-life activities of the NCCB. The ethic claimed that all life was sacred and consequently insisted that a consistently life-enhancing position be taken on all life issues. For Bernardin, these issues included but were not limited to abortion, nuclear war, capital punishment, pornography, euthanasia, hunger, and poverty.[3]

> We believe that life is a gift from God and therefore must be protected and nourished at every stage of development. Furthermore, we believe not only that life is a sacred reality but also that it has social dimensions. People live in communities, which means not only that the *individual* has the obligation to protect life, but that it is also the obligation of *society* to protect life and provide the things needed to enhance that life. That is the theological basis and the starting point of the consistent ethic.
>
> Now the next logical step in applying this principle is to say that everything that protects, enhances, and nourishes life is good, is necessary. Those things, though, that in some way either destroy or diminish life are not good. Using that criterion, it soon becomes evident that all the issues are related. For example, abortion is the direct taking of innocent, unborn life. Nuclear war threatens to destroy life. . . . So any issue that in some way affects human life for better or for worse is a "life" issue.(emphasis in original)[4]

The consistent ethic thus challenges people to decide what kind of a community they wish to build and then provides guidance for their choices. The reader should note that Bernardin is requiring each member of society to accept responsibility for contributing (whether positively or negatively) to the human experience.

The consistent ethic, which expands upon the peace pastoral in its concern to draw the different life issues together, was expected to provide "a more comprehensive theological and ethical basis" for the Respect Life Program of the American bishops. Yet Bernardin also felt that the consistent ethic was relevant to policy debates outside the Roman Catholic Church hierarchy. He predicted that abortion and defense issues would be of critical importance in the 1984 presidential election. Without a "framework or vision" to describe their beliefs to the public, the bishops would be vulnerable to the politicking of single-issue groups.[5] As President of the NCCB during the 1976 presidential elections, Bernardin had personally experienced such pressure politics;[6] he had no wish to endure the loss of credibility and authority that might occur if the bishops were again presented as endorsing a particular platform or candidate. The consistent ethic, therefore, was additionally "meant to shape the public witness of the Catholic Church," revealing the positive commitment of the Roman Catholic Church to all life issues and establishing the independence of the bishops' political voice.[7]

Still, some American bishops maintain that the breadth of the consistent ethic compromises the Roman Catholic commitment to effecting particular policy changes. Archbishop Bernard Cardinal Law of Boston, for example, agrees that the right to life is "not a one-issue tenet" but argues for the centrality of abortion.[8]

> However weighty the urgency of life-related issues such as the right to life of the unborn and the spiraling nuclear arms race, one thing must be clearly noted: Nuclear holocaust is a frightening possibility, but the holocaust of abortion is a present cruel reality and fact. The slaughter of our innocents cannot be dismissed, forgotten or turned away from.[9]

This debate over priorities has been examined in an earlier chapter by Timothy A. Byrnes. As a participant and observer, however, Bernardin must have found the outcome of these discussions curiously ambiguous.

Bernardin's successor as chair of the bishops' committee for pro-life activities is Archbishop John Cardinal O'Connor of New York City. Like Bernard Law, O'Connor believes that abortion is appropriately the first political priority for the American Roman Catholic Church. The implications of this perspective are particularly evident in the responses Bernardin and O'Connor make to the social circumstances surrounding pregnancy.

Bernardin does not confine himself to offering the mother medical services and the child adoption services. His goal is to create a much-needed emotional and medical support system for the woman during and after her pregnancy.

> Our necessary—indeed, essential—public witness in providing a place in the public debate for the moral claims of unborn children can lead to a failure to address the situations faced by pregnant women. We can fail to consider the circumstances of conception—that it can be the result of coercion, ignorance or abuse. We can seem to be unaware that women who want to bear their children are without the social and economic resources needed to sustain new life. We can appear to ignore the fact that pregnancy for women is at least partly the experience of being left alone with the consequences of immoral, irresponsible male behavior—at the point of conception and afterward. These issues, and the circumstances surrounding conception and the resources needed to sustain a pregnancy and support children, are also part of the moral fabric of the abortion debate.[10]

O'Connor also possesses a lively awareness of his pastoral responsibilities to women and their families. Yet his writings and addresses give a stronger emphasis to judging what is right and wrong. While promising to work with women who must "pick up the pieces of their lives after an abortion," he emphasizes the irrationality of abortion in all circumstances.[11]

> We in no way minimize the horror and the trauma of rape. Obviously, whether we are speaking of a thousand cases or one case, a woman's life, a family's future can be virtually destroyed. But, as we have asked before, will violence against an unborn child compensate for the violence against the woman raped or will it in many cases simply increase her suffering? Is it at least possible that bearing a

child, however conceived, and either rearing it or offering it for adoption to the hundreds of thousands of couples pleading to adopt, might bring, even out of the tragedy of rape, a rich fulfillment?[12]

As these representative passages indicate, both Bernardin and O'Connor recognize the complications that surround pregnancy decisions. Bernardin, however, stresses the social context of childbearing; in so doing, he acknowledges the courage with which all life-givers confront life, whether those confrontations involve decisions about nuclear weapons or medical care for the dying or childbirth.[13] Quite clearly, Bernardin also believes that the community has a responsibility to provide the support that will enable each decision-maker to decide for life.[14] While O'Connor is not unaware of the trauma that attends these decisions, his words isolate decision-makers in their choices and so appear to relieve society of any obligations.

This difference of opinion between the two men, and O'Connor's uncompromising insistence that the bishops focus on protesting abortion, led many to question whether O'Connor's leadership was true to the Respect Life Program that Bernardin had directed. In an effort to allay such doubts, Bernardin and O'Connor held a joint press conference to endorse one another's policy perspectives.[15] In 1985, notwithstanding the obvious and on-going differences between the two leaders, the consistent ethic was adopted as the "theological context" for the Respect Life program.[16] Thus the tension over priorities and understandings of public policy was formalized in the institutional church and continued to characterize its pro-life efforts.

For a number of political observers, however, it remains unclear whether a church should be involved in the making of public policy. Bernardin has addressed this concern directly, arguing that the separation of church and state in the American Constitution means that religious institutions "should expect neither favoritism nor discrimination in the exercise of their religious and civic functions." Like other citizens and citizen organizations, the Roman Catholic Church "must earn the right to be heard by the quality of [its] arguments."[17] The church and its leadership must appeal to the intellectual integrity of the general population.[18] Such an approach will—not incidentally—raise the quality of public policy debates and enhance the "capacity" of the American public, enabling it to provide greater guidance to those who write the legislation and implement the programs.[19] With regard to abortion, Bernardin is especially careful to present a strong and precisely reasoned argument. As a result, his political activism has a gentler tone than is often associated with abortion politics,[20] an approach that will be assessed in the next section.

Still, there remains a concern that the Catholic bishops are turning to legislation because their own efforts at moral guidance have failed, that they are seeking to coerce behavior that their teachings are unable to secure.[21] Certainly Bernardin does not deny that the pro-life agenda involves legislation; that is what his speeches, articles, and Congressional testimony have sought to influence. But he does perceive the law as more than a set of punishments. In his view, the law also obliges citizens to assess their role in the society and their responsibilities to one another.[22]

We who support an [Constitutional] amendment are sometimes accused of asking the law to do what we cannot do ourselves. If we cannot convince people by moral suasion to refrain from abortion, isn't it presumptuous of us to ask the law to forbid people to have abortions? And why imagine that coercion will work if people are not convinced that abortion is wrong?

The objection points to a real problem, but it is one that pertains to much besides abortion. Moral argument alone has never been able to prevent much wrongdoing. Underlying all forms of legal constraint is the reality that law, though imperfect, is needed to protect values which are basic to society and to forbid behavior which grossly violates such values. So, if abortion does violate a fundamental value important to society, it is appropriate that it be proscribed by law, just as it is appropriate for law to proscribe other kinds of wrongdoing.

Further, the law itself is a moral educator, one of many agents in society which teach people to distinguish right from wrong. . . . The law now teaches that abortion is morally permissible. Those who disagree desire to change the law in order, in part, to change its moral teaching.

An amendment to the Constitution will reduce the number of abortions in two ways: The existence of legal penalties will deter some abortions, and the educative impact of the law will teach that abortions ought not to be sought or performed.[23]

Bernardin believes that a legislated ban on abortion is appropriate because it will protect the basic human right to experience life. In later passages of the article excerpted above, as in other writings, Bernardin draws parallels between his pro-life efforts and the work of the American civil rights movement. Both were undertaken on behalf of individual rights and both enhance the society by drawing more voices into creative dialogue.[24] Such an outcome is to be valued for, as Bernardin repeatedly notes, human beings are social creatures and much of their growth is in the context of community.

Thus Bernardin links his struggle against abortion with the progressive enfranchisement of all peoples through American history, placing the consistent ethic of life firmly within the American tradition of individual freedom. Freely acknowledging that civil law is not and cannot be coterminous with moral law, Bernardin nonetheless requires civil law to meet its own rights-based standard: The citizen's claim to freedom is properly honored until its exercise impairs the society that would otherwise nurture its expression.[25]

It remains unclear, however, whether the consistent ethic can serve as an ideological link among the various groups that shape abortion policies. This question of practical politics lies at the heart of the following section, which analyzes the politics of abortion in Illinois.

Abortion Politics and Policies in Illinois

Well past the mid-1980s, the Illinois state legislature was decisively pro-life in its politics and policies. The tone of these years is evident in the preamble to the Illinois Abortion Act of 1975, passed in response to the 1973 *Roe v. Wade* decision.

Without in any way restricting the right of privacy of a woman or the right of a woman to an abortion under [the Supreme Court] decisions, the General Assembly of the State of Illinois do (sic) solemnly declare and find in reaffirmation of the longstanding policy of this State, that the unborn child is a human being from the time of conception and is, therefore, a legal person for the purposes of the unborn child's right to life and is entitled to the right to life from conception under the laws and Constitution of this State. Further, the General Assembly finds and declares that longstanding policy of this State to protect the right to life of the unborn child from conception by prohibiting abortion unless necessary to preserve the life of the mother is unpermissible (sic) only because of the decisions of the United States Supreme Court and that, therefore, if those decisions of the United States Supreme Court are ever reversed or modified or the United States Constitution is amended to allow protection of the unborn, then the former policy of this State to prohibit abortions unless necessary for the preservation of the mother's life shall be re-instated.[26]

Although this law recognizes a woman's right to privacy, its greatest emphasis is placed on the personhood of the fetus and the "unborn child's right to life." The circumstances in which an abortion is deemed acceptable—"to preserve the life of the mother"—are extreme; and the final sentence requests that *Roe* be overturned and anticipates the *Webster* decision.

Preambles are frequently the place for rhetorical flourishes. Yet Illinois pro-life legislators were able to act upon the sentiment of this introduction, which was entitled "Legislative intention," and place increasingly strict regulations on abortion procedures. Illinois laws governing minors' access/parental consent to abortion and the provision of abortion in cases of incest and rape are stringent. On several occasions in the late 1980s, the State Attorney General found the laws passed by the General Assembly sufficiently limiting of the *Roe* standards that he enjoined them pending Supreme Court rulings on related cases.[27]

In the years following the *Webster* decision, however, the attitudes of voters and of state legislators underwent a significant change. Acknowledging their failures before 1989, interviewed pro-choice leaders said that state legislators voted pro-life for reasons of conscience but also because the lawmakers felt that *Roe* protected a woman's basic reproductive rights. A pro-life vote in the legislature therefore had little effect but was politically easy to explain to an electorate mobilized largely by pro-life organizations. The *Webster* decision, though, weakened the *Roe* decision—or so it seemed to the Illinois legislators—and forced these representatives to reconsider their views. *Webster* also energized citizens and groups on both sides of the issue, each seeing an opportunity to definitively win (or lose) this public policy debate.[28]

The abortion issue and its associated issue networks are fast becoming a divisive issue in Illinois state elections. Pro-choice PACs in particular have mobilized their resources with some success.[29] In 1990, Personal PAC, the most active of the pro-choice political action committees in the state, could jubilantly issue the following notice to its sponsors.

We won! In every race that Personal PAC targeted as a priority, the pro-choice candidate won! . . . Six formerly anti-choice House seats are now held by six pro-choice legislators for a stunning 12 seat gain by pro-choice forces. . . . Not a single pro-choice incumbent running for re-election was defeated anywhere in Illinois. . . . We are clearly on the road to transforming Illinois into a solidly pro-choice state in the 1990s.[30]

Because Illinois has had no campaign finance ceilings for its state elections, PAC donations become critically important. Personal PAC, for example, ultimately committed $25,000 in financial and service support to each of the three campaigns it sponsored against targeted pro-life legislators.[31] Although pro-life organizations were also active in the 1990 election, the electoral vulnerability of defeated pro-life legislative incumbents had to send a warning to other elected officials. In a few highly publicized instances, state legislators changed their position from pro-life to pro-choice; others, while keeping a lower profile, were unwilling to regulate abortion with the stringency displayed in the 1970s and 1980s.

Other electoral races were also of concern to the pro-life and pro-choice activists, though again the pro-choice efforts seemed more successful. During the 1980s, Republican Governor Jim Thompson vetoed every bill that constrained access to abortions, obliging pro-life organizers to marshall enough votes to overturn a veto.[32] In 1990, because Thompson did not again seek re-election, the gubernatorial candidates were Republican Jim Edgar (Thompson's Secretary of State) and Democrat Neil Hartigan (Thompson's State Attorney General). Neither candidate was endorsed by pro-life organizations: Edgar had supported a number of Thompson's vetoes on earlier pro-life legislation and Hartigan was denounced for his negotiated settlement in *Ragsdale v. Turnock,* an outcome described as a victory for pro-choice views on the licensing standards for abortion clinics. Yet neither candidate was supported by pro-choice organizations, either: Edgar's position on minor access/parental consent was unclear while Hartigan had reservations about public funding. Still, pro-choice activists were not dismayed when Edgar won the election. Thus, in addition to gaining strength in the state legislature, the pro-choice coalition retained its original power base in the Governor's mansion. Pro-choice groups also retained a source of support in the State Attorney General's Office when their favored candidate, Democrat Roland Burris, won a competitive election.[33]

Responding to this change in their political power, Illinois pro-life organizations are no longer seeking to ban abortions in the immediate future. Instead, they are monitoring the outcomes of various test cases in the Supreme Court, intending to push the state law to the most stringent standards for regulating abortion that are already recognized as Constitutional. This strategy allows the Illinois pro-life coalition to conserve its political resources for lobbying on behalf of their agenda within the state as opposed to litigating in the federal courts.[34]

Pro-choice state legislators, though, were far less optimistic than were lobbyists in evaluating their opportunities for legislative gains. Aware of electoral developments, pro-life legislators also pointed out that the 1989–1990 legislative session had not passed any pro-life abortion legislation.[35] In the 1991–1992 session, however, pro-life legislators had again submitted bills regarding minor access/parental consent, fetal tissue experimentation, and gestational viability; harried and weary of the controversies surrounding these issues, pro-choice legislators were uncertain that they could defeat these proposals.

Any action on these matters, however, will probably wait until late 1992 and possibly until the next session of the General Assembly. During 1991, the Illinois legislature will have to pass a budget, revising its fiscal policies to cope with an economic recession. The legislature will also have to construct a redistricting plan for the state, eliminating two Congressional districts and significantly altering others.[36] The political and partisan confrontations surrounding these matters are likely to be so great that legislators will avoid other divisive issues, among them abortion.

Still, the proposed bills—six submitted by pro-life representatives and one by pro-choice representatives—give substance to the broad trends described above. Most obvious is the fact that pro-choice representatives are not writing legislation. Pro-choice lawmakers may submit one additional bill, easing minors' access to abortion by limiting parental consent requirements, but their legislative restraint is part of a deliberate political strategy. Although the tone of the Abortion Law of 1975 is markedly pro-life, pro-choice activists view abortion as "basically legal" in Illinois. As a result of this interpretation, they describe their actions as protecting an established right rather than claiming a new privilege. Their single bill, as of mid-1991, therefore proposes to restore public funding for abortion, an effort which they describe as a moral and fiscal responsibility.[37]

The six bills proposed by pro-life state legislators are briefly summarized below.

- A requirement that the human fetus be cremated, interred by burial, or dealt with as required by the Director of Public Health. These arrangements need not be discussed with the mother.[38]
- A prohibition of all abortions after the point of fetal viability unless "it is necessary to prevent either the death of the pregnant woman or the substantial and irreversible impairment of a major bodily function of the woman."[39]
- A statement that "[n]othing in [the 1975 Act] shall be construed to create a right to an abortion." The bill also bans the use of fetal tissue for research.[40]
- A requirement that doctors performing abortions provide a detailed accounting of the patient's socio-economic status and medical history; the doctor's name, the facility, and the medical procedure must be described in precise terms.[41]
- A prescription for mandatory viability testing when the fetus has a gestational age of 20 weeks or more and the woman requests an abortion. Illinois law already stringently regulates abortions following fetal viability.[42]
- An obligation that the attending or referring physician inform the woman, at least 72 hours before the abortion, of the gestational age of the fetus

and the manner in which the human fetus develops in the womb, the method by which the abortion will be conducted and its attendant dangers; and the availability of public health programs to provide support if the woman wishes to take her pregnancy to full term.[43]

Many of these proposals continue the Illinois pro-life agenda of regulating the performance of abortions as a means of limiting access to the procedure. The reporting requirement legislation, in particular, is proposed because former State Attorney General Hartigan enjoined earlier legislation as unconstitutional, arguing that its detailed statistics compromised the woman's right to privacy. A new development in pro-life legislative proposals, however, is the concern that the woman be educated about the long-term implications of an abortion. Yet the pro-life message about reproduction and responsibility is unclear when the bills are studied as a single package: Some proposals encourage the woman to think critically about her decision and still others exempt her from knowledge, as in directing "the disposal of the remains" of her fetus.[44]

The Catholic Church and Abortion in Illinois

In allowing the states greater freedom to govern in the matter of abortion, the *Webster* ruling also encouraged the legislatures to conduct widely varying conversations. Today, the membership and characteristics of pro-choice/pro-life networks vary greatly from state to state; determining some of the reasons for that diversity gives impetus to this text, which focuses on the role of the Roman Catholic Church in this issue network. In Illinois, one might expect that Archbishop Joseph Cardinal Bernardin's stress on the consistent ethic of life would cause the Catholic Conference of Illinois to undertake extensive pro-life lobbying efforts. That expectation is fulfilled. But Bernardin and the Catholic Conference have a life agenda which extends beyond abortion and is sometimes at odds with the work of other pro-life organizations.

Developing its priorities in consultation with bishops and church personnel throughout the state, the Catholic Conference of Illinois focuses upon quality of life issues, an emphasis entirely in accord with the Cardinal's consistent ethic.[45] In 1991, the concerns of the Illinois Catholic Conference were grouped into eight broad areas: pro-life issues, community affairs, education, social services (especially for children and families), homes for the aging, campus ministry, rural life, and lay organizations.[46] Commenting upon pro-life matters, Executive Director Jimmy Lago made the following statement.

We in the church have got to talk along two lines. We've got to get some restrictions in a legislative way, but we've also got to talk a lot about some programmatic ways that we would consider alternatives to abortion—neonatal care, pregnancy counseling services, single-parent supports and traditional public welfare stuff. . . . But we as a church have a broader perspective. . . . We've got to deal with this in a complex way rather than a simple way. Our vision of pro-life is broader than just antiabortion.[47]

These are words that reflect the goals of Bernardin's consistent ethic, suggesting that the Cardinal is drawing the church in Illinois into an acceptance of his theory. Yet the Conference also expresses some serious differences of opinion with pro-life organizations, most frequently on medical issues surrounding death and dying. The dialogue between the Conference and the coalition is therefore "regular," but does not necessarily conclude in agreement.[48]

The Conference's independent approach to pro-life issues has drawn criticism from those on both sides of the abortion debate. Some observers, while recognizing that the Conference agenda is consistent with the seamless garment argument, conclude that Bernardin is deliberately stepping away from abortion battles. As one pro-choice activist remarked during an interview, "I'm speculating, but it could be because he has ambitions within the church—he doesn't need this conflict—that he is doing more soft pedalling on this issue. Especially given that clergy and laity have such a difference of opinion." This view is more commonly held by pro-life activists who, without necessarily wishing to impugn the Cardinal's character, cannot understand why he is not more outspoken on abortion. Bernardin has, for example, resisted repeated requests that certain state politicians (among them, then-State Attorney General Neil Hartigan for his role in the *Ragsdale* settlement[49]) be excommunicated or censured; the Cardinal has retained his contacts with all levels of state government, with pro-life and pro-choice politicians. Commenting upon this insider approach to influencing state government, one pro-choice lobbyist stressed the professionalism of Bernardin's political performance.

> Bernardin is definitely felt in Springfield. He has written letters to the legislators, the Cook County commissioners, and so on. He also has a lobbyist and can draw on the large Catholic population in the legislature and in Illinois—although there isn't a complete link between the Catholic church and pro-life organizations. [Bernardin is] intelligent and people smart; he handles his public relations in a positive way. But the [consistent ethic of life] is not in the forefront of the debate [over abortion] because it includes health care for the poor and other programs.[50]

Again the breadth of the Catholic Conference agenda is perceived as distinguishing this lobby from others engaged in debating abortion policies. Another pro-choice lobbyist, though, denied that this wider focus diluted its pro-life/antiabortion message although he recognized Bernardin was also interested in other matters.

> Bernardin is not a moderating force—he is pretty clearly antichoice, not questioning the church position. His influence comes through legislators who identify themselves as Catholic and find in that [identity] the genesis of their position. The Catholic Conference also has a lobbyist in Springfield, but he doesn't assume real leadership in this area. . . . Bernardin is pretty clear on his position. He's not into excommunicating people, if that's what you mean by a moderating effect.[51]

Bernardin's standards for public policy have won reluctant respect but have left both sides of the debate somewhat discontented. While this may be the defining characteristic of a true moderate, it also suggests that Bernardin's talents as a mediator have proven less successful in church-state relations than in controversies more internal to the church hierarchy.

Bernardin has, however, proven able to exercise personal influence over the making of abortion policy. In the 1990 elections, Richard Phelan was elected President of the Cook County Board of Commissioners. This Board, as one of its responsibilities, establishes general medical policies for the Cook County Hospital which services the poor and medically uninsured of the Chicago area. Phelan, a pro-choice advocate, campaigned on a promise to restore abortion on demand to the list of services available at the county hospital. Phelan's speeches and subsequent electoral success touched off immediate policy disputes.

During the campaign, Bernardin prepared an editorial for the archdiocesan newspaper that argued against Phelan's proposals without actually mentioning the candidate by name.[52] After the election, Bernardin arranged a meeting with the new President, and counselors from the church and the pro-choice activist conferred on the most appropriate allocation of the limited resources available to the county hospital. Phelan's public position remained pro-choice but he did not bring the abortion issue before his board. Nor did he attempt to change the hospital policies by executive order. That the procedure itself is still not permitted at Cook County Hospital is viewed—at least in part—as evidence of Bernardin's ability to mobilize clergy and laity to conduct a constructive dialogue with Chicago politicians.

Notably, Bernardin's criticism of the Phelan proposal had both theological and political elements. The decision to reinstitute abortions at the hospital was described as "wrong in principle" because the hospital was intended to heal and preserve life, not "to destroy the lives of . . . unborn children." But also, Bernardin contended that the resources Phelan was directing to abortion were needed for trauma and health care clinics, nutritional and educational programs, and care for AIDS patients and for the fragile elderly.[53] As the success of his lobbying attests, Bernardin has a demonstrated ability to analyze public programs and to work with the system on behalf of the community.[54]

This approach to problem solving is perceived by some as a weakness. Testifying to this interpretation is Joseph Scheidler, who has often appeared frustrated by Bernardin's unwillingness to do more for the pro-life effort. Rarely confronting one another in person, their recommendations and counter-suggestions are usually conveyed through articles about abortion politics in the *Chicago Tribune*. Bernardin is generally the respondent, explaining why he will not take the action requested by Scheidler. In light of Bernardin's established political philosophy and behavior, it is not surprising that he has resisted invitations to stage media events or to perform other such actions.

In summary, the *Webster* decision altered the evolution of abortion policies in Illinois. The potential threat to the *Roe* guidelines for abortion mobilized both pro-choice and pro-life organizations; the Supreme Court's willingness to allow the state legislatures to rule on these matters obliged representatives to re-assess their policy positions and the views of their electorates. In the midst of this change, Bernardin held to his conviction that abortion must be considered in the broader context of health and social programming. Always more comfortable as a political insider, he learned the political culture of Illinois and succeeded in establishing a reputation as a thoughtful moderate.[55] This same role also rendered him the target of much criticism. Yet he did contribute to the realization of some immediate pro-life goals, as in the Cook County Hospital confrontation, and continues to be a strong advocate of policy perspectives congruent with the consistent ethic.

Conclusion

Bernardin's consistent ethic of life is a creative synthesis, an alternative vision of policymaking that seeks a liberal and conservative consensus on the value of life. By its author's own admission, the success of this ethic may be judged by its achievement of two goals. First, the consistent ethic is intended to guard the political independence of the American Roman Catholic bishops, protecting them from pressures to endorse or criticize particular candidates or policy proposals. In this respect, the ethic is nonpartisan and perhaps even nonpolitical in character, a statement of moral understanding rather than a legislative recommendation. And yet the consistent ethic is also meant to change the character and quality of the debates that routinely transpire between pro-life and pro-choice activists. This second goal is intensely political and is directed at an audience outside the Roman Catholic Church, Bernardin apparently seeking to mediate between organizations that perceive themselves as polarized opposites. Taking Bernardin's experiences in Illinois as a case study for the impact of the consistent ethic in post-*Webster* abortion politics, it is clear that while his theory is able to present and explain the distinctive perspective of Roman Catholic church leadership, it has not provided a meeting ground for pro-life and pro-choice advocates.

In part, this outcome may reflect the extraordinary and somewhat unrealistic nature of its standards for success. After all, one can scarcely imagine a political statement that allows one group to distinguish itself from all others and yet also enables those same "others" to resolve their differences among themselves. As a bishop, Bernardin's words necessarily appeal to a particular sub-set of the population and he may rightfully reflect that this appeal will be strong and enduring—he has provided his fellow bishops with a new understanding of the relationship that exists among all life issues and, through the peace pastoral and the Respect Life program, his ideals reach congregations nationwide.[56] Perhaps this theological and pastoral accomplishment is sufficient compensation for the ethic's failure in the political realm.

Some analysts have attributed the political inadequacies of the consistent ethic, incidentally dismissing any hope of its eventual political relevance, to its rejection of the established boundaries of liberal and conservative thought in American politics. Politicians cannot combine liberal stances on nuclear disarmament and social programming with vigorous opposition to abortion, these critics maintain, because party organizations and voters will resist such a juxtapositioning of policy stances.[57] This objection, however, seems unnecessarily limiting of elected officials, who may be able to explain their votes on life issues and thereby persuade their constituents to accept the consistent ethic.[58] Pro-choice legislators in Illinois come from both the Democratic and Republican parties; there is no reason to presume that a pro-life stance could not be similarly bipartisan. The conditions for such a development are present in Illinois. As confirmed by an interview with a legislative aide to Democrat Michael J. Madigan, Speaker of the Illinois House of Representatives, the state Democratic Party has resolutely declined to take a unified stand on abortion, allowing each elected official to take the position that she or he considers appropriate.[59] The leader of the Republican Party, newly elected Governor Jim Edgar, is also equivocating about a strong party stand on this issue. Such deliberate lapses in party discipline seem to encourage bipartisan coalition-building on abortion policies, as on other life issues.

The consistent ethic will probably not be realized in Illinois, however, or at least not by the current generation of lawmakers. Activists, lobbyists, and legislators in Illinois do not embrace the consistent ethic as a "framework" for abortion policymaking because the theory draws their efforts away from a relatively narrow and definable policy area into a broad expanse of social planning and programming possibilities.[60] In an era when political campaigns are dominated by the technology of the mass media, and expect that little real political learning will occur during an election, candidates are unwilling to adopt complex concepts in lieu of established pro-choice or pro-life stances. Then, too, the breadth of the consistent ethic ensures that its impacts will necessarily be indirect. Its proposals, for example, would make it economically feasible for a woman to carry her pregnancy to full term and to deliver a healthy child. But there are no guarantees that women will make this choice, a reality that motivates Bernardin to advocate legislation explicitly prohibiting abortion. For legislators on a two-year election cycle, though, there is a need to point to more immediate and direct accomplishments—and so they relegate the social programs to the background and stress the impact of regulations which they impose directly on abortion.

Even assuming that the voting population could be educated to the pro-life philosophy of the consistent ethic, the theory remains an unlikely base for policy resolutions among pro-life and pro-choice advocates in Illinois. In breadth the consistent ethic rivals the platforms of the Republican and Democratic national political parties; activism on this scale would require resources beyond the dreams of most interest groups or even of most interest group coalitions.

Bernardin himself has recognized this irony—that the limitless quality of the consistent ethic is a powerful limitation to its real political contribution—and has made some efforts to render the ethic more accessible.

Now it is very important to understand that even though all these issues are linked, nonetheless each is distinct; each requires its own moral analysis. And the solution for one may not be the solution for the other. Moreover, at any given point, all may not be equally important. One issue might be more urgent or need greater attention at a particular moment than another one.[61]

Even as he admits of different emphases within the ethic, however, Bernardin is drawing greater numbers of more widely varying perspectives into his dialogue. Such an acceptance of complexity and diversity precludes the setting of absolute rules and clear priorities; Bernardin's philosophy will always be a disappointment to those who favor the pronouncements of a Cardinal Archbishop Bernard Law or John O'Connor. And insofar as politics is the realm of establishing obligations rather than realizing aspirations, Bernardin's political philosophy may indeed be politically unrealizable. Yet upon reflection, it is difficult to decide whether "politics as usual" is a pastoral failure for Bernardin or a powerful rejection of unknown possibilities by established political actors.

Notes

1. *Current Biography Yearbook, 1982,* Joseph Louis Bernardin; *New York Times,* 20 November 1974, p. 26; *New York Times,* 25 August 1982, p. 4; "Religion: Defense of a 'Seamless Garment,'" *Time* 122 (19 December 1983), p. 62; Thomas H. Stahel, "A Report: Cardinal Bernardin on the 'Forgotten Factor' and Other Gaps in the Abortion Debate," *America* 162 (7 April 1990), pp. 354–356.

2. Joseph Bernardin, "*Pacem in terris:* Twenty Years Later," *Bulletin of the Atomic Scientists* 40 (February 1984), pp. 11–14; *Origins,* 1 March 1990, pp. 629–631.

3. Thomas G. Fuechtmann, ed., *The Consistent Ethic of Life* (Chicago: Sheed and Ward, 1988), passim; *New York Times,* 7 December 1983, pp. 1, B8; *Origins,* 29 December 1983, pp. 491–494; *Origins,* 5 April 1984, pp. 705–709; *Origins,* 29 November 1984, pp. 397–398; *Origins,* 12 April 1990, pp. 741–748.

4. "The Consistent Ethic, An Interview with Joseph Cardinal Bernardin," *Second Opinion* 8 (February 1988), pp. 104–105.

5. *Origins,* 25 October 1984, pp. 289–291; *Origins,* 30 October 1986, p. 347.

6. *New York Times,* 1 September 1976, pp. 1, 44; *New York Times,* 11 September 1976, pp. 1, 20; *New York Times,* 17 September 1976, pp. 1, D12; *New York Times,* 26 September 1976, p. 28; *New York Times,* 3 March 1977, p. 16.

7. *Origins,* 8 November 1984, pp. 321–328; *Origins,* 29 November 1984, pp. 397–398; *Origins,* 1 September 1988, pp. 186–189.

8. "Abortion, Politics and the Bishops," *Commonweal* 111 (23 March 1984), pp. 163–165; *Origins,* 6 September 1984, pp. 184–186.

9. *Origins,* 6 September 1984, p. 185; *Origins,* 1 November 1984, p. 311.

10. *Origins,* 12 April 1990, p. 745.

11. *Origins,* 25 October 1984, pp. 291–301.

12. *Origins,* 25 October 1984, p. 298.

13. See *New York Times,* 4 May 1987, p. 21; *Origins,* 28 May 1987, pp. 21–26; "The Consistent Ethic, An Interview with Joseph Cardinal Bernardin," *Second Opinion,* p. 112.

14. Joseph Bernardin, "Religion and Politics," in Richard McMunn, ed., *Religion in Politics* (Milwaukee, Wisconsin: The Catholic League for Religious and Civil Rights, 1985), p. 68.

15. *New York Times,* 2 October 1985, p. 12.

16. *New York Times,* 15 November 1985, p. 19; *Origins,* 30 October 1986, p. 347.

17. Joseph Bernardin, "Dialogue With World Aids Renewal," *New World*, 18 May 1990, page unknown; *Origins*, 2 May 1985, pp. 759–761.

18. *Origins*, 17 October 1985, pp. 306–308; *Origins*, 30 October 1986, p. 349.

19. *Origins*, 2 February 1984, p. 568; *Origins*, 22 October 1987, pp. 348–349; *Origins*, 12 April 1990, p. 747.

20. Joseph Bernardin, "Abortion: Catholics Must Change Hearts As Well As Laws," *U.S. Catholic* 54 (December 1989), p. 33.

21. For an illustration and analysis of this debate, see *Origins*, 27 September 1984, pp. 234–240; *Origins*, 25 October 1984, pp. 291–301; *New York Times*, 21 March 1990, p. 24.

22. Joseph Bernardin, "Address for National Consultation on Obscenity, Pornography, and Indecency," in Fuechtmann, ed., *Consistent Ethic of Life*, pp. 31–32; *Origins*, 12 July 1984, pp. 120–122; *Origins*, 9 August 1984, 154–158.

23. *New York Times*, 26 February 1977, p. 19.

24. *Origins*, 26 January 1984, 545–549; *Origins*, 12 April 1990, p. 746.

25. *Origins*, 30 October 1986, pp. 347, 349; *Origins*, 12 April 1990, p. 746.

26. Illinois Statutes, Chapter 38, paragraph 81–21.

27. Michael D. Klemens, "Abortion as State Issue: Pro-Life and Pro-Choice Forces Prepare for General Assembly Vote," *Illinois Issues* 15 (October 1989), p. 15.

28. Pam Sutherland, Illinois Planned Parenthood lobbyist; telephone interview conducted by MaryAnne Borrelli, 13 April 1991.

29. Terry Cosgrove, Director of Personal PAC; telephone interview conducted by MaryAnne Borrelli, 11 April 1991; Marcie Love, Founder and Chair of Personal PAC, Board Member of Illinois NARAL; telephone interview conducted by MaryAnne Borrelli, 11 April 1991.

30. Memo, To Board of Directors and Special Friends [of Personal PAC], From Marcie Love and Terry Cosgrove, November 1990.

31. "The 1990 Illinois Elections Are About Choice . . ." Personal PAC campaign brochure, 1990; Memo, To Board of Directors and Special Friends [of Personal PAC], From Marcie Love and Terry Cosgrove, November 1990.

32. George J. Church, "Five Political Hot Spots," *Time* 128 (17 July 1989), p. 64; Klemens, "Abortion as State Issue," p. 15.

33. *Chicago Tribune*, 23 November 1989, pp. 1–24; *Chicago Tribune*, 8 November 1990, p. 21; *Ragsdale v. Turnock* 841 F.2nd 1358; Interviews with Cosgrove, Love Sutherland; Confidential interviews with several pro-life activists.

34. Jimmy Lago, Executive Director of the Illinois Catholic Conference; telephone interview conducted by MaryAnne Borrelli on 16 April 1991; Ralph Rivera, Chair of the Illinois Pro-Life Coalition; telephone interview conducted by MaryAnne Borrelli on 25 January 1991.

35. Several confidential interviews were conducted with pro-life and pro-choice state legislators. See also Klemens, "Abortion as State Issue," pp. 13–15.

36. James D. Nowlan, "Redistricting: The Politics," *Illinois Remap '91*, March 1991; "Hardball Time in Windy City," *National Journal* 23 (4 May 1991), p. 1031.

37. House Bill 2083, proposed to the 87th General Assembly of the State of Illinois; "*Choice* Facts: House Bill 2083," Bulletin prepared by Planned Parenthood Federation of America, [1991]; Interview with Sutherland.

38. House Bill 0612, proposed to the 87th General Assembly of the State of Illinois.

39. House Bill 0622, proposed to the 87th General Assembly of the State of Illinois.

40. House Bill 0709, proposed to the 87th General Assembly of the State of Illinois.

41. House Bill 1202, proposed to the 87th General Assembly of the State of Illinois.

42. House Bill 2265, proposed to the 87th General Assembly of the State of Illinois.

43. House Bill 2624, proposed to the 87th General Assembly of the State of Illinois.

44. House Bill 0612.

45. *Origins*, 6 June 1985, p. 38.

46. "Priorities, 1990–91," Catholic Conference of Illinois brochure, 1990.

47. Quoted in Michael J. Behr, "With Defeat, Abortion Debate Back to 'Grass Roots,'" *New World*, 20 October 1989, page unknown; Interview with Lago.

48. Joseph Bernardin, "Don't Play God on Life, Death Issues," *New World*, 22 June 1990, page unknown; Joseph Bernardin, "Don't Play God with End-of-Life Issues," *New World*, 29 June 1990, page unknown; *New York Times*, 27 May 1988, p. 12; Interviews with Lago and Rivera.

49. *Chicago Tribune*, 23 November 1989, p. 24.

50. Interview with Love.

51. Rob Schofield, Illinois American Civil Liberties Union lobbyist; telephone interview conducted by MaryAnne Borrelli, 22 January 1991.

52. Joseph Bernardin, "County Weighs New Abortion Policy," *New World*, 1 June 1990, page unknown.

53. "Abortion Pending at County, Alternatives Offered," *New World*, 16 November 1990, page unknown; Jay Copp, "Abortions at County Unlikely, Opponents Say," *New World*, 21 December 1991, p. 3.

54. *Origins*, 31 January 1985, pp. 543–548.

55. Jeff Brady, "Readers' Choice: Top 10 Illinoisians of the Decade," *Illinois Issues* 11 (August-September 1985), p. 16; Monsignor John Egan, Archbishop Cardinal Bernardin's former Director of Human Relations and Ecumenism for the Archdiocese of Chicago; telephone interview conducted by MaryAnne Borrelli, 11 April 1991.

56. For a discussion of Bernardin's work as representing a prophetic tradition of leadership, see: J. Stephen Cleghorn, "Respect for Life: Research Notes on Cardinal Bernardin's 'Seamless Garment,'" *Review of Religious Research* 28 (December 1986), pp. 129–142.

57. David R. Carlin, Jr., "Patchy Garment: How Many Votes Has Bernardin?" *Commonweal* 111 (10 August 1984), pp. 422–423.

58. Sidney Callahan and Daniel Callahan, "Breaking Through the Stereotypes," *Commonweal* 111 (5 October 1984), pp. 520–523.

59. Klemens, "Abortion as State Issue," p. 15.

60. Interview with Rivera.

61. "The Consistent Ethic, An Interview with Joseph Cardinal Bernardin," *Second Opinion*, p. 105.

5

The Abortion Control Act of 1989: The Pennsylvania Catholics

Thomas J. O'Hara

In November of 1989, the Pennsylvania legislature passed what was then the nation's most restrictive abortion law. The legislation was quickly signed by Governor Robert Casey, a Democrat. This paper is an investigation into that legislation. In and of itself, an analysis of the actions of the legislature, interest groups, and the governor on this sensitive and controversial public policy issue, presents an interesting case study of policy formulation. Beyond that, however, there are several implications that can be drawn from this case study. One, the sensitive nature of this policy issue and the actions of the political actors can be understood within the framework developed by Murray Edelman. Secondly, Allen Hertzke has produced some ground breaking analysis of the role of the religious lobbies in the policy process and this paper follows on the insights developed by Hertzke. This paper will have as a major emphasis the role of the Catholic community in the passage of the Abortion Control Act. However, such analysis can only be undertaken if there is a wider discussion of the issues and actors involved in the formation of the legislation.

Two additional points need to be made before beginning the analysis. First, in this highly emotional public policy issue even the names attached to the opposing sides are rather sensitive issues. Very often when I spoke with representatives of the side favoring abortion restrictions, they would call the opposing side "pro-abortion." When I spoke with representatives of those opposed to abortion restrictions, they would call the other side "anti-choice." Wording is clearly significant and highly charged. Who wants to be tabbed, in a land that cherishes freedom and choice, as "anti-choice?" Who wants to be tabbed, in a country that attempts to promote human life and dignity, as "pro-abortion?" The use of language is not an insignificant issue. How groups are named is in itself a political issue. Edelman helps us to understand this point very well. The symbolic power of language cannot be ignored within the political arena. For Edelman when the issue is highly sensitive, "language sanctifies action. Through language a group can achieve an immediate result. It evokes a response and is an index of the groups norms."[1] If one group can successfully tab the other group with a name that seems to run contrary to the norms of society, then political power is exerted. Conversely, if you can name your own group signifying a value that is widely held by all of society, political capital is gained. Therefore, for purposes of this paper, the forces on each side of the issue will be referred to by the name they optimally prefer, i.e., "pro-choice" for those opposed to abortion restriction laws, and "pro-life" for those in favor of abortion restriction legislation.

Secondly, this chapter investigates *policy formation.* It attempts to identify the actors and assess the strategies of these actors leading to the passage of significant legislation. This paper is not a commentary on the moral implications of the issue at stake nor on the ethics of the legislation. It does not attempt to make value judgments on the correctness of those who argue for the rights of women's reproductive freedom as opposed to those who argue for the right of human life as they see it, to be protected. Thus when this chapter addresses the activities of the Roman Catholic Church in Pennsylvania with regard to this legislation, there will be no attempt to discuss important theological and ecclesiological questions. Rather, the analysis will focus on the church as a *political actor* in the policy issue of abortion in the state of Pennsylvania.

The importance of this legislation is obvious. On July 3, 1989, the Supreme Court allowed for state restrictions on abortion in its *Webster v. Reproductive Health Services* decision. This seemed to give the signal to other states that challenges to *Roe v. Wade,* in the form of state legislation, would be entertained. Pennsylvania was one of the first states to pick up on this Supreme Court signal by attempting to legislate new abortion restriction legislation. That Pennsylvania was quick to respond was not surprising for Pennsylvania is a state with a history of antiabortion legislation. In the last fifteen years the state has passed eight antiabortion amendments. Most of these amendments have been blocked by the courts. The most prominent restriction that remains in effect is the provision that bars Medicaid funding of abortion except in cases of rape, incest, or a threat to a woman's life. In effect, before *Webster* the legislature would routinely pass abortion restriction legislation knowing that the courts would probably enjoin the legislation because of its unconstitutionality. The significant difference with this particular piece of legislation was that because of the *Webster* ruling, there was a greater likelihood that the legislation could indeed take effect.

The chief sponsor of the legislation, Rep. Steve Friend, a Republican from suburban Philadelphia, was a long time proponent of abortion restriction legislation. Friend stated, "We view the *Webster* decision as a window of opportunity. As soon as it came down, we began to work on new legislation."[2] Further, Rep. Friend was interested in challenging the concept of legalized abortion by testing how much the legislature could restrict abortions in Pennsylvania. He stated, "If you look at the *Webster* decision, the Supreme Court appears to be inviting state legislatures to pass additional legislation that will permit the court to look at the fabric of *Roe v. Wade.*[3] The chance to pass legislation that would directly challenge *Roe v. Wade* obviously heightened the intensity of the legislative battle, bringing national attention to Harrisburg. The national media turned its institutional eyes upon Pennsylvania and seemed to escalate even more the intensity of the legislative battle. The media speculated that the legislature would pass very significant restrictions on abortion. In fact, the ultimate piece of legislation was less dramatic than the media had led most to believe. During interviews I conducted for this research, representatives on both sides of the issue complained that the media had a tendency to distort the reality of the situation. Nevertheless, the Pennsylvania legislature responded to the power of the media in that for the first time in the history of the legislature, proceedings in the General Assembly were covered by live television.

Edelman gives us insight into why this policy discussion assumed the importance it did and why the media were inextricably involved in the process. Abortion is one of those policy issues that for Edelman reaches to the "deepest expressions of meaning" for a given society. The practical battle of what type of legislation would be produced was far from the whole story. The issue was more than legislation, for there was a far deeper *symbolic* battle that was occurring. "The formal categories that name political goals are to be understood as expressions of created values. They tell us something about the prevailing values in society."[4] The case can be made that the legislation became symbolic, and specifically in Edelman's terms a condensation symbol. Such a symbol, "evokes a quiescent or an aroused mass response because it *symbolizes* a threat or a reassurance."[5] Thus for pro-life forces the legislation symbolized a reassurance and for pro-choice forces the legislation symbolized a threat. Significantly, Edelman states that when such a symbolic point is at stake "every day intensive reporting by mass media is drunk up by the public as drama, for such reporting is the raw material of symbolization."[6] Thus, it is important to realize that this issue was not simply about the practical details of passing legislation; there was a deeper symbolic issue at hand, and the media helped sustain that symbolic battle.

On October 3, 1989, the abortion restriction legislation with eighty co-sponsors was submitted to the House Judiciary Committee. The committee approved the legislation 20–2, clearing the way for a vote on the House floor. Extensive committee hearings were not held. Opponents of the bill accused Rep. Friend of trying to railroad his bill through the legislature. Rep. Lois Hagerty, a Republican and pro-choice leader complained, "We are rushing to an uneducated vote on the floor."[7] Rep. Friend countered that the issue of abortion had already been extensively debated in previous legislative sessions claiming, "No more talk is needed for I want to deal with this in a prompt, expeditious manner."[8] As that legislation was sent to the floor of the House the principal aspects of the legislation were as follows (using terminology of the bill):

1. No abortion, at any stage of pregnancy, is allowed for the purpose of sex selection.
2. At least twenty-four hours prior to an abortion, the doctor performing the abortion or the referring physician must inform the woman of: (a)

risks and alternatives to the abortion, (b) probable gestational age of the unborn child, (c) risks associated with carrying the child to term. Also, the doctor must inform the woman that printed materials are available that describe the unborn child, list agencies which provide alternatives to abortion, and provide information on medical assistance benefits. A copy of the materials will be provided to her free of charge if she chooses to review them.

3. The doctor performing the abortion upon a married woman must obtain a signed statement from the woman that she has notified her husband of the impending abortion except for the following reasons: (a) spouse is not the father of the child, (b) the woman could not locate her husband after diligent effort, (c) the pregnancy resulted from spousal sexual assault, (d) the woman has reason to believe she is likely to have bodily injury inflicted upon her if she notifies her spouse.

4. The bill prohibits the performance of an abortion when the woman is twenty-four or more weeks pregnant, unless a doctor reasonably believes that the abortion is necessary to prevent death or substantial and irreversible impairment of a major bodily function. Where an abortion is permitted and no medical emergency exists, the doctor must also comply with the following: (a) obtain a second physician's opinion which concurs with his assessment of the necessity of the abortion, (b) terminate the pregnancy in a manner which is safest for the child unless that would significantly increase risk to the mother, (c) arrange for a second doctor to be present and care for the child in case it survives.

5. The bill regulates the circumstances under which experimentation and transplant of fetal tissue may be used.

6. The bill provides the Attorney General of the state of Pennsylvania concurrent jurisdiction to investigate and institute criminal proceedings for violations of any provision of this Act.

7. The bill provides stiff penalties for doctors who violate the provisions of the law, up to seven years in prison and $1500 in fines.

After nine hours of debate on the House floor, the House considered more than twenty-five amendments attempting to weaken the bill. Almost all of those amendments failed. An amendment to substitute the term "viability" for the term "gestation age" and use viability rather than twenty-four weeks as the point at which abortion would be prohibited, failed 47–152. An amendment to substitute broader health language for abortion after twenty-four weeks such that abortion would be allowed for "substantial risk of death, serious physical illness, *or* protracted loss or impairment of bodily function," failed 70–131. An amendment to add an exception for fatal fetal anomalies after twenty-four weeks failed, 73–126. Rape and incest exceptions after twenty-four weeks failed 63–137, a suicide exception failed 49–151. An amendment to strike the spousal notification section of the bill failed 75–126. An attempt to put the issue to a state wide popular referendum failed 64–137.

The final consideration of the bill led to adoption 143–58. Despite overwhelming defeats on most issues, the pro-choice forces did score some successes. The House voted 122–79 to ease the restrictions on the use of fetal tissue for experimentation. In addition, an amendment passed which allows doctors to talk to women about donating fetal tissue for research *before* they have an abortion. Rep. Friend wanted to restrict any discussion to after the abortion was complete. The pro-choice forces passed by 188–10 an amendment that the Commonwealth of Pennsylvania would not interfere with the use or methods of contraception. In addition, the section of the bill that gave the Attorney General concurrent jurisdiction in abortion violations was deleted. In the end, though, it was a major victory for the pro-life forces. This led Rep. Karen Ritter, Democrat and leader of the pro-choice forces to say, "This bill is cruel and mean spirited. The polls tell us that the tide is turning on the abortion issue and my colleagues are about to miss the boat."[9]

If that were the case, it did not deter Rep. Ritter's colleagues in the Senate. Since the legislation was so soundly passed in the House, approval in the Senate seemed certain. This time there was no television, less drama, and less debate. Indeed, the sponsors attempted to move to vote on the legislation without debate. That move was overturned by a vote of 26–24, giving a temporary measure of success to the pro-choice forces. But each subsequent amendment to weaken the legislation was defeated, and after five hours of debate, the bill passed the Senate 33–17.

Finally, with little fanfare, the governor signed the legislation. He had indicated previously that he would not sign any legislation he felt to be unconstitutional. In signing he stated, "I believe this bill is consistent with the law and does not act as a so called test case. These provisions are appropriate and reasonable given the enormity of the decision any woman faces when she considers having an abortion."[10]

Actors and Strategies

For purposes of analysis, interviews were conducted with key actors involved in this legislation. The principal legislators on either side, aides to the governor, and representatives of key interest groups, were all interviewed so as to present a complete picture of the policy formation stage.

Legislators

The principal legislative force behind the bill was Rep. Steve Friend.[11] A Republican from suburban Philadelphia, Friend has over the years championed the pro-life cause in the Pennsylvania legislature. He is a hard driving legislator who is not deterred easily in his crusade against abortion. Friend has never been deceptive about his ultimate goal; there was no hidden agenda. He made it quite clear that it was his intention to chip away at *Roe v. Wade* step by step. This legislation was just one more step toward that goal. Clearly, he wanted to produce a test case for the Supreme Court to review. Although Friend is a Catholic, in the interview he was careful not to term abortion an essentially religious issue. He insists, "This is not a religious issue but clearly an issue of human rights." Indeed, he readily admits that different religions have differing perspectives on abortion.

Friend sees himself as the legislative coordinator of all the pro-life forces. Each year, at the beginning of the legislative session, Friend pulls the leaders of all the pro-life groups into his office for a conference. He feels the need "to tell them what is possible and what is not possible. Although I oppose abortion philosophically, one needs to be practical. One does not win legislation based on philosophical principle." For this reason, Friend has found it necessary at times to inform the pro-life groups of the realities of the political situation. Indeed, he even expressed some frustration with some of the more ardent pro-lifers who seem to be more concerned with protest and civil disobedience than "practical" political action such as electoral politics.

Although his detractors accuse him of being an ideologue, Friend has shown he will bend when it is clear he is not in a winnable situation. For instance, he compromised on the fetal tissue experimentation aspect of the legislation before it hit the floor. His legislation originally called for a complete ban on all experimentation, but realizing the votes were not there, he reworded the legislation so as simply to impose guidelines (on the floor, he subsequently had to settle for an amendment that made the guidelines even less rigid). When asked about his willingness to compromise he once again spoke of the need to be practical and be willing to attain what is winnable. Friend's advice to activists sums up his apparent legislative strategy, "Success is not measured by input but by outcome. It is not a measure of passion alone but political savvy." On this policy issue, even his detractors agree Friend is passionately committed but also very politically adept.

Rep. Jerry Kozinski was a major Democratic leader of the legislation.[12] Kozinski, like Friend, is blunt enough to say his ultimate goal is to challenge *Roe v. Wade*. Like Friend, he also adheres to a practical strategy. For Kozinski in 1989, that meant constructing a bill that the governor would sign. Since Casey vetoed an abortion restriction act in 1987 because he felt it was unconstitutional, Kozinski felt it was imperative that mistake not be repeated. He stated, "A bill that won't be signed or a law that is ruled unconstitutional doesn't help us." There is an irony here, of course. Kozinski and Friend clearly wanted a bill that tested the limits of the court. The governor wanted no part of a test case. However, since each side wanted some form of legislation, careful negotiation was necessary between the legislative leaders and the governor's office. Kozinski faulted his colleagues in the Idaho and Louisiana legislatures for not employing the same careful strategy with the executive. Kozinski took personal pride in the fact that the Pennsylvania legislation was carefully planned and written. After the *Webster* ruling came down, there was some pressure to call a special session for the purpose of immediately passing restrictive legislation. Kozinski fought that call stating that the legislative pro-life forces needed time to construct the proper legislation, legislation that he freely admits does not please all the pro-life activists. However, he stated that his primary responsibility was not to please the activists but to write and defend legislation that can "survive the legislature and be upheld by the courts." As a result,

Kozinski feels it is not the role of activists to dictate the tone of the legislation. "I vote on the bill so I pay the consequence with my constituents. Therefore I control the legislation."

Rep. Karen Ritter was the chief legislative voice for the pro-choice forces.[13] A second term representative and a Democrat, Ritter is as committed to her position as Rep. Friend is to his. She is clearly a crucial asset of the pro-choice forces. In the years when the Pennsylvania legislature was passing abortion restriction measures easily, there was no "insider" voice to coordinate a counter argument. It was left to the activists to try to influence the legislators from the outside. Such a strategy of relying on only external pressure was not effective. Said one pro-choice activist, "Prior to Rep. Ritter there was no one to lead the way as Rep. Friend did for the other side. We desperately needed a legislator to take control."[14]

In the interview with Rep. Ritter, she described herself much as Friend did, as the legislative coordinator for the activists. But like Friend, she is not totally captured by the activists on her side. Although she has been the champion of the pro-choice forces, she sees herself as a skilled politician and not an ideological activist. She sent a memo to all of her Democratic colleagues, for example, stating that she would not actively oppose any incumbent Democrat in the upcoming elections, regardless of his or her position on abortion. (This is particularly important because those elections chose the legislature that will reapportion Pennsylvania's legislative districts.) Even when speaking at pro-choice rallies, she is careful not to align herself with any one group. Says Ritter, "I am really a moderate, I do not want to be tied to NOW."[15] In the personal interview, Ritter conceded that many of the activists do not consider her liberal enough. For instance, at the point of viability she feels the state has a compelling interest in protecting fetal life.

A second important strategy employed by Ritter was simply to respond to Friend in an official manner within the legislature, by using all the privileges afforded a House member. For instance, when Friend sent her a rather strong letter and sent copies to all the legislators, Ritter responded in kind. She penned an equally strong response and sent copies to all legislators. This helped insure that Friend could not monopolize the legislative dialogue on abortion.

A third strategy was to help prepare challenges for the courts. Whereas Friend had the objective of presenting a test case for the courts, Ritter simply coordinated an attempt to soften the legislation as much as possible and then to challenge in the courts those provisions that they could not defeat on the floor. For example, Ritter saw the sex selection clause as a direct assault on *Roe* because it gives the state permission to outlaw abortions even at an early stage of pregnancy. Whereas Friend looks to the courts with optimism, Ritter is concerned about future judicial rulings on this legislation. (At the time of these interviews Justices Brennan and Marshall had not yet resigned. No doubt Ritter's concern has escalated). After the bill was passed, the pro-choice forces, in a suit filed by the ACLU, challenged the spousal consent and twenty-four hour waiting period provisions of the legislation. The court subsequently enjoined those two provisions, pending a trial. The twenty-four weeks provision and the sex selection provision were not challenged. Some have charged that the pro-choice forces were afraid to challenge those provisions because they feared they could lead to a direct test for the dismantling of *Roe*. Ritter denies that, saying they are simply searching for a plaintiff and it is not always easy to find a woman who is willing to serve as the plaintiff. In any event, Ritter clearly places less confidence in the courts, especially after *Webster*.

The Governor's Office

Governor Casey's chief counsel discussed the governor's approach to this legislation.[16] The governor made it clear to all sides that he would only sign legislation he deemed constitutional. He also did not take the lead on this issue nor make it a priority item on his agenda. In 1987, he vetoed abortion legislation because of concerns about a parental consent provision. In 1988, he worked with Friend and others to produce acceptable legislation. In 1989, in early dialogues with Rep. Friend's office, Casey made it clear he was not in the business of supporting test cases. Therefore, the dialogue centered on those issues that conceivably went beyond what the courts would find constitutional. The governor made it clear, for example, that he was more comfortable with a twenty-four week ban as opposed to a twenty week ban that was being discussed. Also, the original provision concerning spousal consent included a court bypass provision for women who were unable to inform their husbands. The governor's staff successfully argued for simple written notice to the doctor, thereby lessening the chance the courts would rule that spousal consent placed an "undue burden" on women. The governor's office is quite confident that the Pennsylvania law can withstand judicial scrutiny. The fact that the pro-choice forces challenged neither the sex selection provision nor the twenty-four week provision led Casey's advisers to feel vindicated in their view that this law is not "terribly restrictive" and that it is within the bounds of acceptable law.

The governor was on a political tight rope. He hoped to be able to sign legislation that would not be used for purposes of a test case. But Friend and Kozinski clearly felt they had produced just such a test. In the end, Casey signed because he was convinced the legislation would not present the dramatic test case that the Supreme Court would use to review *Roe*. Defending its legislation through to the Supreme Court would be costly for the state. In addition, Casey faced re-election in November of 1990. His opponent was the State Auditor General, Barbara Hafer. The fact that Hafer, the Republican, was running on a pro-choice platform, and Casey, the Democrat, on a pro-life platform, put the Democratic pro-choice coordinator, Karen Ritter, in a peculiar situation. Ritter, however, made it clear she supported Casey. In our interview, Ritter said, "Casey is a man of integrity and principle. I truly think he believes the bill to be constitutional. Clearly, I disagree with the governor on this issue. But I think the governor has an excellent record in many other areas of importance."[17] Casey in fact easily won re-election.

Interest Groups

Mary Beliveau is the chief lobbyist for the Pro-Life Federation, a non sectarian, non denominational, composite of pro-life groups.[18] This group is an umbrella organization and very much stresses grass roots organization. Included in this federation are both the Catholic Conference and fundamentalist groups. Beliveau credited Friend for his co-ordinating role and stated that the federation's chief goal was to maintain constituent support for the legislation. In light of the post-*Webster* mobilization of pro-choice forces, Beliveau said it was imperative that the legislators were made aware of constituent preference for this legislation. Beliveau complained that the media had a tendency to exaggerate the scope of the legislation. The federation, therefore, focused on educating the public as to the actual restrictions contained in the bill. Apparently, some constituents were initially opposed to the legislation because they thought abortion was to be outlawed completely. After the Abortion Control Act was passed, the Pro-Life Federation's grass roots strategy became more electoral, concentrating on the election of pro-life candidates to the state legislature.

Morgan Plant was the chief lobbyist for Planned Parenthood.[19] In an interview, she agreed with Rep. Friend that this legislation was a direct challenge to *Roe. v. Wade,* and she argued that the governor had violated his pledge not to sign unconstitutional legislation. Planned Parenthood's chief strategy was to educate the legislators as to the nature of the legislation. For example, legislators had to be made aware of the fact that the health exemption for abortions after twenty-four weeks was so restrictive that many serious health problems or evidence of fetal deformity would still not allow for an abortion to take place. Ms. Plant took little consolation in the few pro-choice amendments that were successful. For example, she stated that the "apparent" victory on fetal experimentation really was based on political considerations of the individual legislators and not on the issue itself. She felt many legislators were privately much more amenable to pro-choice legislation, but the political climate did not allow it. For this reason, her long term strategy is to work for the election of pro-choice candidates in Pennsylvania so as to "change the political landscape on this issue." Her immediate strategy is to challenge all the provisions of the legislation, including the sex selection and the twenty-four week provisions.

The Catholic Community

The only way for us to truly understand the role of the Catholic Church on this policy issue is to place it within the broader perspective that was developed in the first section of this chapter. In order to assess the role the church took on this policy issue, the unit of analysis will be the institutional church, focusing on (1) the Pennsylvania Catholic Conference and (2) the Pennsylvania bishops.

The Pennsylvania Catholic Conference, like its parent organization in Washington, D.C., the United States Catholic Conference, functions as an arm of the Catholic bishops (in this case the bishops of Pennsylvania). Among other functions, the PCC in effect serves as an interest group and a voice for the Catholic Church in the state policy arena. Therefore, this organization represents the church's position on such diverse issues as health care, aid to private schools, capital punishment, and in this case, abortion. The PCC represents one of the strongest and most effective state Catholic conferences in the country. It is well regarded within the church and seen by political analysts in Harrisburg as an effective lobby organization. Almost without exception, in the interviews conducted for this paper, the PCC was raised by the interviewee. One legislator stated, "When the PCC speaks on any issue in this state, they carry considerable clout. They speak as a moral and political force." Another stated, "The PCC was clearly one of the strongest forces behind this legislation." A lobbyist noted, "The Catholic conference clearly is the most significant lobby on this legislation. It is extremely sophisticated, extremely powerful and well regarded."

It is clear that on the passage of the Abortion Restriction Act, the PCC was a major actor. PCC representatives were part of the early consultations with Rep. Friend's office as the bill was being formulated. They were also part of the negotiations with the governor's office trying to produce legislation that could be signed. At each step of the policy formation stage, the PCC was kept abreast of legislative strategies and of changes in the bill.

Howard Fetterhoff is the executive director of the PCC and Francis Viglietta is its chief lobbyist. In separate interviews, they discussed the formation of this legislation and the role of the PCC in this policy battle.[20] Although the PCC has a long history in Pennsylvania politics of participating in the formation of abortion legislation, they indicated that the many abortion restriction amendments passed over the years were not primarily because of any special clout of the PCC. Rather, the legislature itself is more or less predisposed to pass abortion restriction laws. In fact, there was a conscious effort not to term this policy issue an essentially "Catholic" issue. Sensitive to the charge that the church is trying to impose its own morality, PCC officials insist they were merely trying to participate in the policy process. For this reason, the PCC generally tried to maintain low visibility on the issue. However, when the American Catholic bishops termed abortion the critical moral issue of our times, the PCC was compelled to take a strong active interest in this type of legislation.

After the *Webster* ruling, the political stakes rose because legislation passed in Pennsylvania might actually be upheld by the courts. Additionally, in the eyes of the PCC, the pro-choice side was much more organized this time around since they too realized the significance of the 1989 version of the abortion battle in the legislature. Ultimately, "The victory this time was not so much in the reach or depth of the legislation rather in the fact that both sides pulled out all stops. Each year the stakes have gotten higher and higher and this year it was a significant victory for the pro-life forces in Pennsylvania."[21] Thus, although the PCC deliberately tried to stay in the public background on this issue, it was absolutely clear the bill was very important to the Catholic Church in Pennsylvania.

What were the strategies employed by the PCC? First, despite the absolute position of the Church on abortion, it is clear the position of the PCC was somewhat practical and accommodating to political feasibility. For example, the PCC would have wanted to continue to keep in the legislation the complete ban on all fetal tissue experimentation. However, it was clear that it would be a major political fight to keep that provision. Therefore, a calculated gamble was made on the part of the PCC to accommodate the legislature on this issue so as not to lose broad support for other issues. Therefore, even without the fetal experimentation ban, the PCC urged passage of the legislation. Secondly, the PCC is astute enough to understand how far elected politicians can be pushed, especially in an election year. After this legislative success, there does not seem to have been any pressure applied by the PCC to begin work on more restrictive legislation. "It is not good politics to force the legislature to vote on abortion too often. They hate to vote on this issue."[22] Thirdly, the PCC seems to be quite willing to enter into alliance with other pro-life groups in the state (including other pro-life groups that formed the Pro-Life Federation). This is a rather significant strategy because many Catholic groups are uncomfortable joining with pro-life groups that may be much more conservative politically on other issues and more fundamentalist theologically. Other state Catholic conferences and indeed the national Catholic conference have often been accused of shying away from right to life groups. Not so the PCC. "These groups are very well organized at the grass roots level. Since we do not do a lot of that, we are grateful that they are there. They save us a lot of work and we do not want to alienate them."[23]

Not only did the Catholic strategy include alignment with conservative and fundamentalist churches, the Catholic Church was careful not to publicly challenge more liberal churches that opposed the legislation. On September 26, 1989, over fifty ministers and rabbis signed a document issued jointly by People for the American Way and the Religious Coalition for Choice. In part it said, "America's religious diversity is reflected in the diversity of views that Americans hold on the issue of abortion, we believe that this issue should remain what it has essentially been since the Supreme Court decision of 1973: a matter of individual conscience, not governmental coercion."[24] In an even more pointed reference to the Catholic Church, the Rev. Ron Sell, leader of the Lutheran Coalition on Public Policy stated, "There is no religious consensus on this issue," and questioned "the appropriateness of making one's religious perspective into law." In a specific challenge to the Catholic community, Sell referred to a 1988 study that found Catholic women more likely to have abortions than Jewish or Protestant women.[25]

The PCC did not respond publicly to these direct and indirect challenges. The PCC lobbyists belong to an ecumenical policy group that meets once a month in Harrisburg. It was a deliberate strategy not to respond to these statements but to concentrate on policy issues on which there was a greater consensus. Said one PCC lobbyist, "There will be other issues in the future in which we will want to join forces. From a practical point of view and in the name of ecumenism, we don't want to disrupt these meetings."[26] That strategy seemed to be appreciated by some. One participant in that group, Fitzgerald Reist, Executive Director of A United Methodist Witness in Pennsylvania, is a clear proponent of the pro-choice position. He noted that the PCC was extremely effective with this legislation and "very difficult to defeat." However, Rev. Reist found that it was much easier to maintain a working relationship with the PCC than with single issue pro-life groups. In his words, "Single issue groups are destructive of the democratic process because they leave little room for disagreement."[27] Thus the PCC successfully pulled off a strategy of co-operating with more conservative and fundamentalist church groups with whom they agreed on this issue, while not alienating lobby groups of mainline churches opposed to the legislation.

While the Pennsylvania Catholic Conference set the tone for the official Catholic approach to the legislation, they are but an arm of the bishops. It is really the bishops of Pennsylvania who direct the official public policy position of the Catholic Church in Pennsylvania. The PCC is in place to implement the overall position of the church as articulated by the bishops. In this legislative initiative, the bishops adopted a strategy of allowing the PCC to work with the legislature without publicly interfering in that discussion. Consistent with the approach of the PCC, the Catholic bishops tried to avoid a public and direct challenge to the legislature. In a pastoral letter on abortion, the Pennsylvania Catholic bishops stated:

> We address the issue of abortion not as a narrow sectarian concern, but as a fundamental issue that touches every person of any or no creed. To speak out against racial discrimination, social injustice or abortion is not to force values upon society, rather it is to call to the attention of our society its long accepted moral principles and commitment to defend basic human dignity and rights.[28]

Clearly, the bishops tried to phrase their opposition to abortion in a manner that would not highlight a single issue. They wanted to place this issue among many other social issues in which they have involved themselves in recent years. To name racial discrimination, for example, highlights a social policy issue on which the bishops have taken a "liberal" position.

While proclaiming the right of Catholics to speak on abortion, the bishops at least recognized the pluralistic nature of American society and the democratic manner in which public policy is formulated:

> No religious group has the right or power to impose its own views on others. In our pluralistic democracy, public policy on abortion and other controversial issues is decided when a majority of citizens of whatever conviction determines the policy. Catholics, along with others must present their views and participate in the public debate with courage and conviction.

Finally, on behalf of their own right to speak, the bishops stated:

> When we speak as citizens, we bishops make no claim other than our right to speak to public policy. We tell no person for whom to vote. But we do have a duty to proclaim the right of every human being, born and unborn.

While not lessening their *moral* objections to abortion, the bishops in these statements exhibited a moderate tone as they recognized that it is ultimately the *political* process that will decide this issue.

A final question that needs to be addressed is whether or not the PCC specifically targeted Catholic legislators to vote for the Abortion Restriction Act. Officials at the PCC stated that there was no such strategy. Said one official at the PCC, "We send the same material, the same information to all legislators. It may be that Catholic legislators give more weight to our material, but there is no separate strategy."[29] Several Catholic legislators confirmed that to be the case.

On this point of pressuring Catholic legislators, the bishops did not single out politicians but they did issue a general statement as part of their pastoral letter on abortion:

> Catholics who are recognized as public figures and enjoy a place of prominence within the community and even within the Church, have a special duty to be faithful in both word and action to the faith they profess. True conviction will not allow itself to be emptied when challenged in public life. One cannot claim to be a Catholic in good standing in the Church while publicly rejecting and advocating the abandonment of its teaching.[30]

In the end, Catholic legislators did not universally support the legislation. However a very high percentage did; in fact, a considerably higher percentage of Catholics than non-Catholics supported the legislation. Seventy-six of eighty-six Catholic members of the House of Representatives voted in favor of the final bill, while fifty-one of ninety-six non-Catholic members did so. In the Senate, fully twenty of twenty-one Catholics supported the measure, while only ten of twenty-six non-Catholics did so.

Obviously, Catholic legislators strongly supported the Abortion Control Act. However, there is no evidence to suggest that the PCC was directly responsible for this high correlation. Presumably, legislators were responding to their own privately held positions, constituent preferences, political considerations, or perhaps indirectly to church statements at the local level.

Conclusions

There are a number of implications that can be drawn from this case study, both with regard to the discussion of the passage of the restrictive abortion law itself as well as the participation of the Catholic Church in that decision-making process.

First, the national discussion of abortion is very intense in the United States. The tendency for polarization, exaggerated claims, and ideological posturing is the result of the personal and emotional nature of this issue. Even the language used is of great symbolic significance. Both sides claim to be representing an essential American and universal right, either the right to freedom of choice or the right to life. One side contends that life that is born has precedence over life that is still of questionable viability. The other side counters that life in the womb needs state protection in the name of protection for the most defenseless members of society. Obviously, the premises on which the two sides base their arguments are very different. Therefore, the discussion that proceeds from those premises demonstrates little convergence. Any attempt to bring this issue to the political realm will either threaten or reassure deeply felt value systems. Murray Edelman's analysis helps us to understand the symbolic nature of each and every legislative battle. Each piece of legislation, each consideration of legislation is *more* than just legislation. The Pennsylvania case demonstrates this point, and it could be generalized to every state or national legislature that discusses abortion.

Secondly, despite the divergent premises of each side, the legislation ultimately produced in Pennsylvania was neither an overwhelming approbation of the pro-life position or a rejection of the pro-choice position. The media, both sides agree, heightened and perhaps even distorted the reality of the legislation. Again, Edelman helps us to understand why we should not be surprised to see that happen. The point is that this law does not outlaw abortion, nor does it outlaw *most* abortions. Sex selection is the only case in which abortion is illegal at any stage of pregnancy. However, if the woman proceeds with an abortion and does not cite sex selection as the reason, the law does not interfere. The spousal notification is philosophically repugnant to many, but practically it is a notification, not a consent, and the exceptions are significantly broad. The twenty-four hour delay is seen even by opponents to the legislation as more of an added price and burden, but probably not one the courts will rule an "undue" burden. It makes abortion more costly, both in real and emotional terms. However, it is not clear that it will ultimately eliminate many abortions. Finally, the twenty-four week provision does not affect a significant number of abortions. In 1988, of 50,000 abortions in the state of Pennsylvania, only 128, or .002 percent, were performed after twenty-three weeks.[31] Pro-life people say even one life is significant, pro-choice people say complete restriction at twenty-four weeks is unwarranted. The point remains, however, that this provision affects very few women contemplating abortion.

Thus, this legislation, as significant as it is, is not a complete victory or defeat for either side. The most ardent pro-life activist cannot really feel this legislation is ideal. And even the most ardent pro-choice person feared far worse legislation. In a day when we are led to believe that the abortion issue as a policy question is all or nothing, I see evidence of the political process in Pennsylvania producing modified legislation. The question remains: at what point will the politically optimum position for legislation or rejection of legislation be reached?

There are several conclusions to be drawn about the role of the Catholic Church and community in this process. Allen Hertzke, in his groundbreaking analysis, said this about the Catholic lobby in Washington:

> The United States Catholic Conference presents one of the more intricately textured lobby groups. On economic policy and foreign military policy it has aligned itself with the 'peace and justice groups' but on social issues it has found itself aligned with those groups concerned with 'traditional values.'"[32]

What Hertzke observed at the national level in Washington, I observe at the state level in Pennsylvania. The PCC, like its parent organization the USCC, takes a wide range of positions, some considered to be on the liberal side of politics and some on the conservative side. At the same time I was interviewing the officials of the PCC on their role in the abortion legislation, for example, they were also appealing to Gov. Casey not to sign the death warrant for an inmate on death row. This attention to a broad spectrum of issues seemed to work to the PCC's advantage. It enabled the church to assume a posture of more than a single issue lobby. They worked with fundamentalist groups on abortion and "peace and justice" groups on capital punishment. Thus their political alliances are more fluid, and they are less likely to be dismissed as an ideological or closed lobby.

Secondly, with regard to strategy, Hertzke distinguishes religious groups which rely on the grass root approach from religious groups that rely on a more direct strategy. He found that the fundamentalist churches seemed to concentrate on grass roots mobilization more so than the main line churches, which concentrated on direct lobbying, elite mobilization, and key contacts. Hertzke placed the USCC in the latter category. Again, what Hertzke found in Washington, I discovered in Harrisburg. The PCC readily admitted that they concentrate on the key contact approach or what Salisbury termed "elite interaction" strategy. However, there is a significant and interesting point to be made in this case study. The PCC, utilizing the elite interaction method, acted in concert with the more fundamentalist groups that mobilized the masses. On this policy issue, it was a conscious strategy for the PCC not to duplicate strategies but to rely on the strengths of the other religious lobby groups with which it had aligned itself. Clearly, the PCC demonstrated a willingness to act politically and not theologically. This type of sophistication is not always in evidence with other religious lobby groups (Catholic conferences included) that act solely on theology or in principle refuse to work with other religious lobby groups. In Pennsylvania, grass roots mobilization is clearly not a principal strategy of the PCC, so they were able to engage in direct lobbying knowing full well the legislator was receiving constituent pressure back home, very often directed by fundamentalist groups.

Pennsylvania's bishops demonstrated a similar measure of political sophistication when they entered the policy debate knowing full well there was no chance of truly "translating moral teaching into public law." In their pastoral letter, the bishops admitted that no church has a right to demand church teaching be translated into public law. What they argued was that all churches have the right to enter into the public dialogue that leads to policy formation, as long as that participation does not involve direct intervention in electoral politics.

I am not arguing that the bishops did not make abortion a priority issue, nor that the bishops did not exert full pressure in influencing this legislation. However, I do offer the following propositions:

1. The bishops in Pennsylvania allowed the PCC to work directly with the legislators. This method of elite interaction allowed lobbyists to work

directly with legislators, without public interference by the bishops. The dialogue took place in the *policy* arena, between policy experts.
2. The PCC worked on behalf of the bishops for a law that is clearly *less than ideal* from a church teaching or moral point of view.

The PCC exhibited a sophistication that most efficient lobby groups demonstrate. They treated the legislation in a *practical* manner, realizing what was doable and what was not. They showed real signs of *compromise*, sacrificing certain aspects of the legislation in order to get a final bill that met most of their requirements. Clearly, the PCC would have liked the legislation to mirror the church's moral teaching as much as possible; yet they enthusiastically worked for what was politically feasible. They were willing to take the cues from Friend and Kozinski, and face the political reality of the difficulty of passing abortion legislation, even in a state like Pennsylvania. It was clear that officials of the PCC realize the situation legislators are placed in when confronting this type of legislation. The PCC made it clear they do not want to initiate this battle too often because, "they (legislators) hate to have to vote on it."

Finally, the bishops themselves stayed for the most part on the teaching side of the issue of abortion and did not interfere in the policy side. Cardinal Bernadin from Chicago has urged Catholic bishops to teach on the issues of abortion rather than threaten public officials with punitive measures. We have observed the actions of Bishop Maher in California, Bishop Gracida in Texas, and the words of Cardinal O'Connor in New York that either speak of excommunication or follow through on such a punitive measure. There was no such pronouncement on the part of Pennsylvania's bishops. To be sure, they said a Catholic politician who rejects church teaching cannot consider him or herself to be a Catholic in "good standing." But not being a "Catholic in good standing" is ecclesiologically significantly different from being an excommunicated Catholic. The rhetoric was not inflammatory; it exhorted rather than threatened. Significantly, without threats, the overwhelming percentage of Catholic legislators voted as the bishops had hoped they would. There is also absolutely no evidence that the church pressured the Catholic governor to expand his stand beyond his willingness to sign legislation that he deemed to be constitutional.

In sum, there is substantial evidence that the Catholic bishops in Pennsylvania were willing to be practical, to allow the policy experts to negotiate, and to refrain from publicly threatening Catholic politicians. The end result was a bill, that though it does not mirror church dogma, is a *political* success.

In the end, Friend, Kozinski, Ritter, and Casey were the principal actors in this process. The Catholic Church was far from a silent participant in the political dialogue, but as Kozinski said, "I control the legislation." That legislation was the product of a *political* process. Without abandoning its moral stance in this highly symbolic battle, the Catholic Church in Pennsylvania showed a willingness to submit to that process. They remain a powerful voice in a state that is over 35 percent Catholic. No doubt there are many direct and indirect ways the church can exert political muscle. Yet in the 1989 Abortion Control Act, their influence was rather measured.

Epilogue

After losing the legislative battle, the pro-choice forces focused their strategy on the courts. Several groups, including The American Civil Liberties Union, Planned Parenthood of Pennsylvania, and The Women's Law Project of Philadelphia sought a court injunction delaying implementation of the law. U.S. District Judge Daniel Huyett issued the temporary injunction just five days before the law was to take effect. The judge blocked the sections that required spousal notification and a twenty-four hour waiting period. The provisions banning "sex selection" abortions and banning abortions after twenty-four weeks were not challenged.

Some weeks after the injunction, in early August 1990, a four day trial took place in Reading before Judge Huyett. At the end of the month Judge Huyett ruled unconstitutional the two contested provisions. It was clear, however, that this judicial decision was far from the last word on the Abortion Control Act. Pennsylvania Attorney General Ernest Preate stated immediately that he would appeal the ruling to the U.S. Court of Appeals. Preate's spokesperson called the law "a reasonable, responsible approach to a very difficult question."[33] Judge Huyett disagreed, stating, "the state's lawyers seemed to argue that the constitutional standard applicable to the judicial review of abortion has somehow been modified by recent Supreme Court decisions. I most respectfully disagree."[34]

All the actors in this policy battle fully expected the case to proceed through the federal court system. Judge Huyett was not optimistic that his decision would be upheld. "Individuals can no longer feel secure," he said, "that abortion rights will be protected by the judiciary."[35] A spokesperson for the ACLU was similarly apprehensive, fearing, "This case could provide the U.S. Supreme Court with the opportunity to overturn *Roe v. Wade.*"[36]

Pro-life forces in Pennsylvania were optimistic. Mary Beliveau of the Pro-Life Federation said Judge Huyett's ruling was "clearly erroneous," and felt "confident the law would be upheld on appeal."[37] Howard Fetterhoff of the Pennsylvania Catholic Conference took his consistently pragmatic position. He said he was not "surprised or disappointed by Judge Huyett's temporary injunction. "If we're going to make progress in modifying *Roe v. Wade,* this is how it has to be done."[38]

As of this writing, the law is still being contested in the courts, with all sides expecting it to make its way to the Supreme Court. The policy arena has switched, as it often does on this issue, from the legislative to the judicial. Unless the Supreme Court makes a sweeping decision, no doubt the strategy will switch back to the state legislatures, and the cycle will continue.

Notes

1. Murray Edelman, *The Symbolic Uses of Politics* (Urbana: University of Illinois Press, 1967), p. 114.

2. *Christianity Today,* November 3, 1989, p. 36.

3. *Harrisburg Patriot News,* October 4, 1989, p. A2.

4. Edelman, *The Symbolic Uses of Politics,* p. 161.

5. Ibid.

6. Edelman, *The Symbolic Uses of Politics,* p. 8.

7. *Harrisburg Patriot News,* October 18, 1989, p. A2.

8. Ibid.

9. *Harrisburg Patriot News,* October 23, 1989, p. A1.

10. *Harrisburg Patriot News,* November 18, 1989, p. A1.

11. Interview conducted, Office of Rep. Friend, Pennsylvania Capitol Building, June 25, 1989.

12. Interview conducted, Office of Rep. Jerry Kozinski, Pennsylvania State Capitol, June 29, 1989.

13. Interview conducted, Office of Rep. Ritter, Pennsylvania State Capitol Building, June 29, 1990.

14. *The Reporter,* October 14, 1989, p. A5.

15. Ibid.

16. Interview with James Haggerty, Chief Counsel to the Governor and Richard Spiegelman, deputy chief counsel, State Capitol Building, Harrisburg, Pa., June 28, 1990.

17. Interview with Rep. Ritter.

18. Interview conducted with Mary Beliveau, York, Pennsylvania, June 29, 1990.

19. Interview conducted with Morgan Plant, Harrisburg, Pa., June 29, 1990.

20. Interview conducted with Howard Fetterhoff, Executive Director of Pennsylvania Catholic Conference, Harrisburg, PA, June 25, 1990. Interview with Francis Viglietta, Director, Department of Justice and Rights, Pennsylvania Catholic Conference, June 21, 1990.

21. Ibid.

22. Ibid.

23. Ibid.

24. Statement released by Religious Coalition for Choice and People for the American Way, Harrisburg, Pennsylvania, September 26, 1989.

25. *Harrisburg Patriot News,* October 24, 1989, p. A3.

26. Interview at Pennsylvania Catholic Conference.

27. Interview conducted with Rev. Fitzgerald Reist, Executive Director, A United Methodist Witness in Pennsylvania, Harrisburg, Pennsylvania, June 25, 1990.

28. Pastoral letter of the Pennsylvania Catholic Bishops, *The Church, Public Policy and Abortion,* April 6, 1990.

29. Interview at the Pennsylvania Catholic Conference.

30. *The Church, Public Policy and Abortion.*

31. Commonwealth of Pennsylvania, Department of Health, 1988 abortion statistics.

32. Allen Hertzke, *Representing God in Washington,* (Knoxville: University of Tennessee Press, 1988), p. 36.

33. *Washington Post,* August 25, 1990, p. A2.

34. Ibid.

35. Ibid.

36. *New York Times,* August 25, 1990, p. A8.

37. *Washington Post,* August 25, 1990.

38. *Washington Post,* January 12, 1990, p. A20.

6

Abortion and Religious Coalitions: The Case of Louisiana

Christine Day

One year after the Supreme Court handed down its decision in *Webster v. Reproductive Health Services,* the Louisiana state legislature passed a bill that banned nearly all abortions.[1] The bill's sponsors had pushed for the most restrictive bill possible, with an eye towards challenging and eventually overturning *Roe v. Wade* in the courts. Both that bill and another, slightly less restrictive bill, were vetoed by the governor, and the legislature failed to override either veto. The vote to override was very close, however, and the governor has indicated a willingness to sign into law some future bill outlawing all abortions except in cases of rape, incest, or to save the life of the mother. Thus, the politics of abortion is likely to spawn vigorous debate once again during the Louisiana state legislative session of 1991.

In many ways, Louisiana is a likely candidate to produce the nation's most restrictive antiabortion laws. The state has a strong religious base for its pro-life movement: predominantly Catholic in the south, and predominantly fundamentalist Protestant in the north. Traditionally, Louisiana antiabortion laws have been strict; a state law that was declared unconstitutional in 1976 made abortion a crime punishable by ten years' imprisonment at hard labor.

The Catholic Church is a major power base within the Louisiana pro-life movement, as it is nationally. The church enjoys certain political advantages in Louisiana relative to most other states: a large population base with concomitant grassroots support, and an adeptness at building coalitions with fundamentalist Protestant and other pro-life groups. In addition, Catholic

In late June 1991, after this chapter was completed, the Louisiana state legislature passed over Governor Buddy Roemer's veto a law that outlawed all abortions except (a) to save the life of the mother, (b) in cases of incest when the crime is reported to the police and the abortion is performed within thirteen weeks of conception, and (c) in cases of rape when the crime has been reported to the police within seven days, the woman has been examined within five days by a doctor other than the doctor who will perform the abortion, and the abortion takes place within thirteen weeks of conception.

political activists in Louisiana seem more willing than their fundamentalist counterparts to accept limited exceptions to the ban on abortion. This stance may help the Catholic lobby achieve results with the legislature and the governor in the future, despite complaints from some officials that it is inconsistent with the church's moral absoluteness in declaring that human life begins at conception. All of these advantages were evident during the 1990 legislative session.

Religion and Political Culture in Louisiana

One-third of Louisianans are Catholic, and they are concentrated in the southern part of the state. At the time of the Louisiana Purchase in 1803, the southern part of the territory was inhabited primarily by Catholic Creoles of French and Spanish descent. In addition, a French-speaking immigrant group expelled by the British from Canada in 1755 had found refuge and settled in the southern part of Louisiana territory. Known as the Cajuns—a name derived from their Canadian home, Acadia—they became fishermen, hunters, trappers, and farmers in the swampy areas outside of New Orleans. Later immigrant groups included Protestants and Catholics of various nationalities, but the southern half of the state remains predominantly Catholic today.[2]

Meanwhile, the northern half of the state developed a political and religious culture similar to that of the rest of the Deep South: fundamentalist Protestant and socially conservative. The two Louisianas have often clashed, culturally and politically, throughout the state's history.[3] The religious cleavage has been evident in such political activities as Catholics' support for funding of non-public schools, and fundamentalists' opposition to sex education. In the abortion controversy, however, Catholic and evangelical Protestant political activists have finally merged in pursuit of a common goal.[4] As we shall see, the two groups worked in coalition with other pro-life organizations throughout most of the 1990 legislative session. A disagreement over exceptions for rape and incest began to drive the coalition partners apart, however, toward the end of the session.

The Post-*Webster* Abortion Controversy in the State Capital

The first legislative session after the *Webster* decision produced two bills restricting abortion. The first one, banning all abortions except to save the life of the mother, cleared both houses of the legislature by large margins in 1990 but was vetoed by Governor Buddy Roemer. The House voted quickly to override the governor's veto, but the Senate failed to override by three votes. The following day, on July 9, with only two days left in the legislative session, the Senate passed a new bill which added exceptions for rape and incest; the House followed suit; and the governor vetoed the second bill eighteen days later. In Louisiana, the legislature can elect to hold a special session after adjourning in order to consider veto overrides; no such special session was called, however, and the abortion issue was dead for a year.

The Senate's passage of that second bill is a fascinating story of legislative maneuvering. With only two days left in the session after the failure to override the first veto, there was no time to craft a new antiabortion bill and send it through committee to the floor. Instead, pro-life legislators found the only bill still pending on the floor which dealt with amending the state's criminal code: a bill which would have made assault on anyone burning a U.S. flag a simple battery punishable by a $25 fine. This "beat-the-flag-burner bill" evidently stood little chance of passage in the Senate (although it had already passed the House), and it seemed an appropriate vehicle for a quick new antiabortion bill. All references to beating up flag burners were simply removed, and replaced with language criminalizing abortion.[5]

Governor Roemer, despite having declared himself in favor of an antiabortion law with the added exceptions for rape and incest, said he vetoed the second bill for three reasons: it contained inadequate protections for rape victims; it had not been properly debated and scrutinized by the legislature; and it may have violated procedural rules requiring that amendments be germane to the original contents of the bill.[6] Many observers, in addition, questioned the constitutionality of the second bill because it mandated severe penalties—ten years in prison and a $100,000 fine—for a "simple battery."[7]

The role of the Catholic Church throughout this process was substantial, and although it is difficult to gauge the influence of one among several pro-life forces, it is possible to examine the various sources of the church's power. First, religious organizations in general, when they become involved in matters of public policy, possess the power of grassroots. Most Americans claim some religious affiliation, and more Americans are members of religious groups than of any other type of group. "Organized religion is thus the premier voluntary association in the country," Allen Hertzke pointed out, "an association particularly important to those historically excluded from participation elsewhere."[8]

In the case of the abortion issue, a high degree of commitment enhances grassroots support for the pro-life positon; at least one study has found that "opponents of abortion are far more likely than proponents to regard the abortion issue as important."[9] Indeed, journalistic accounts of demonstrations around the state Capitol spoke of "corridors filled with an unlikely alliance of Roman Catholics and Bible-toting Protestant fundamentalists," while at some committee meetings, "pro-choice lobbyists [were] either voluntarily retreating in the face of overwhelming odds, or being deliberately hampered by state officials."[10] "They can pull out three to five thousand people just like that," said one pro-choice activist.[11]

The mass base of support, then, is a political resource possessed by all religious groups involved in the pro-life movement, Catholic and fundamentalist Protestant alike. An additional resource of the Catholic Church but not, evidently, of the Protestant pro-life churches is a staff of professional lobbyists. The only organizations associated with the pro-life cause which had lobbyists registered with the Louisiana state legislature in 1990 were the Louisiana Catholic Conference and the Louisiana Federation of Right to Life; a few other activists and attorneys worked with them as well. There were no registered lobbyists officially connected with the fundamentalist Protestant churches; nor were such professional lobbyists visible in the Capitol, according to one legislator.[12]

The Louisiana Federation of Right to Life has no official religious affiliation, although Catholics took the lead nationally in forming right-to-life organizations beginning in the 1960s, when states began relaxing abortion restrictions.[13] Religious and secular pro-life activists alike have publicly downplayed the religious aspect of pro-life political activity. "[R]ight to Life has taken the position that this is a civil rights issue," said a lobbyist for the Louisiana Federation for Right to Life. "There is no organized lobbying effort by a quote unquote church for this bill."[14] The position that abortion is a civil rights, not a religious, political issue was echoed by the executive director of the Louisiana Pro Life Council, which is affiliated with the Archdiocese of New Orleans.[15]

Coordinating resources and working in coalition have not been easy for national pro-life forces. This is partly because secular groups do not wish to be perceived as pushing a religious cause, and partly because the religious groups themselves—Catholics and fundamentalist Protestants—have differed on other issues. Pro-choice organizations around the country were faster and more effective in forming coalitions than were pro-life groups.[16] In Louisiana, however, many observers, including activists on both sides of the issue, perceived an unusually high degree of coordination between the Catholic and the fundamentalist Protestant churches in pushing for antiabortion legislation in 1990.[17] Catholic political activists themselves, furthermore, seem unusually united on the abortion issue. Neither journalistic accounts nor interviewees mentioned or perceived the organized presence of such pro-choice Catholic organizations as Catholics for a Free Choice.[18]

Within the legislature, although the two sponsors of the first and most restrictive bill—Representative Louis "Woody" Jenkins and Senator Mike Cross—are both Protestant, they were joined by several Catholic and Protestant co-sponsors. All of them were united on the goal of passing the strictest bill possible in order to challenge *Roe v. Wade* in the courts.[19] They achieved their goal: passage of a bill allowing no abortions except when necessary to save the life of the mother.

Once that bill had been vetoed and the override attempt failed, however, the coalition shattered. Pro-life legislators and activists disagreed over whether to try passing another bill permitting abortions in cases of rape and incest, or to cling to the no-exceptions position. The revamped "beat-the-flag-burner bill," which became the antiabortion bill allowing exceptions for rape and incest, was sponsored by Catholic Senators John Saunders and John Hainkel; attorney Robert Winn of the National Right to Life Committee board helped to write the new bill; and Catholic Senator Samuel Nunez, President of the Senate, allowed the new bill to be introduced on the floor by ruling that the abortion amendment was germane. Many Catholic legislators received telephone calls from Catholic bishops and priests, "releasing" them to vote for the new bill despite the rape and incest exceptions.[20] Peg Kenny of the Pro-Life Council defended the new bill even though it was "imperfect" (i.e. containing exceptions) and hastily crafted from another bill; the church she said, will accept imperfect legislation that will "chip away at *Roe* [and] save babies' lives."[21]

Meanwhile, many fundamentalist Protestant leaders were unhappy with the effort to quickly pass a bill allowing exceptions. Activists with the Eagle Forum, a conservative organization with fundamentalist Protestant ties, seemed uncomfortable with the new bill and unsure whether to support it.[22] Representative Woody Jenkins himself—who was not only the prime sponsor of the first bill, but also a major leader of the fundamentalist grassroots and primary media spokesman for the pro-life position—refused to vote for the new bill.

Half of the Louisiana state legislature is Catholic, and the question arises: Are Catholic public officials vulnerable to pressure from the Catholic hierarchy? Bishops and priests are citizens, of course, and thus have every right to express their opinions to public officials and to speak out on the issues. On the other hand, religious organizations that try to influence public policy are often criticized for overstepping the "wall of separation" between church and state. For this reason, most elected officials who are Catholic are reluctant to admit to bowing to church influence, and in fact often vigorously deny such influence. At any rate, there is little evidence that Catholic politicians in the U.S. change their positions on issues under the direction of the church hierarchy.[23]

Anecdotal evidence of church officials' influence on the votes of Catholic legislators is, in Louisiana as elsewhere, difficult to verify. Politicians do not want to give the impression that they have breached the "wall of separation" between church and state; furthermore, it is difficult for any politician to analyze precisely the complex influences on his or her own votes. But such anecdotal evidence did arise out of the 1990 legislative session. There were stories of Catholic legislators who, after voting against antiabortion legislation, were called before their own church committees or entire congregations to answer for their votes, prohibited by church officials from speaking publicly at any church-sponsored forum, and even threatened with excommunication.[24] The most-publicized such story was that of Catholic Senate President, Samuel Nunez, who voted against the first, no-exceptions bill, despite a petition from his mother's church, a letter and a phone call from his mother at the urging of her church's priest, and even a phone call from a women claiming to represent the Vatican (a claim not verified). Nunez went on to support the second antiabortion bill, however. Answering to the complaints of pro-choice activists who felt he had abandoned them, he said he had always supported such a bill as long as there were exceptions for rape and incest.[25]

Finally, perhaps the most dramatic account of pressure from the Catholic Church on the abortion issue occurred during Senate debate on the first, most restrictive bill. Pro-life senators waved an advertisement appearing in the New Orleans *Times-Picayune* and containing an open letter from Nobel Peace Prize laureate Mother Teresa urging passage of the legislation. The origin of the message was unclear, as it turned out; Mother Teresa, in a telephone interview, did not recall sending any such message directly to Louisiana.[26]

The Catholic lobby's support for the second, less restrictive bill, and the general position that legislation containing exceptions is better than no abor-

TABLE 6.1   Louisana State Legislators' Votes on Proposed Antiabortion Bills, by Religion, 1990 (percent)

	Fundamentalist Protestant	Catholic	Mainstream Protestant
First antiabortion bill			
yes	66	75	62
no	34	25	38
N =	(44)	(69)	(21)
Second antiabortion bill (rape, incest exceptions)			
yes	78	84	73
no	22	16	27
N =	(46)	(70)	(22)

Source: *State of Louisiana 1989 Roster of Officials* and *Baton Rouge Morning Advocate,* 15 June 1990, 22 June 1990, and 7 July 1990.

tion restrictions at all, has been a two-sided coin for Catholic pro-life forces. On the one hand, legislation containing exceptions for rape and incest clearly has a better chance of eventually becoming law, while a rigid, no-exceptions position may never achieve results. On the other hand, many legislators, including those who are Catholic, perceive an inconsistency in the church's position when the church defines abortion as murder and yet allows exceptions to the abortion ban. The inconsistency, they feel, leaves them free to make their own political choices without violating the church's moral doctrine. Even Representative Sam Theriot, an ordained deacon in the Roman Catholic Church and strong pro-life supporter who said, "I'd never make a vote I'd have to explain to my God," admitted that the second bill placed him and others "in a position where we may be eating a little crow."[27]

Turning from anecdotes to aggregate votes, Catholic legislators were slightly more likely than both fundamentalist Protestant and mainstream Protestant legislators to vote for both antiabortion bills.[28] (See Table 6.1.) The differences between the three religious groups are not statistically significant, however. Furthermore, substantial majorities of all three groups—even mainstream Protestants—voted for both bills.

If the legislature did not divide neatly along religious lines in their votes on the abortion issue, they divided even less along partisan lines. Large majorities of both Democrats and Republicans (between 70 percent and 83 percent) voted in favor of each antiabortion bill, and there was no significant difference between the two parties. This was true despite clear differences between the two major national parties on the same issue. In their 1984 national platforms, for example, the Democratic party supports "reproductive freedom" and opposes an antiabortion amendment to the Constitution, while the Republican party proclaims that "the unborn child has a fundamental individual right to life" and supports such an amendment.[29]

The abortion issue did generate racial and gender cleavages within the state legislature. Both women and African Americans in the legislature were significantly more likely to vote the pro-choice position. All three women voted against the first, most restrictive bill; two out of three voted against the second. Sixteen out of the twenty African American legislators also voted against both bills. There are so few women and blacks in the legislature, however, that their solid majorities against the antiabortion bills made no difference in the actual vote results; both bills passed both houses overwhelmingly.

In conclusion, it is difficult to gauge the amount of influence that the Catholic Church, its activists, and its lobbying organizations exercised over individual state legislators on the abortion issue in 1990. However, in a state legislature that is half Catholic, representing a state population that is one-third Catholic, the substantial resources of the Catholic Church and the potential for influence on public policy are important political considerations. We turn now to the question of representation, with an examination of attitudes toward abortion among the citizens of Louisiana.

Politics, Religion, and Public Opinion: The Constituency Connection

In this section we will address two questions about representation:

1. Does the Catholic Church represent Louisiana Catholics in its support for antiabortion legislation?
2. Does the Louisiana state legislature reflect the attitudes of the people of Louisiana in its actions on the abortion issue?

Neither question has a simple answer. Although both pro-life and pro-choice activists often present abortion as a black-and-white issue with no middle ground, it is in fact highly complex, and so are people's attitudes. Most people, nationally and in Louisiana, are neither against abortion nor pro-choice in every conceivable situation.

There are many different types of restrictions and exceptions that have been proposed or written into the laws of the states. Analysts have generally divided the reasons for having an abortion into two types: "health" reasons, including rape, incest, health or severe disabilities of the unborn child, and health or life of the mother; and "personal" or "economic" reasons, including financial difficulties and the high cost of raising a child, interruption of school or career, and general use of abortion as a means of birth control. Americans are generally more willing to accept the pro-choice position for health reasons than for personal or economic reasons, but surveys display a great deal of variety and ambiguity in public attitudes.[30] Similarly, majorities of Louisianans have expressed support for legal restrictions on abortion when the mother cannot afford a child, does not want to interrupt her career, or wants a child of the opposite sex; while most Louisianans oppose a ban on abortion in cases of

TABLE 6.2   Attitudes Toward Abortion by Religion in Louisiana (percent)

	Fundamentalist Protestant	Catholic	Mainstream Protestant	Other	None	Total
Legalize abortion:						
under any circumstances	17	20	31	50	42	22
under certain circumstances	55	60	54	50	39	56
never	28	20	15	—	20	22
N =	(306)	(334)	(125)	(6)	(41)	(812)

$p < .01$

Source: University of New Orleans Survey Research Center, Louisiana Senate Race Survey, September 1990.

rape, incest, severe deformities in the unborn child, or danger to the life or health of the mother.[31]

Louisianans' support for or opposition to legalized abortion is related to their religious affiliations. Louisiana Catholics tend to be significantly more pro-life than mainstream Protestants, but significantly more pro-choice than fundamentalist Protestants, according to a survey conducted by the University of New Orleans Survey Research Center (hereafter referred to as the UNO Poll").[32] Table 6.2 shows that a majority of all three religious groups take the middle position that abortions should be "legal under only certain circumstances." The remaining Catholics are evenly divided between those who oppose all legal abortions and those who oppose all abortion restrictions. The remaining mainstream Protestants are more likely to oppose all restrictions, while the remaining fundamentalists are more likely to oppose legalizing any abortions at all.

These significant differences among religious groups in Louisiana reflect the religious differences on the abortion question that have been found in nationwide studies. Among Christians, fundamentalist Protestants tend to be most opposed to legalized abortion, mainstream Protestants tend to be the most pro-choice, and Catholics are somewhere between the two Protestant groups.[33]

Within each religious group, African Americans, conservatives, and people with less education and lower incomes tend to oppose legalized abortion more than whites, liberals, and people at higher education and income levels. This appears to be the case for Louisianans as it is for Americans generally.[34] Even across education and income levels, racial and gender groups, and ideologies, the relationship between religion and attitudes toward abortion among Louisiananans remains the same; that is, fundamentalists oppose abortion the most, mainstream Protestants the least, and Catholics are in the middle.

Younger people also seem more supportive of legalized abortion than older people. Interestingly, however, this relationship varies somewhat across religious groups. Middle-aged and older Catholics and fundamentalists in Loui-

TABLE 6.3 Regression of Abortion Attitudes on Religion, Ideology, and Demographic Variables

	B	Beta	T-ratio	Significance
Fundamentalist (age)	.005	.153	3.06	.00
Catholic (age)	.003	.113	2.32	.02
Ideology	.211	.225	5.27	.00
Education	−.082	−.128	−2.99	.00
Race	.176	.110	2.44	.01

R^2 = .11, constant = .053, N = 868

Source: University of New Orleans Survey Research Center, Louisiana Senate Race Survey, September 1990.

siana are more opposed to legalized abortion than mainstream Protestants in their age groups. Among younger people—under forty-five years, and especially under thirty—there is much less difference among religious groups in their attitudes toward abortion. Benin found the same interaction effect between religious preference and age in her analysis of 1982 national-level data. She attributes this effect to either greater religiosity and religious influence among older people, or greater salience and personal relevance of abortion to younger people, or both.[35]

Multivariate analysis further confirms the significant relationship between religious preference and attitudes toward abortion, when other factors related to abortion attitudes are taken into account. The three-point abortion attitude scale from the UNO Poll (−1 = legal under any circumstance; 0 = legal under certain circumstances; 1 = never legal) is regressed on religious preference (dummy variables for Catholics and fundamentalist Protestants), demographic variables (education, income, gender, race, age), political party, and ideology. The resulting regression coefficients indicate that both Catholicism and fundamentalist Protestantism are significantly related to the pro-life position, as are conservatism, low education, and African American ethnicity. However, when interaction terms combining religion and age are introduced into the equation, religious preference by itself is no longer statistically significant. When nonsignificant variables are dropped through backward regression, the resulting equation, shown in Table 6.3, contains the following significant independent variables: ideology, education, race, and the two interaction terms. Thus, religious preference is indeed related to Louisianans' attitudes toward abortion—but primarily among middle-aged and older Louisianans, and not so much among the young.

Returning to the question of representation, it is clear that most Louisiana Catholics support at least some legal restrictions on abortion, and in that sense the Catholic Church represents their views in pushing for such restrictions. It is also clear that most Louisianans in general support some restrictions, as does the majority of state legislators representing them. On the other hand, fewer than a fourth of the Catholics and of the general Louisiana population surveyed would support a total ban on all abortions. When asked about specific restrictions, Catholics and Louisianans in general are quite closely divided on many of them. The push by the Catholic Church and by some legislators for a total abortion ban is probably more restrictive than most Louisianans desire; the details of the abortion legislation that would come closest to pleasing everyone remain obscure.

Conclusion

Although often presented as morally simple by pro-life and pro-choice advocates alike, the abortion issue is complex. The abortion attitudes of Louisianans, Catholic and non-Catholic, are ambiguous and deeply divided. The Catholic Church and its lobbying organizations have often been criticized for overstepping the "wall of separation" between church and state, as they have sought to incorporate the church doctrine that life begins at conception into state law. At the same time, the church has indicated a willingness to permit exceptions to the ban on abortion, a willingness apparently shared by most Louisiana Catholics and the general population.

This leads to another type of criticism often leveled at the Catholic Church: that it is inconsistent in proclaiming that abortion is murder, while accepting the legality of abortion in limited circumstances. Such acceptance may be necessary in order to pass any kind of antiabortion legislation in Louisiana. Thus, the church's position on abortion is both a strength and a weakness in dealing with the state government: a weakness in that some legislators denounce the perceived inconsistency, and a strength in that it may eventually lead to the passage of at least some legal restrictions on abortion in Louisiana.

The Catholic Church's combination of absolute moral pressure and limited political compromise is quite common among religious organizations in the United States. As Hertzke has noted:

> Religion, at its heart, requires a radical commitment from its adherents, which explains in part the temptation of some religious leaders to embody a "prophetic" militancy in their public rhetoric. Yet the congressional milieu, with its emphasis upon consensus and strategic compromise, demands that groups articulate their concerns on *its* terms.[36]

The Catholic Church commands potent political resources and claims many adherents in Louisiana. The church has every right to lobby for the strongest antiabortion laws possible, just as the state government has the responsibility to ensure that the wall of separation between church and state is not breached.

Notes

1. I wish to acknowledge the helpful suggestions and research assistance of Charles D. Hadley and John Cosgrove. I am also grateful to Terri Bartlett, executive director of Planned Parenthood of Louisiana; Peg Kenny, executive director of the Louisiana Pro-Life Council; and the Honorable Mitchell J. Landrieu, Louisiana House of Representa-

tives, for cheerfully taking a few hours out of their busy schedules to discuss the issue and the events of the 1990 Louisiana legislative session.

2. Charles D. Hadley and Ralph E. Thayer, "Louisiana: The Unfolding of its Political Culture." (Paper delivered at the annual meeting of the American Political Science Association, Washington, D.C., August 31–September 4, 1988), 1–10.

3. Hadley and Thayer, "Louisiana: The Unfolding of its Political Culture," 21–22.

4. Dawn Ruth, "State's Catholics, Protestants Join Forces in War on Abortion," New Orleans *Times-Picayune,* June 26, 1990.

5. See Doug Myers and Bill McMahon, "New Anti-abortion Bill OK'd," Baton Rouge *Morning Advocate,* July 9, 1990.

6. Ed Anderson, "Roemer Rejects Abortion Bill," New Orleans *Times-Picayune,* July 28, 1990.

7. John LaPlante and Doug Myers, "Pro-choice Forces Say New Measure Flawed; Anti-abortion Side Subdued," Baton Rouge *Morning Advocate,* July 9, 1990.

8. Allen D. Hertzke, "The Role of Religious Lobbies," in Charles W. Dunn, ed., *Religion in American Politics* (Washington D.C.: CQ Press, 1989), 126. See also Hertzke, *Representing God in Washington: The Role of Religious Lobbies in the American Polity* (Knoxville: University of Tennessee Press, 1988).

9. Jacqueline Scott and Howard Schuman, "Attitude Strength and Social Action in the Abortion Dispute," *American Sociological Review* 53 (October 1988): 785–793.

10. Ruth, "State's Catholics, Protestants Join Forces in War on Abortion," A-4. See also Doug Myers, "Abortion Override Fails," Baton Rouge *Morning Advocate,* July 8, 1990.

11. Interview with Teri Bartlett, executive director of Planned Parenthood of Louisiana, February 1, 1991.

12. Interview with State Representative Mitchell J. Landrieu, February 7, 1991. See also Ed Anderson, "Roemer: No Abortion Ban," New Orleans *Times-Picayune,* March 28, 1990; Iris Kelso, "Lots of Fallout from Legislative Abortion Bombshell," New Orleans *Times-Picayune,* July 15, 1990: Ruth, "State's Catholics, Protestants Join Forces in War on Abortion."

13. Kenneth D. Wald, *Religion and Politics in the United States* (New York: St. Martins Press, 1987), 232.

14. Ruth, "State's Catholics, Protestants Join Forces in War on Abortion," A-4.

15. Interview with Peg Kenny, executive director of the Louisiana Pro-Life Council, February 5, 1991. For more on the ties between the Catholic Church and the secular right-to-life movement, see Wald, *Religion and Politics in the United States,* 232–233; Alissa Rubin, "Interest Groups and Abortion Politics in the Post-*Webster* Era," in Allan J. Cigler and Burdett A. Loomis, eds., *Interest Group Politics,* 3d ed. (Washington D.C.: CQ Press, 1991): 239–255.

16. Rubin, "Interest Groups and Abortion Politics in the Post-*Webster* Era."

17. Interviews with Terri Bartlett and Peg Kenny; Ruth, "State's Catholics, Protestants Join Forces in War on Abortion."

18. For a discussion of the diversity of Catholic organizations, see Thomas J. O'Hara, "The Multifaceted Catholic Lobby," in Carles W. Dunn, ed., *Religion in American Politics* (Washington D.C.:CQ Press): 137–144.

19. Ed Anderson, "Abortion Foes Want a Bill to Challenge Court," New Orleans *Times-Picayune,* June 7, 1990.

20. Myers and McMahon, "New Anti-abortion Bill OK'd"; Kelso, "Lots of Fallout from Legislative Abortion Bombshell"; interviews with Terri Bartlett and State Representative Mitchell J. Landrieu.

21. Interview with Peg Kenny. See Also Richard Meek, "Louisiana Pro-lifers Optimistic for This Year," *Clarion Herald,* January 17, 1991. (The *Clarion Herald* is the newspaper of the Archdiocese of New Orleans.)

22. LaPlante and Myers, "Pro-choice Forces Say New Measure Flawed; Anti-abortion Side Subdued."

23. Wald, *Religion and Politics in the United States,* 236–238;

24. Interviews with Terri Bartlett and the State Representative Mitchell J. Landrieu.

25. Myers, "Abortion Override Fails"; Kelso, "Lots of Fallout from Legislative the Abortion Bombshell": interview with Terri Bartlett.

26. James Varney, "Mother Teresa's Role in Ad Unclear," New Orleans *Times-Picayune,* June 12, 1990.

27. Ed Anderson, "Abortion Foes Want a Bill to Challenge Court," New Orleans *Times-Picayune,* June 7, 1990; Myers and McMahon, "New Anti-abortion Bill OK'd"; interview with State Representative Mitchell J. Landrieu.

28. In the analyses of both state legislators' votes and public opinion, Protestant denominations are classified as follows: (1) Fundamentalist Protestant: Baptist, Pentecostal, Assembly of God, Seventh Day Advetnist, Church of God, Christian Scientist, Mormon, Jehovah's Witness; (2) Mainstream Protestant: Methodist, Episcopalian, Lutheran, Presbyterian, United Church of Christ.

29. Everett Carell Ladd, *The Ladd Report #8: Abortion: The Nation Responds* (New York: W.W. Norton, 1990), 18.

30. See, for example, Charles H. Franklin and Liane C. Kosaki, "Republican Schoolmaster: The U.S. Supreme Court, Public Opinion, and Abortion," *American Political Science Review* 83 (September 1989): 751–771; Ted G. Jelen, "Respect for Life, Sexual Morality, and Opposition to Abortion," *Review of Religious Research* 25 (March 1984): 220–231; Clyde Wilcox, "Race Differences in Abortion Attitudes: Some Additional Evidence," *Public Opinion Quarterly* 54 (1990): 248–255; Mary Holland Benin, "Determinants of Opposition to Abortion," *Sociological Perspectives* 28 (April 1985): 199–216; Ladd, *Ladd Report #8: Abortion: The Nation Responds.*

31. These were the findings of the two surveys: one conducted in September 1990 by Mason-Dixon Opinion Research, Inc. and reported in Jack Wardlaw, "Voters, State Legislators and the Abortion Question," New Orlrans *Times-Picayune,* September 12, 1990; and the other conducted in Septenber 1989 by Southern Media and Opinion Research and reported in "Poll: La. Generally Against Abortion," New Orleans *Times-Picayune,* October 1, 1989.

32. The data for the public opinion analysis presented here come from a survey conducted by the University of New Orleans Survey Research Center under the direction of Dr. Susan Howell, September 4–12, 1990. 868 registered voters in Louisiana were interviewed by the telephone: the sampling error is plus or minus 3.4 percent. The text of the question about abortion is as follows: "Do you think abortions should be legal under any circumstances, legal under only certain circumstances, or never legal under any circumstances?" The UNO Survey Research Center is not responsible for the analyses or interpretations presented here.

33. See, for example, Wald, *Religion and Politics in the United States,* 75–76; Hertzke, "The Role of Religious Lobbies," 131–132; Benin, "Determinants of Opposition to Abortion." Some studies have shown that indicators of religiosity—for example, frequency of church attendance—are at least as important as religious denomination in predicting attitudes toward abortion; see, for example, Ross K. Baker, Laurily K. Epstein, and Rodney D. Forth, "Matters of Life and Death: Social, Political, and Religious Correlates of Attitudes on Abortion," *American Politics Quarterly* 9 (January 1981): 89–102; Larry R. Peterson and Armand L. Mauss, "Religion and the 'Right to Life':

Correlates of Oppositionto Abortion," *Sociological Analysis* 37 (Fall 1976): 243–254; Franklin and Kosaki, "Republican Schoolmaster." Unfortunately, there is no measure of religiosity in the UNO Poll being analyzed here.

34. See Baker et al., "Matters of Life and Death"; Benin, Determinants of Opposition to Abortion"; Wilcox, "Race Differences in Abortion Attitudes"; Peterson and Mauss, "Religion and the 'Right to Life'"; Franklin and Kosaki, "Republican Schoolmaster." Nearly all studies of abortion attitudes find that men and women differ very little, if at all, in their support of or oppositon to legalized abortion, although the issue is evidently more salient to women than to men; see Scott and Schuman, "Attitudes Strength and Social Action in the Abortion Dispute."

35. Benin, "Deteminants of Opposition to Abortion," 208–211.

36. Hertzke, "The Role of Religious Lobbies," 133.

7

Leading the Nation After Webster: Connecticut's Abortion Law

Spencer McCoy Clapp

Introduction

In 1990, Connecticut, the third most Catholic state in the nation,[1] became the first and only state to guarantee a woman's right to abortion as a matter of law. The operative language of the statute is in essence a codification of the United States Supreme Court standard enunciated in 1973 in *Roe v. Wade* and reads as follows: "The decision to terminate a pregnancy prior to the viability of the fetus shall be solely that of the pregnant woman in consultation with her physician."[2]

Immediately following the enactment of the new law, pro-choice activists in Connecticut, and nationally, hailed the law as a high water mark for the political organizing ability of the pro-choice movement following the Supreme Court's decision in *Webster v. Reproductive Health Services*. As Dawn Johnson, legal director of the National Abortion Rights Action League (NARAL), said in a *New York Times* article: "It's a very important victory, this is the first state law that says a woman has a right to choose an abortion, not under the Constitution, but under state law."[3] The practical significance for pregnant women in Connecticut is that access to abortion services would be unaffected if the Supreme Court overturns *Roe v. Wade*.

The new law was passed by Connecticut's legislature because it was the product of pragmatic compromise and delicate negotiations. The result was a bill that both the pro-choice and pro-life factions, including the Catholic Church, could agree upon. As a result of this broad base of support, the bill was approved by both chambers of the legislature by overwhelming margins.

The pro-life forces were satisfied in seeing limits put on the right to abortion, including a mandatory counseling provision for girls under sixteen years old, and in preventing the pro-choice movement from enacting its ideal bill which would have given a woman an absolute right to abortion throughout the entire pregnancy. The language pro-life supporters point to as a beachhead for further pro-life modifications states: "No abortion may be performed upon a pregnant woman after viability of the fetus except when necessary to preserve the life or health of the pregnant woman."[4]

The statute "acknowledges that Connecticut has a definite interest in protecting the life of the unborn," according to Regina Smith, the executive director of the Pro-Life Council in Connecticut and the vice chairwoman of the National Right to Life Committee in Washington, D.C. Smith sees the new law as a beginning for the pro-life movement in Connecticut, which has been unable to pass any restrictions on abortion. Smith maintains this position even though the new law does not require viability testing nor does it define when viability begins. Nonetheless, after the bill was passed Smith declared in a *New York Times* op-ed piece:

> Not one piece of legislation to protect the unborn child or to limit abortion has passed in this state since the 1973 Roe decision. Pro-abortion advocates have had a free hand in their operations with no government interference. This has ended with the law that embodies an important principle that recognizes the right of the unborn child to be protected. It acknowledges that all is not well with abortion on demand, and legislators are willing to restrict abortion. We had nothing in place to protect the unborn or women; now we have something. And although not the ideal bill we proposed, the new law offers us a solid base on which to build.[5]

One thing that both sides could agree on was the repeal of mid-19th century laws that made abortion a crime.[6] These laws, which were effectively voided by *Roe,* were considered some of the harshest laws in the country.[7] The laws, some dating from just after the Civil War, provided penalties of up to five years in prison for anyone performing an abortion and two years in prison for any woman receiving an abortion.[8] Prior to the start of the legislative session in which the new law was passed, the repeal of the criminal statutes was the only thing that both the pro-choice and pro-life forces could agree on.[9] In fact, in order not to offend, or appear to favor one side or the other, the drafters of the bill gave it the innocuous title of "An Act Concerning the Repeal of Certain Statutes."

How Connecticut ended up with this new law is a fascinating political story, involving key legislators, lobbyists, the Catholic Church, timing, and more than just a bit of luck, fate, or perhaps divine intervention. What follows is a description of the key factors which shaped the new law. This chapter will conclude with some thoughts on how passage of the Connecticut law could be emulated in other states with similar demographics and a similar political landscape.

Connecticut Politics and the Catholic Church

Connecticut has approximately 1.3 million Catholics out of a population of just over 3 million.[10] The state contains three major dioceses, Hartford, Bridgeport, and Norwich. The largest and most active politically is Hartford, which encompasses about half the state's population, contains over 800,000

Catholics, and is headquartered in the state's capital. The spiritual leader of all Connecticut Catholics is Hartford's Archbishop John Whealon.

For the past twenty years, Whealon has been a respected and much-loved leader. He maintains regular communication with the faithful through a weekly column in the *Catholic Transcript,* the state's only weekly Catholic newspaper. He also appears regularly on a Catholic-owned radio station, WJMJ, and he films inspirational spots for television.[11]

The archbishop's time is primarily taken up with administrative duties. "I'm the president of, I suppose, 500 corporations," Whealon has said. "We have meetings that go on constantly and problems that come up, and I'm the one to make the decisions."[12] In addition, Whealon teaches a scriptural course once a week, continues his work as a biblical scholar, and manages to find the time to chair the Faith and Order Committee of the Christian Conference of Connecticut. The group's executive director, the Rev. Stephen Zidorak, a United Methodist minister, calls Whealon "the most ecumenically committed Catholic leader in Connecticut and one of the most ecumenically minded of the American Catholic hierarchy."[13]

People who know Whealon say that while he is politically conservative, he is not dogmatic; he is willing to engage in debate. "He's conservative, but he's not a hard-liner in the mold of (Cardinal John) O'Connor in New York or (Cardinal Bernard) Law of Boston," according to the Rev. Richard McBrien, a theologian at the University of Notre Dame and a part-time Connecticut resident.[14]

It may be fair to describe Whealon as a moderate within the ranks of the National Conference of Catholic Bishops. He has made it clear, for example, that he would not take retribution against Catholic legislators who did not follow the church's position on pending legislation. At a customary luncheon given by Whealon for legislative leaders prior to the start of the 1990 session in which the new abortion law was passed, the archbishop, through his chief lobbyist William J. Wholean, made it clear that "it was a matter of conscience on the part of the legislator."[15] It was clear to all who attended the luncheon that Whealon would not follow the lead of bishops who have treated harshly pro-choice Catholic politicians.

The Bishops of Bridgeport and Norwich were also present at the luncheon. Representative James T. Fleming, a Republican from the wealthy suburb of Simsbury, and a Catholic, said the bishops were "pretty open on the issue politically, and Catholic legislators certainly would not be treated any differently than anyone else. That, I thought, the Archbishop made pretty clear."[16]

Considering the fact that everyone in Connecticut politics was well aware that the 1990 session would be addressing the abortion issue in some manner, the decision by the Connecticut Catholic hierarchy not to browbeat legislative leaders was an important signal that the Catholic Church would not threaten legislators in order to move the pro-life agenda. After all, the church had experienced lobbyists working for it and their track record was quite respectable.

In 1989 and 1990 the Catholic Church was credited by many with the defeat of a bill which would have extended civil rights to homosexuals and lesbians, the so-called "gay rights bill." Betty Gallo, principal lobbyist for the gay rights bill, believes that were it not for the opposition of the Catholic Church, the legislation would have passed. "I think that the archdiocese is one of the most powerful lobbying forces in the General Assembly." Gallo says. "They speak for the church, and the church has a very large membership in the state."[17]

The chief lobbyist for the church is William Wholean, executive director of the Connecticut Catholic Conference and an archdiocesan lobbyist since 1969. Wholean is proud of the clout that he has been able to bring to bear at the state Capitol. "The archbishop might get involved with an issue, but very seldom. That's why they have me," Wholean says. "The only time I remember the bishops getting involved was in the early 1970s, when there was an attempt to minimize the tax-exempt status of non-profit institutions, including churches," he recalls. "I don't remember who the speaker (of the House of Representatives) was at the time, but I told him I was calling out the troops, and that they didn't want that. He withdrew the bill."[18]

Although Wholean claims that the archbishop seldom gets involved in a legislative issue, abortion appears to be the exception to the rule. In August, 1988, in the middle of the presidential race, Archbishop Whealon declared in one of his weekly columns in the *Catholic Transcript* that he was renouncing his lifelong affiliation with the Democratic Party because it "officially is in favor of executing unborn babies."[19] He did not say at the time that he was joining another political party, but his registration the previous week as a Republican was subsequently reported in the press. Both Catholics and non-Catholics charged that the archbishop, who agreed the following month to meet with presidential candidate George Bush, had violated the constitutional separation of church and state. The state's largest daily paper, *The Hartford Courant,* while defending the archbishop's First Amendment right to speak freely, also wondered if he was not crossing the line separating church and state by exerting undue influence on his flock.[20] In addition, the newspaper criticized him for fostering single issue politics, a charge he readily accepts. If the Democratic Party had a change of heart on abortion, he says, he would return to its ranks. He says that he simply believes that the issue of abortion is more important than all others and he calls it a more serious moral question than slavery.[21]

Whealon defends his right to damn the Democrats. "In 1980, the Democrats first said they were open to abortion and supported abortion rights, and they did it again in 1984," he says. "In 1988, I felt they were showing no signs at all of straightening themselves out. So the only way that I could see to help my own Democratic Party was to say I couldn't stand them anymore, and for that reason."[22]

While noting his respect for the archbishop and his opinions as a leader of Connecticut's Catholics, the chairman of the state Democratic Party, John F. Droney, who describes himself as a practicing Catholic who is personally opposed to abortion, but who does not support legislation to restrict it, disagrees with Whealon:

The archbishop also has an opinion with regard to contraception, which I think you should understand very clearly: He is 100 percent opposed to contraception, just as he is 100 percent opposed to abortion. And it is his personal opinion that everyone should feel the same way. Now I will suggest to you that there are not too many people in this state who are not practicing some form of contraception, despite the archbishop's opinion in regard to it. But he has the right and duty to express that opinion insofar as it mirrors the teachings of the Roman Catholic church. Catholics have to decide: one, how to govern their personal lives in light of those teachings; and two, how to govern their political and governmental lives, if they happen to be in those positions.[23]

It would be interesting to know how Archbishop Whealon feels now that the national Republican Party has decided that its "tent is big enough," in the words of former party chairman Lee Atwater, to accommodate Republicans who are pro-choice.[24]

The archbishop also became personally involved briefly during the 1990 state legislative session when he wrote a letter to the *Hartford Courant* after it had published an editorial which advised legislators to concentrate on balancing the state budget and to avoid a battle over new abortion laws. Titled "No New Abortion Laws," the editorial supported the repeal of the criminal statutes, a position that both pro-choice and pro-life forces held prior to the session. The editorial also advised the repudiation of laws favoring viability testing, saying such laws are designed "to intimidate doctors and pregnant women—to warn them that they could be charged with murder unless they tried to save a 'viable' fetus." The editorial also opposed parental notification, would-be father notification, the elimination of Medicaid funding, and the banning of abortion as a means of sex selection.[25]

The editorial appeared during a critical period of the legislative session, just a week after the legislature's Judiciary Committee had conducted a major public hearing on the various pro-choice and pro-life bills. Apparently the archbishop felt that the paper's editorial, published at such a crucial time, called for a response from him. The response took the form of a letter to the editor which appeared on March 27th. The letter castigated the paper for being "pro-abortion," and in a twisted interpretation of the editorial, accused the paper of "supporting abortion as a means of sex selection." The letter ended on a philosophical bent, unrelated to any pending legislative proposals:

The editorial surprised the most by failing to ask three basic questions that must bring concern to any legislator: 1. In an abortion, is there the elimination of a separate, unborn, innocent human life? 2. In the United States, is not all human life to be guaranteed life, liberty and the pursuit of happiness? 3. Is not the protection of innocent human life the major responsibility of every legislator, regardless of polls, votes and euphemisms?"[26]

The same day that the paper printed the archbishop's letter, it also printed a two paragraph mini-editorial entitled "Abortion Semantics" in which the paper explained that saying the banning of abortion for sex selection purposes would be unenforceable was not the same thing as endorsing abortion for the purpose of sex selection. "The *Courant* doesn't 'support' abortion. It respects the constitutional right of a pregnant woman to choose. Opponents of abortion do not accept such distinctions, but most people do."[27]

Aside from his regular column in the *Catholic Transcript*, the letter in the *Hartford Courant* appears to be the archbishop's only public comment on abortion legislation during the historic 1990 session. Pro-choice supporters were probably quite pleased that the archbishop decided to attack the state's most influential newspaper, and to focus his attention on the most peripheral of the then-pending bills—the banning of abortion for sex selection. This rather inept attempt to influence opinion and lawmakers may be precisely why the hierarchy in Connecticut delegates its legislative agenda to its full-time lobbyists and paid consultants.

The Key Players: Legislators, Lobbyists, and the "God Squad"

After any major political event commentators frequently try to determine whether the result was due to the powerful women and men who were in control of the issue or whether the larger forces of public opinion dictated that the time had come for such a result. The new Connecticut abortion law was subjected to this after-the-fact analysis, and the overwhelming majority of political observers agreed that there were a few key players without whom there would not be a new abortion law in Connecticut.

This is not to say that the timing of the issue and other exterior forces did not influence the tone of the debate and perhaps even the ultimate outcome; however, many of these same forces were at work in other states in the spring of 1990, yet only Connecticut passed a law guaranteeing a woman's right to abortion.

The person most responsible for hammering out a compromise and bringing the warring forces to the same table was State Representative Richard Tulisano. Tulisano, who calls himself pro-life, is the cochairman of the powerful Judiciary Committee, a civil libertarian, and a Catholic. He was joined in the quest for consensus legislation on abortion by his co-chairman on the Judiciary Committee, State Senator Anthony Avallone. Soon after the Supreme Court decided the *Webster* case on July 3, 1989, Avallone, who is also Catholic, but pro-choice, called Tulisano to discuss the impact of *Webster* on Connecticut. Avallone reminded Tulisano that 1990 would be an election year, that the legislative session was a short one, and that a protracted battle over abortion could draw energy and attention away from the important business of adopting a state budget. Avallone suggested to Tulisano that they, as co-chairs of Judiciary, take the initiative on the issue before it took control of them and the entire legislative session.[28] Tulisano was not exactly thrilled by Avallone's suggestion and initially he thought that the safest course might be to do nothing.[29]

"It's one of the most difficult issues I've ever dealt with," said Tulisano, who is no stranger to explosive issues like capital punishment and gay rights (he opposes the former and supports the latter).[30] He knew that abortion was one of those issues that can bring a politician down; he said that his wife was just one of the many people who told him he was "crazy" for thinking about taking on the abortion issue directly.[31]

But Tulisano is known as a contemplative and independent lawmaker. He often looks to European laws (he owns a house in Italy) for inspiration on how to solve state problems. Although in the summer of 1989 he had no particular agenda on abortion, he did have, along with Avallone, faith that something could be worked out. "Richard and I believed that there was a consensus possible on abortion," said Avallone. "Nobody else but he and I believed that."[32]

The impact of *Webster*, which sent a clear message that the battle on abortion would increasingly be fought at the state level, was understood by both pro-choice and pro-life groups in Connecticut. They both knew that the upcoming legislative session would be a test of their political strength, and each side began in earnest to advance its respective legislative agenda.

The pro-choice forces organized into the Connecticut Coalition for Choice, an umbrella organization representing dozens of groups including Planned Parenthood, the National Abortion Rights Action League (NARAL), the National Organization for Women, Connecticut Catholics for Choice, and the Religious Coalition for Abortion Rights (RCAR). The Coalition's point person was Betty Gallo, a veteran lobbyist with a long list of liberal clients. Considered one of the most skilled lobbyists at the Capitol, Gallo had in previous years succeeded in eliminating pro-life bills at the early stages of the legislative process. By intensely working the key members of the Judiciary Committee, Gallo was often able to prevent a pro-life bill from getting the "JF" or joint favorable recommendation needed for the bill to be raised for a public hearing. The practical result was that many pro-life bills never saw the light of day.[33]

Gallo, who was raised in a devoutly Catholic family, was part of a tactical committee of the Coalition which included Deborah MacDonald of Planned Parenthood and Kim Harrison, a full-time lobbyist for the United Church of Christ and one of the newest members of the "God Squad"—full-time religious lobbyists.[34] According to Gallo, the *Webster* decision convinced the Coalition it had to act fast to protect abortion rights should *Roe* be overturned. In addition, the Coalition felt it would be better to act before the 1990 state elections. "We knew the legislature we had. We didn't know the legislature we might have or the governor we might have," MacDonald of Planned Parenthood said.[35]

The Coalition decided in the early fall that it would seek a trio of new laws it called the Reproductive Health Equity Acts of 1990.[36] One bill sought expanded school sex education programs and another would have guaranteed poor women access not just to abortion, but to all aspects of maternal health care, including birth control, prenatal care, day care, and substance-abuse treatment. The third bill said: "The State of Connecticut and all political subdivisions and agencies thereof, shall not interfere with a woman's personal decision to prevent, commence, terminate or continue a pregnancy."[37]

The language was absolute, even extreme some might say, and it meant that every woman had the right, in theory, to obtain an abortion as late as nine months into her pregnancy. Leaders of the Coalition defended the language by saying that no sane woman would end a normal pregnancy at such a late date, and that late term abortions are extremely rare and only done if the woman or the fetus is gravely ill.

It seemed as though the Coalition was committed to standing on principle even if it meant that most legislators would never vote for such a bill. Considering the fact that nationally only 1 percent of abortions are performed after the twentieth week, and that more than 90 percent of the nearly 20,000 legal abortions done annually in Connecticut occur at twelve weeks or less, it is clear that "the principle" at stake was overwhelmingly symbolic.[38] Some observers felt that by insisting on the right to very late-term abortions, the Coalition was jeopardizing its entire legislative package. On the other hand, one could see their position as a calculated political tactic to stake out an extreme position in order to give away something in negotiations, something that had little chance of passing but which could be traded for a specific pro-life proposal.

While the Coalition was preparing its legislation, the Pro-Life Council of Connecticut was doing likewise. The key figure for the Council, which claims a membership of 70,000 statewide, is Regina Smith, a lobbyist who was a member of the State Senate from 1978 until 1984. Smith is a moderate in a movement dominated by extremists. A mother of seven children, she was a founder of the Pro-Life Council and is a vice chairwoman of the National Right to Life Committee based in Washington, D.C.[39]

While the Council is technically nonsectarian, it clearly has the blessing of the Catholic Church. In addition to her duties as a lobbyist for the Council, Smith is also a paid consultant to Connecticut's Catholic bishops. Joining Smith at the Capitol were the dean of the God Squad, William J. Wholean, executive director of the Connecticut Catholic Conference, and Father Thomas Berry, Archbishop Whealon's executive secretary.

The Pro-Life Council intended to sponsor five bills during the 1990 legislative session. Those bills would require:

1. parental notification when minors seek abortions
2. notification of the would-be father
3. a ban on abortion as a means of sex selection
4. prohibition of Medicaid funding for abortions
5. viability testing for abortions sought after the twentieth week

The last bill was modeled after the Missouri statute which was upheld in *Webster.*[40]

A common denominator of all the Council's bills was that they sought limits on the fringes of abortion policy—there was no direct frontal assault on the basic right to have an abortion early in the pregnancy. Apparently Smith and the Council saw no point in pushing a bill that would embody the pro-life creed that life begins at conception and that abortion is wrong in all but the most extreme circumstances. It was clear that such a bill, if it could get passed at all, could not survive a constitutional challenge as long as *Roe* was the law of the land. Smith was not interested in futile gestures, and she knew from past experience that such a bill probably would not even survive the committee process. Instead, Smith chose a pragmatic approach from the beginning. She concentrated on chipping away at the unfettered right to abortion in Connecticut by pushing bills that just might have a chance of passing the legislature.

The Right to Abortion Under State Law: The 1990 Session

It is very important to appreciate the political climate which surrounded the abortion issue in late 1989 and early 1990, just prior to the start of the legislative session. In mid-October 1989, in a much publicized shift of position, Connecticut Congressman John Rowland modified his long-held opposition and voted for limited federal funding for abortions.[41] Three days later he announced his candidacy for governor of Connecticut. Rowland, a Republican, had been the only member of Connecticut's Congressional delegation who opposed abortion. While changing his position, he argued that abortion would not be a pivotal issue in his race for governor, but the timing of his "conversion" was thinly veiled.

Another member of Connecticut's Congressional delegation, Rep. Nancy L. Johnson, is a leading Republican spokeswoman for abortion rights. She said that she would not have been able to support Rowland if he had not softened his opposition to abortion.[42] Because both U.S. Senators in Connecticut are Democrats, Johnson is the state's leading Republican.

In the elections of November 1989, Douglas Wilder of Virginia and James Florio of New Jersey won the governorship of their respective states while campaigning for abortion rights. The general belief at the time was that the *Webster* decision, by showing the public that the loss of abortion on demand was a potential reality, had galvanized many pro-choice voters out of their complacency. Meanwhile, the national Republican Party, through its chairman Lee Atwater, was reading the public opinion polls and trying to distance itself from its antiabortion wing as quickly as possible. This move created considerable tension within the party nationally, and did not go unnoticed by Connecticut's Republican legislators as they returned to Hartford in early February 1990.

Approximately two weeks before the start of the session, both sides of the abortion issue previewed their legislative programs. On January 23rd, the Pro-Life Council sponsored a rally at the Capitol which drew only about 200 supporters.[43] At that rally, timed to coincide with the seventeenth anniversary of *Roe v. Wade,* the Council publicly stated its intention to focus on prohibiting abortions after viability and to seek viability testing. Even though abortions after viability are extremely rare, State Representative Benjamin DeZinno, a

Democrat, told the supporters at the rally, "If we can save one life, we have accomplished God's will."[44] In an effort to soften up the rank-and-file to the Council's legislative agenda, which did not seek the perennial ban on abortion, Lieutenant Governor Joseph Fauliso told the protesters to be realistic and support the Council's goals. "Anything we can do to reduce the number of abortions is a step in the right direction," Fauliso told the crowd.[45]

Ten days later the pro-choice forces held their own rally at the Capitol, attracting more than 3,000 people despite freezing rain and slush.[46] While the Pro-life Council had tried to raise support for pragmatic goals, the Coalition for Choice speakers focused on old-fashioned hardball politics. "Our state legislators must be told they must support freedom to choose or they will not be our legislators much longer," Irene Senter, a member of the Coalition told the crowd. One familiar placard in the crowd read, "Read Our Lips—Vote Pro-choice or Lose in November."[47] About a dozen state legislators attended the rally, as did Congressman Bruce Morrison, a gubernatorial candidate. The leadership of the Coalition unveiled the Reproductive Health Equity Acts of 1990, putting emphasis on the bill that would ensure a woman's right to terminate her pregnancy at any point.

This, then, was the political landscape in Connecticut as the legislative session was about to begin in 1990. The pro-choice forces wanted to pass an extreme bill, while the Pro-Life Council sought to establish a beachhead with viability testing, and perhaps parental notification. The Catholic Church had spoken to the legislative leadership at the annual pre-session luncheon, but it was clear there would be no retribution for legislators, Catholic or otherwise, who voted their conscience. In addition, in light of national developments, no Republican legislator could expect to gain points with the state party leadership by carrying the antiabortion ball during the session.

One final factor in the legislative process was the governor, William O'Neil. At the start of the session, O'Neil, a conservative Democrat and a Catholic, had not decided whether or not to seek reelection. Pro-choice Congressman Bruce Morrison had already decided to challenge O'Neil for the Democratic party's nomination. No one knew what O'Neil, who had sat in the governor's chair since 1980, would do if presented with a new abortion law. No significant piece of abortion legislation had come across his desk in ten years. But the governor's silence on abortion was in stark contrast to his much-publicized oath to veto an income tax, should the legislature attempt to pass one. That silence, concerning the issue on everyone's lips at the start of the session, was taken as a weak signal that he would abide by the will of the legislature, provided he was not asked to sign a bill that could become a political liability for him or the Democratic party in 1990.

Once the session began, Rep. Tulisano and Senator Avallone implemented a strategy designed to maintain communications with both the Coalition for Choice and the Pro-life Council, while at the same time making clear that they were the ones in charge of their Judiciary Commitee and the legislative issue of abortion. A key test of their authority came when they decided to hold a public hearing on all of the proposed bills having to do with abortion. Betty

Gallo and the pro-choice forces had successfully stopped antiabortion bills prior to the public hearing stage in other years, and they did not want the antiabortion bills to get a public hearing this time. Tulisano and Avallone insisted. Their even-handed treatment at all stages of the process, exemplified by this decision, was designed to protect their credibility with all sides. When Gallo began pressuring individual members of the Judiciary Committee to squash the antiabortion bill, for example, Tulisano and Avallone read her the riot act.

Gallo remembered that Avallone told her, "How do you negotiate if everybody's not at the table and you don't want the other side at the table?" Gallo recalled that she did not argue the point with Avallone. "He yelled at us," she said.[48]

In the end, all the bills got a public hearing in one, long session that lasted from late in the morning until early evening. Everyone got their chance to comment as nearly 190 people signed up to testify.[49] Asked after the hearing which of the bills had the best chance in the Judiciary Committee, Rep. Tulisano said "We are still in the process of discussion and are working to reach a consensus, a position that a majority of the legislators can agree on."[50] Despite the inclusion at a single hearing of both pro-life and pro-choice activists there were no incidents or outbursts. Tulisano and Avallone had successfully maintained control, and with it their authority.

Some members of the committee, notably Representatives George Jepsen, Doug Mintz, and Nancy Wyman were strong allies of the pro-choice movement. They wanted to see a pro-choice bill voted out of the committee, but they all felt that the Coalition's Reproductive Health Equity Act, with its absolute right to abortion throughout a pregnancy, had no chance of passing the legislature.[51] Deborah MacDonald, a Coalition co-chairwoman, remembered a confrontation between Mintz, the Judiciary Committee's vice-chairman, and Shelley Gaballe, the Connecticut Civil Liberties attorney who drafted the Coalition's legislative package. "Doug thought our position was too strident," MacDonald said. "We thought that Shelley, another attorney, could explain it to him. It was incredibly tense. I found it intimidating just to listen. The difference of opinion was very startling, especially since we were all pro-choice."[52]

"When I sit down with a client I say 'Tell me what your ideal bill is. . . . Now tell me what you can live with,'" said Gallo, who knew the Coalition would have to compromise and soften the bill to assure the support of even pro-choice legislators. In the end, MacDonald said, the Coalition retreated gradually. "It was a major philosophical concession. What we wanted was an expansion of *Roe*. . . . But there was no history of that in any other state. We met every week as the session went on. Our bottom line kept changing. It was very fluid."[53]

The bottom line the Coalition finally settled on was a refusal to give up any rights that they already had; in essence, their baseline was a codification of *Roe v. Wade* into state law. But if restrictions on abortion, such as parental notification were added to a codification bill, the Coalition stood prepared to fight the whole package. Whether they could make good on their promise to defeat it was another story.

Meanwhile, in early March, after the public hearing, Rep. Tulisano decided that he did not like any of the existing bills, and started writing his own.[54] He knew that both sides had previously agreed to repeal the old unconstitutional antiabortion statutes which contained criminal penalties. He also knew that both sides had tentatively agreed that some sort of counseling for minors could be included. This was no concession for the Coalition for Choice because clinics were already doing such counseling on their own.[55]

Another important consideration for Tulisano was how to "wrap" his bill in such a way that it would not be offensive to either side. For guidance he looked to abortion laws in Western Europe, in particular to a French law that talks about the sanctity of life as state policy while still permitting abortion. With help from a legislative staff attorney, Tulisano drafted a bill in three days, and then distributed it to Mintz, Jepsen, and a few other key legislators.[56]

Tulisano's bill offered something to both sides. It contained a pro-life preamble which referred to the state's "interest in the preservation of life in all its stages" and in "protecting the potentiality of human life." But it also contained a section which could be considered a codification of *Roe v. Wade*, except that it said no abortions may be performed after viability unless necessary to prevent "significant" impairment of the mother's health.[57]

Predictably, there was a fight in the Judiciary Committee over viability. Tulisano wanted it put at twenty-two weeks. The Coalition for Choice's allies on the committee wanted it set at twenty-eight weeks. In addition, Rep. George Jepsen said hours were spent in committee searching for a way to define what sort of threat to a mother's health would justify an abortion after viability; no acceptable definition was found.[58]

According to Jepsen, the legislators were stuck on the health and viability questions as the deadline neared for reporting bills out of committee. Since they could not agree on the health and viability sections they were dropped, and the bill was left with only the repeal of the criminal statutes and the counseling for girls under sixteen.

Meanwhile, Betty Gallo, the pro-choice lobbyist, and Regina Smith, the Pro-Life Council's representative, were out counting heads for the amendments they each intended to propose. Gallo had an amendment codifying *Roe*, and Smith was ready with amendments calling for parental notification and viability testing. This was precisely the kind of situation that Rep. Tulisano wanted to avoid. Amending the bill on the floor of the House of Representatives promised to be a rancorous event at best, and it was possible that each side could muster enough support to defeat the other side's amendment. The result would be no statutory standards for abortion at all. Jepsen tried to convince Tulisano that if that were to occur and *Roe* were to be overturned, then it would be possible that an absence of statutory standards on abortion would allow a woman to seek an abortion in Connecticut at *any* time in her pregnancy. Tulisano was not sure that he agreed with Jepsen's analysis, but he conceded that it was a possible scenario.[59]

This may have been the impetus for Tulisano to contact his colleague on the Judiciary Committee, Doug Mintz and tell him, "We're still missing a piece."[60] Tulisano wanted to include viability language in order to appeal to the Pro-life Council. On the other hand, Mintz knew that the Coalition for Choice wanted codification language, and would settle for nothing less. Tulisano and Mintz, working toward a bill that could be passed, agreed the bill would offer no definition of viability and would not require viability testing. Basically the bill would just say that abortions were available up to viability and after that point only to preserve the health of the mother, which they also agreed would remain undefined.[61] This agreement between Tulisano and Mintz may well have been the magic moment that allowed Connecticut to pass a law that both sides could claim as a victory.

Mintz said that there was an implicit understanding that each side would refer to the amendment by a different name. Pro-choice legislators and lobbyists would call it the "codification" amendment, while pro-life supporters would refer to it as the "viability" amendment.

The vote in the House of Representatives on the unamended bill was scheduled for the next day. Tulisano had already planned to meet with the Pro-Life Council's Regina Smith the next morning to discuss her plan to have a parental notification amendment offered from the floor during debate on the bill. The meeting was held at Tulisano's law office at eight-thirty in the morning and included, in addition to Rep. Tulisano and Ms. Smith, the Rev. Thomas J. Barry of Archbishop Whealon's office and Benjamin DeZinno, co-chairman of the Public Health Committee and a strong pro-life legislator.

Smith recalled that "We were not aware that he (Tulisano) was sitting there with any amendment. I asked him if we could strengthen the language and he said 'This is what the other side agreed to.'" Smith had to decide quickly what to do. Pro-life legislators were waiting at the Capitol to meet with her, and the House of Representatives was due to convene at eleven o'clock. She had wanted a viability amendment herself and that was what Tulisano was calling the one on the table. She accepted his logic that the amendment was "a foot in the door," giving the state the right to restrict abortion, and allowing Smith and her allies to try for tougher limits in subsequent years.[62]

Smith decided to trust Tulisano's judgment that no other viability language stood a chance of passing.[63] It was this or nothing, he said. She asked him if, in addition to his amendment, he would support a parental notification amendment. He declined, citing a lack of votes for it in the legislature. His pro-life colleague, Rep. DeZinno, agreed with that judgment.[64]

Father Barry, who said little during the meeting, felt that Tulisano was presenting a done deal. Later he said that he did not think that anyone had agreed to anything in the meeting, but both Ms. Smith and Rep. DeZinno acknowledged that they had.[65] In any event all three were in the office when Tulisano called Doug Mintz at the Capitol and told him to go ahead with the codification/viability amendment they had discussed the day before. Mintz immediately notified Rep. Jepsen and then Betty Gallo. All three of them were very surprised to learn that Tulisano had been able to bring Regina Smith, and the Catholic Church, on board.[66] The die was cast.

Later that day at the Capitol Rep. DeZinno introduced the bill and yielded the floor to Tulisano. Only three substantive amendments were offered. One, submitted by Rep. Anthony Nania, did not stand a chance. With severe restrictions and penalties for having an abortion, it went down on a voice vote. Next came a parental notification amendment that the legislators debated for more than an hour. In the end, however, it got only 48 votes out of 149 voting members present that day. Tulisano had been right—the votes were not available for parental notification. Finally, Tulisano introduced the critical viability/codification amendment, and it passed on a voice vote, signifying the overwhelming support it enjoyed. The vote on the final amended bill was 136–12 in favor of passage, an astonishing margin for any piece of significant legislation, and an unheard of majority for a bill dealing with an issue as controversial as abortion.[67]

After the vote, Tulisano asked to meet with Betty Gallo and her group of lobbyists and Regina Smith and her group of insiders. In the hall of the House of Representatives, Tulisano opened a large pastry box which contained a cake shaped like a paschal lamb. He cut the lamb, a Christian symbol of Easter and peace, and offered slices to each side. They took them. The *Hartford Courant,* in reporting the lopsided vote and the claim of victory by both sides, referred to the bill as a "political miracle."[68]

However, the bill still needed to pass the State Senate. Anthony Avallone had said the Senate would pass the bill as long as no changes were made by the House. Still, it took ten days for the Senate to vote on the bill, in part because Avallone came down with chicken pox. Senate leaders considered delaying the vote until his return, but finally they decided not to let the bill linger.[69]

Rep. Mintz said that the Senate may have been influenced in this decision by a rumor that Archbishop Whealon had been convinced by a group of pro-life legislators that the bill was a disaster and had to be stopped. In fact, Anthony Nania and a handful of other lawmakers did get an audience with Whealon after the House vote. But while Whealon was disappointed with the vote he thought it best to leave the bill alone.[70] Had Whealon agreed with Nania, he might have been able to stop the bill in the Senate. It would definitely have been an uphill battle, however, because the Senate is generally regarded as more liberal than the House.

Rep. Nania thinks that the Senate misread his meeting with the archbishop. "The church was protecting Regina (Smith)," Nania said.[71] Later that week Nania called for Smith to resign from the Pro-life Council, and said that the Council leadership had gotten "snookered." Smith, charged Nania, gave away everything "for a seat at the table" with Tulisano.[72]

Regina Smith, who takes credit for stopping the Coalition for Choice's sweeping abortion rights bill, insists that the final bill represents a pro-life victory because, for the first time, it places limits on abortion. A few weeks after the bill became law, Smith wrote op-ed pieces for both the *Hartford Courant* and the *New York Times* putting her spin on the legislation.[73]

The bill was finally brought before the Senate where it passed 32-3.[74] The next day, without the usual fanfare associated with the signing of a major piece of legislation, Governor William O'Neil quietly signed the bill into law. In a written statement issued by his office, O'Neil praised the legislation as "a compromise forged between many groups concerning one of the most explosive social issues facing us. . . . Overall, I believe this measure strikes a balance between a person's right to privacy and the state's interest in protecting the fetus after viability."[75]

After O'Neil signed the bill into law, the attempts at spin control continued. The pro-choice forces were unanimous in their praise for the bill, and they highlighted the fact that Connecticut was the first state to guarantee a woman's right to abortion as a matter of state law. They were, understandably, silent about the pragmatic decision to jettison the more expansive Reproductive Equity Act bill. For their part, the pro-life forces were split. Smith called the law a victory and held a press conference to announce a public-awareness campaign to inform people about the new law's provision for counseling minors and its prohibition of abortions after viability. Rep. Nania, on the other hand, called the new law a "tragedy" and dismissed Smith's press conference as "an attempt to put dentures on a toothless dog."[76] This split in the pro-life forces made it more difficult for them to claim an unqualified victory, whereas the united front presented by the pro-choice forces added credibility to their claims.

Richard Tulisano, the acknowledged godfather of the new law, would still like to see a more restrictive law. But he also believes it is futile and wrong to try to stop abortion until society can offer women better alternatives. His original version of the bill had provisions for prenatal and postnatal care, but they did not survive the legislative process. Tulisano's perspective reflects the concerns of a caring, pragmatic, yet moral politician who knows the difference between the way things are and the way that people would like them to be. Connecticut has the highest per capita income of any state in the country, but at the same time it contains three cities, Hartford, New Haven, and Bridgeport, that are among the ten poorest in the country.[77] Tulisano knew all that and designed a bill to capture what he saw as a "middle ground" on abortion. Only time will tell whether Connecticut's experience with resolving the abortion dilemma will be emulated by other states.

Conclusion

Every state in our country has its own political landscape and no two states are alike in this respect. It is obvious that the Connecticut experience cannot be cloned or replicated in Ohio, New Mexico, or Iowa. The players are different, the timing is different, and the church is often different. But the issue, abortion, is the same.

Perhaps there are some lessons to be learned by the experience in Connecticut. When looking back on what happened in Connecticut one can see certain broad outlines or elements which may in fact assist those who are working legislatively on the abortion issue in other states. What follows is a brief list of some of those elements.

Find Some Common Ground

In Connecticut's case the common ground was the repeal of the old 19th century criminal statutes. Later, both sides found that they could agree on counseling for girls under sixteen. Establishing some common ground early means that there is something which can be enhanced, broadened, or built upon through negotiation or compromise.

Work with the Catholic Church
Early in the Process

The Connecticut bill sailed through both chambers of the legislature because in large part it was perceived to have the imprimatur of the Catholic Church. Seek out the most moderate or pragmatic voice in the church and bring that person into the loop of negotiations early in the process. Connecticut is blessed and fortunate to have an intelligent archbishop who is, if not a moderate, at least willing to let Catholic legislators make up their own minds without fear of excommunication.

Work with Moderate Pro-Life Activists

This may sound like an oxymoron to some people. But Connecticut was fortunate to have a leader of the Pro-Life Council who was pragmatic. This may be in part because the leader was a former legislator and therefore knew first-hand that politics is the art of the possible. Try to identify the moderate pro-life leaders, if there are any, and bring them into the negotiation process. Once they are brought in and made a part of the process they will have an investment in the final proposal which emerges.

Find Lawmakers Who Are Respected by Both Sides

The Connecticut experience reveals how important powerful legislators on key committees can be in the lawmaking process. Rep. Richard Tulisano was the right person, in the right spot, at the right time. He was respected by both sides, although he was probably trusted more by the Pro-Life Council than he was by the Coalition for Choice. The latter group, however, did not put all its faith in Tulisano but instead developed a handful of other legislative allies on the crucial Judiciary Committee.

Eliminate the Sticking Points

Start with the points that can be agreed upon and then slowly work toward the most difficult issues. If after several reasonable attempts to work through the hard points there is no agreement, then see if the sticking points can be eliminated. In the Connecticut case there was no agreement on when viability begins and on what constitutes a serious enough threat to the mother's safety to warrant a post-viability abortion. Since there was no agreement on these two points, they were taken out of the final bill.

Never Underestimate the Power of Language

One side called it the "viability" amendment and the other side called it the "codification" amendment. The language was identical, but people saw it according to the label with which they felt most comfortable. The Connecticut law was three pages long and all but two sentences dealt with the counseling of minor girls. The bill was encased in language which pleased the Pro-life Council, but one of the two sentences codified *Roe v. Wade* into state law. That single sentence assured Connecticut a place in history as the first state to do so.

Notes

1. J. Lang, "The Green Light," *Hartford Courant*, 12 August 1990, Northeast Magazine, pp. 12–20.
2. "An Act Concerning the Repeal of Certain Statutes," Public Act No. 90–113, Section 3(a).
3. "Connecticut Acts to Make Abortion a Statutory Right," *New York Times*, 27 April 1990.
4. Public Act No. 90–113, Section 3(b).
5. "Who Won on Abortion Law?" *New York Times*, 3 June 1990.
6. Lang, "The Green Light," p. 14.
7. "Connecticut Acts," *New York Times*, 27 April 1990.
8. Ibid.
9. Lang, "The Green Light," p. 14.
10. D. Holahan, "Hard Days for the Archbishop," *Connecticut Magazine*, November 1989, pp. 85–91.
11. Ibid.
12. Ibid., p. 86.
13. Ibid., p. 91.
14. Ibid.
15. "Catholic Legislators Caught Between Sacred, Secular," *Hartford Courant*, 3 February 1990.
16. Ibid.
17. Holahan, "Hard Days," p. 88.
18. Ibid.
19. Ibid., p. 89.
20. Ibid.
21. Ibid.
22. Ibid., p. 91.
23. Ibid.
24. "G.O.P. Blurs Abortion Focus, Dismaying Some in the Party," *New York Times*, 18 January 1990.
25. "No New Abortion Laws," *Hartford Courant*, 11 March 1990.
26. "Paramount Concerns About Abortion," *Hartford Courant*, 27 March 1990.
27. "Abortion Semantics," *Hartford Courant*, 27 March 1990.
28. Lang, "The Green Light," p. 14. Connecticut has a bicameral legislature identical to the federal Congress with its Senate and House of Representatives. Unlike Congress, however, Connecticut has a joint committee system which has co-chairs, one each from

the Senate and the House. Membership on the important Judiciary Committee consists of both state senators and state representatives.

29. Ibid.

30. Ibid.

31. Ibid.

32. Ibid.

33. Ibid., p. 15. Proposed legislation starts in the committee which has jurisdiction over the subject matter of the bill. A simple majority vote of the committee is necessary to raise a bill for a public hearing, a process known as "JFing" a bill or giving it a joint favorable recommendation. Failure to get a bill "JFed" means that it effectively dies in committee.

34. Ibid.

35. Ibid.

36. Ibid.

37. "Late Abortions Rare, Studies Show," *Hartford Courant,* 10 July 1989.

38. "Abortion-Rights Advocate Views a Victory," *New York Times,* 13 May 1990, Connecticut section.

39. Lang, "The Green Light," p. 15.

40. Ibid.

41. "Abortion Debate Gives Rise to Political Realignments," *Hartford Courant,* 12 February 1990.

42. Ibid.

43. "Abortion-decision Anniversary Marked by Opposing Groups," *Hartford Courant,* 23 January 1990.

44. Ibid.

45. Ibid.

46. "Abortion Activists Rally at State Capitol," *Hartford Courant,* 5 February 1990.

47. Ibid.

48. Lang, "The Green Light," p. 16.

49. "Foes Converge for Abortion Hearing," *Hartford Courant* 3 March 1990.

50. Ibid.

51. Lang, "The Green Light," p. 16.

52. Ibid.

53. Ibid.

54. Ibid.

55. Ibid.

56. Ibid.

57. Ibid.

58. Ibid.

59. Ibid., p. 17.

60. Ibid.

61. Ibid.

62. Ibid.

63. Ibid.

64. Ibid.

65. Ibid.

66. Ibid.

67. "State House Passes Abortion Rights Bill," *Hartford Courant,* 18 April 1990.

68. "Abortion Bill Pleases Both Sides," *Hartford Courant,* 22 April 1990.

69. "Senate Backs Abortion Bill," *Hartford Courant,* 28 April 1990.

70. Lang, "The Green Light," p. 20.

71. Ibid.

72. "Abortion Foes Irate at Leader," *Hartford Courant,* 27 April 1990.

73. "Who Won on Abortion Law?" *New York Times,* 3 June 1990; *Hartford Courant,* 6 May 1990, editorial.

74. *Hartford Courant,* 28 April 1990.

75. "Abortion-Rights Bill Becomes State Law," *Hartford Courant,* 1 May 1990.

76. *Hartford Courant,* 27 April 1990.

77. "Hartford, New Haven in Top 10 of Impoverished Cities," *Hartford Courant,* 4 February 1983.

8

The Cardinal and the Governor: The Politics of Abortion in New York State

Timothy A. Byrnes

The law and politics of abortion have changed substantially in many of the states covered in this book. In some, restrictive legislation has actually been passed. In others, great battles have taken place in the state legislature, creating new political alliances or causing new rifts and controversies. In still others, abortion has played a crucial role in statewide campaigns, splitting electoral coalitions and moving candidates in one direction or another. In comparison to these other states, the law and politics of abortion in New York have not been particularly dramatic. As of spring 1991 there had been no significant change in the state's laws governing either the availability or funding of abortion. And though it was a significant issue in the 1990 legislative campaign, abortion has not been as politically explosive in New York as it has been elsewhere.

Despite this relative stability, New York merits inclusion in a book on the Catholic Church and abortion for a number of reasons. It is, after all, a very large state with a sizable Catholic population; roughly 40 percent of New York's seventeen million people are Roman Catholic. In addition, New York has played a central role in the history of abortion in the United States. New York's early and expansive liberalization of its law on abortion in 1970 earned it the title, "abortion capital of the nation." That distinction lost much of its meaning after *Roe v. Wade,* but *Webster* may draw national attention back to New York's particularly firm commitment to the ready availability of legal abortion.

More than any other reason, however, New York merits inclusion in this book because it is home to John Cardinal O'Connor and Governor Mario Cuomo. These two articulate Catholics, each with ready access to the national media, have been locked in public debate for years over questions such as: What particular responsibilities do Catholic politicians have when it comes to abortion? What is the difference between a moral teaching and a legal strategy?

Is public funding of abortion governmental support for murder or nothing more than a manifestation of simple fairness? This debate has always held the interest of a wide audience well beyond the borders of New York State. In fact, it is fair to say that O'Connor and Cuomo, more than any other two individuals, have defined the terms and set the parameters of the "Catholic" politics of abortion in America.

Background

New York has been and continues to be a solidly pro-choice state. In 1970, three years before *Roe v. Wade,* New York's legislature left the decision on abortion to a woman and her doctor during the first twenty-four weeks of pregnancy. That highly controversial law, establishing so-called "abortion on demand," was repealed by the legislature in 1972, but the act of repeal was then vetoed by Governor Nelson Rockefeller. When the Supreme Court handed down its landmark decision in 1973, New York had one of the nation's most permissive policies on abortion.

Since *Roe,* New York has continued to guarantee ready access to legal abortion. Public funding of abortions for poor women continues in New York. Parental notification, introduced in committee the last several years, had not, as of spring 1991, made it to the floor of the Assembly for debate. And state courts have stoutly defended the right to abortion through reference to provisions of New York's state constitution. These pro-choice policies are apparently consistent with public opinion in New York. Support for abortion varies depending on the circumstances prompting it, but according to one poll 46 percent of New Yorkers support access to abortion in *all* circumstances, and 47 percent support access to abortion in some circumstances.[1] However, at the same time, fully 82 percent of those polled agreed that "even if a woman wanted to have an abortion for reasons I disagreed with, I don't think the government should intervene in the decision."[2] By all measures, then—legal, political, and attitudinal—the right to abortion is well protected in New York State, and all indications are that it will continue to be so in the foreseeable future.

At the same time, perhaps in response to these factors, New York has been the site of a vital and active pro-life movement. The New York Right to Life Committee, formed in 1967, offered a model for other states to follow. One of its leaders, Edward Golden, served as the first head of the National Right to Life Committee. The Right to Life Party was founded in New York State. And Randall Terry's Operation Rescue, a group of antiabortion activists who specialized in blocking entry to abortion clinics, was headquartered in Binghamton, New York. Right to Lifers are a minority in New York; but they are a well-organized and very vocal one.

The Catholic Church has been deeply involved in antiabortion politics in New York from the beginning. In the words of its current executive director, the New York State Catholic Conference was "instrumental" in the founding of the New York Right to Life Committee.[3] Other observers have described the church as the "major opponent" of liberalization of abortion law in 1970 and the "backbone" of the effort over the next two years to have "abortion on demand" repealed.[4] New York was the national center of Catholic opposition to abortion in the early 1970s largely because of the leadership of Cardinal Terence Cooke, Archbishop of New York. Cooke actively opposed liberalization of New York's law in 1970 and publicly campaigned for repeal in both 1971 and 1972. In addition, he strongly denounced the Supreme Court's decision that rendered moot the debate in New York. Terming *Roe v. Wade* a "horrifying decision," Cooke called on the American people to "rededicate themselves to the protection of the sacredness of all human life" and to do "all in their power to reverse this injustice to the rights of the unborn child."[5]

Until his death a decade later, Cardinal Cooke remained a leading figure in the church's antiabortion effort at both the national and local levels. He was the first chairman of the National Conference of Catholic Bishops' committee on pro-life activities. And in New York he inaugurated the "canister collection," a practice whereby the New York State Right to Life Committee collects funds outside Catholic churches one Sunday each year. After his death, Cooke's right-to-life commitment was affirmed and perhaps even deepened by the Catholic hierarchy of New York State. Cooke's successor as Archbishop of New York, John O'Connor, is also a successor to the chairmanship of the bishops' national committee on pro-life affairs. The canister collection continues to be taken annually in a number of dioceses in New York. And the staff of the New York State Catholic Conference, the bishops' collective body, continues to play a leading role in lobbying the legislature to restrict access to legal abortion.

The Effects of *Webster*

In July 1989, of course, the Supreme Court of the United States redrew the national debate over abortion by stepping back from *Roe v. Wade* and accepting restrictive provisions of Missouri's abortion law. State legislatures throughout the country reacted by debating a wide variety of new restrictions on abortion. A few states, such as Pennsylvania and Utah, mounted frontal assaults on *Roe*. Others followed Missouri's lead and restricted abortion at *Roe's* margins. *Webster* did not affect directly the law in New York, but the court's decision did lead to renewed fervor on all sides of the issue. Antiabortion forces were encouraged; pro-choice forces remobilized; and Catholic leaders were moved to restate their opposition to abortion and to redouble their efforts to have it restricted in New York.

Brooklyn's Bishop Francis Mugavero's reaction was typical of New York's bishops. "I am heartened by the Court's decision," Mugavero said. "It is a victory for life. The court has affirmed the authority of the states to recognize and protect unborn human life. We encourage new legislation by our elected officials that will protect unborn children to the maximum degree possible."[6] The New York State Catholic Conference characterized the court's action as a "challenge for positive change here in New York. We will be working with members of the New York State Legislature in the near future to introduce and advocate proposals which will protect the unborn child to the maximum degree now allowable by the Supreme Court of the United States."[7] Those proposals, when formally presented, called for

1. restrictions on the use of state Medicaid funds for abortion
2. enactment of the right of parents to be involved in their child's abortion decision
3. prohibition on the performance and funding of sex selection abortion
4. enactment of measures to provide for the true health care needs of poor women, including increased financial support for pre-natal and post-natal services, child care, nutrition, and public assistance[8]

The problem with this agenda, from the perspective of the Catholic Conference anyway, was that items 1–3 on it had very little chance of actually being passed into law. With the State Assembly and the governor's mansion in the hands of pro-choice Democrats, even Kathleen Gallagher, the Catholic Conference's Associate Director for Pro-Life Activities, admits that "the climate is not good" for changing abortion law in New York anytime soon.[9] Indeed, over the last several years, it has been difficult for pro-lifers to get abortion-related bills onto the floor of the legislature where they could be voted on and where the position of each legislator could be recorded. Cardinal O'Connor expressed the official church's frustration at these circumstances at a public policy forum in January 1990. "Nobody leaves me off the hook about where I stand on anything," O'Connor said, "why shouldn't legislators have to go on record on this most critical issue."[10]

The New York State Catholic Conference, like other state conferences, is guided in its antiabortion efforts by the *Pastoral Plan for Pro-Life Activities,* a document first released by the National Conference of Catholic Bishops in November 1975. The plan proposed a three-pronged strategy for battling abortion. First, the bishops called for a "public information/education program" involving a campaign designed to create "awareness of the threats to human dignity in a permissive abortion policy," and a long range educational effort to lead people to "a clearer understanding of the issues, to firm conviction, and to commitment."[11] Second, the plan envisioned a greater emphasis on "pastoral care," including "moral guidance and motivation . . . service and care for women and unborn children . . . [and] reconciliation" between the church community and women who have had abortions.[12] Finally, and most controversially, the bishops offered a blueprint for a "legislative/public policy effort" based on "well-planned and coordinated political action by citizens at the national, state, and local levels."[13]

Given the political realities it faces, the New York State Catholic Conference has had very little success in its "legislative/public policy" efforts both before and subsequent to *Webster.* For that reason, the conference's pro-life office has concentrated much of its efforts on the *Pastoral Plan*'s first dimension, "public information/education." This is not to say that staff members do not lobby for changes in public policy; they do. But according to Ms. Gallagher, they concentrate the bulk of their efforts on "[educating] the constituency out there which can then in turn pressure the representatives."[14]

As I indicated in chapter one, however, there is one dimension of the Catholic bishops' antiabortion effort that is not covered in the *Pastoral Plan*. That dimension is the pressure bishops apply to Catholic politicians who either actively support legal abortion or who refuse to take steps to prevent it. In New York, as in other states, bishops have been applying this pressure with renewed emphasis and energy since *Webster*.

The Cardinal

Cardinal John O'Connor is particularly forthright in his opposition to abortion and unmistakably clear in his expectation that Catholic politicians will do all they can to restrict access to it. O'Connor's very active efforts in this regard pre-date the court's decision in *Webster*. In 1984, shortly after he was installed as Terence Cooke's successor as Archbishop of New York, O'Connor publicly criticized vice presidential candidate Geraldine Ferraro for what he called her misstatement of Catholic teaching:

> Geraldine Ferraro has said some things relevant to Catholic teaching which are not true. . . . The only thing I know about her is that she has given the world to understand that Catholic teaching is divided on the subject of abortion. . . . As an officially approved teacher of the Catholic Church all I can judge is that what has been said about Catholic teaching is wrong. It's wrong.[15]

"Given the world to understand that Catholic teaching was divided on the subject of abortion" referred to Ferraro's signature on a letter from Catholics for a Free Choice inviting members of Congress to a briefing on the particular problems associated with abortion for Catholic politicians. The section to which O'Connor objected asserted that the "Catholic position on abortion is not monolithic and there can be a range of personal and political responses to it."[16] Once Mrs. Ferraro learned that O'Connor's objections related to this passage, she pointed out that she had taken the term "monolithic" to refer to the views of individual Catholics rather than to Catholic doctrine as such. O'Connor was not impressed with this distinction. "The teaching of the Catholic Church is monolithic on abortion," he declared, "and it is stated in a letter signed by Ferraro that it is not monolithic. Now that, to me, is a pretty basic disagreement."[17] In response, Ferraro conceded that "the Catholic Church's position on abortion is monolithic. But," she added, "I do believe that there are a lot of Catholics who do not share the views of the Catholic Church."[18]

In this case, Cardinal O'Connor argued that Geraldine Ferraro had *misstated* the church's *moral* position on abortion. Two years later, however, in 1986, his vicar general in the archdiocese of New York challenged politicians who *disagreed* with the church's position on the *legal* status of abortion. Such politicians, announced Bishop Joseph O'Keefe, would no longer be welcome to speak at official Catholic events in the archdiocese. "It is not only inappropriate, it is unacceptable and inconsistent with diocesan policy to invite those individuals to speak at such events whose public position is contrary to and in opposition to the clear, unambiguous teaching of the church."[19] Cardinal O'Connor called his vicar general's directive "common sense" and argued that "the church's support, or seeming support, perceived support of a speaker who was explicitly supporting abortion . . . would be a scandal."[20]

Assemblyman John Dearie, included in the ban because of his support for public funding of abortion, charged that the cardinal was acting "in anticipation of the [1986] election," to try to put pressure on Catholic candidates and Catholic voters.[21] O'Connor rejected this charge as "grossly untrue, deeply insulting and morally libelous."[22] But regardless of the cardinal's intentions, the archdiocese's ban did find its way into the gubernatorial contest between two Roman Catholics, incumbent Mario Cuomo and his challenger Andrew O'Rourke. Cuomo expressed his great disappointment in the ban and claimed that "lay people have a right to be heard."[23] For his part, O'Rourke offered that "if [Cuomo] doesn't want to be a Catholic, he shouldn't be one."[24]

The Governor

Mario Cuomo, of course, has emerged as a central player in the Catholic politics of abortion. He is a leading spokesman for a national Democratic party that strongly supports a woman's right to terminate her pregnancy. As governor of New York he has consistently supported public funding of abortions for poor women in his state. And, in the face of vocal opposition from Cardinal O'Connor and others, he has frequently asserted his right as a Catholic layman and a public official to dissent from what he defines as particular legal and political *applications* of his church's moral teaching on abortion.

Cuomo's public dispute with members of the Catholic hierarchy over abortion began in 1984 when Archbishop O'Connor remarked that he could not see how "a Catholic in conscience could vote for an individual explicitly expressing himself or herself as favoring abortion."[25] While accepting the archbishop's right to articulate Catholic teaching on abortion, Governor Cuomo claimed O'Connor had stepped over the line of appropriate behavior for an American religious leader. "Now you have the Archbishop of New York," Cuomo charged, "saying that no Catholic can vote for Ed Koch, no Catholic can vote for Pat Moynihan . . . or Mario Cuomo—anybody who disagrees with him on abortion."[26]

For the first, and perhaps last, time O'Connor retreated in the face of Cuomo's rejoinder. "It is neither my responsibility nor my desire," O'Connor said, "to evaluate the qualifications of any individual of any party for any public office or of any individual holding public office. My sole responsibility is to present as clearly as I can the formal official teaching of the Catholic Church. I leave to those interested in such teachings whether or not the public statements of officeholders and candidates accord with this teaching."[27] At the time, Cuomo declared himself "delighted to have the clarification,"[28] but I doubt either man realized this was only the first skirmish in a long battle over the responsibilities of Catholic politicians to translate their church's moral opposition to abortion into a legal prohibition of it. Cardinal O'Connor believes this responsibility is a simple matter of moral consistency and political courage. Governor Cuomo, to say the least, believes it is much more complicated.

On September 13, 1984, Cuomo gave a speech at the University of Notre Dame in which he expanded on the sensitive subject of Catholic politicians and abortion.[29] He began by laying out a series of questions: "Must politics and religion in America divide our loyalties? Does the 'separation between church and state' imply separation between religion and politics? . . . Even more specifically, what is the relationship of my Catholicism to my politics? When does the one end and other begin?"[30] Cuomo's answers to these questions were based on what he called the "special responsibility" of a "Catholic who holds political office in a pluralistic democracy. . . . The Catholic public official," he argued, "lives the political truth most Catholics throughout most of American history have accepted and insisted on: the truth that to assure our freedom we must allow others the same freedom even if occasionally it produces conduct by them we would hold to be sinful."[31]

Turning specifically to his duties as both a Catholic and a governor, Cuomo said "I believe I have a salvific mission as a Catholic. Does that mean I am in conscience required to do everything I can as governor to translate all my religious values into the laws and regulations of the state of New York or the United States? Or be branded a hypocrite if I don't?" Holding that "there is no church teaching that mandates the best political course for making our beliefs everyone's rule," Cuomo claimed the right as a faithful Catholic to

> accept the bishops' position that abortion is to be avoided [and] after careful consideration of the position and arguments of the bishops [conclude] . . . that the approach of a constitutional amendment is not the best way for us to seek to deal with abortion. . . . I believe that legal interdiction of abortion by either the federal government or the individual states is not a plausible possibility, and even if it could be obtained it wouldn't work. . . . The bald truth is that abortion isn't a failure of government. No agency or department of government forces women to have abortions but abortion goes on. . . . The failure here is not Caesar's. This failure is our failure, the failure of the entire people of God.[32]

This speech has become a rather famous one in the ensuing years, and the governor often answers questions concerning his views on abortion with an admonition to read the "Notre Dame speech." Cuomo's supporters believe he laid out a carefully constructed argument that affirms his religious loyalties, his own moral convictions, his responsibilities as a public official, and reconciles all these values with the political reality in which he finds himself. To many of Cuomo's opponents on this issue, however, especially within the Catholic Church, his speech at Notre Dame was, at best, an exercise in self-deception, and at worst, a monument to political calculation. To these critics, Cuomo's position has come to be known as "personally opposed but. . . ," a stand Cardinal O'Connor has termed "equivalently a pro-choice position,"[33] and therefore inconsistent with Catholic teaching. The cardinal has also said that politicians taking such a stand "have the obligation to demonstrate that their position is not rooted in political expediency."[34] Governor Cuomo's critics have also dismissed his position as obfuscation and rhetorical gymnastics. Bishop Joseph O'Keefe, for example, by way of explicitly including Cuomo in his ban on pro-choice speakers, said the governor was "so smart he would confuse young people" at a Catholic graduation ceremony.[35]

This dispute over the "special responsibilities" of Catholics "holding public office in a pluralistic democracy" continues in New York State, and I think it is very unlikely it will be significantly ameliorated any time soon. The two sides disagree on fundamental points of definition and principle, and I can scarcely imagine either side changing its position on the central questions involved. That is not to say, however, that the debate is static; it is not. For as I said in chapter one, debates such as this take place within particular political and legal contexts that shape both the political significance of abortion and the practical meaning of the "personally opposed but . . ." position. Those contexts were fundamentally altered by the Supreme Court's decision in *Webster v. Reproductive Health Services, Inc.*

The Politics of Abortion in New York

Mario Cuomo's strongest argument for not taking a more active role in seeking to limit abortions in New York has been his claim that as governor of a single state he has had no direct role in determining abortion's legal status. "We must keep in mind always that we are a nation of laws," Cuomo said at Notre Dame, "when we like those laws, and when we don't. The Supreme Court has established a woman's constitutional right to abortion."[36] So long, he argued, as a woman's right to abortion is protected as a fundamental liberty by the United States Constitution then it is pretty much irrelevant whether or not Mario Cuomo or any other state official thinks it ought to be. As Governor of the state of New York, Cuomo has taken an oath to uphold the Constitution and that means, among many other things, upholding a woman's right to terminate her pregnancy if she sees fit to do so.

It was precisely this argument, however, that was undercut when the Supreme Court upheld Missouri's restrictions on abortion and at least implicitly invited other states to send up their own restrictions for judicial review. After July 1989, it was more difficult for Mario Cuomo or any other state official to claim that he or she was bound by federal constitutional law to uphold access to abortion in virtually all circumstances. Indeed, such a claim can fairly be termed disingenuous. If Mario Cuomo, as Governor of New York, wants to place restrictions on a woman's access to abortion in New York, he can propose a bill in the state legislature so stating. Such a bill would not be passed in the New York legislature at the moment. Also, it might, as I will demonstrate shortly, run afoul of New York's state constitution and state court rulings. But following *Webster* it is no longer clear that the Supreme Court or lower federal courts would hold that such a bill is inconsistent with the United States Constitution. The federal judiciary's doctrine on abortion is evolving, and *Roe v. Wade* is no longer a safe haven for state officials seeking protection from the perils of abortion politics.

In light of this retreat from *Roe,* of course, activists on both sides of the issue have turned with renewed interest to governors and state legislators. Pro-life groups, in New York and elsewhere, have asked state officials to do *something* to restrict access to abortion, now that the court has signaled acceptance of such restrictions. And pro-choice groups have pressured those same officials to state in clear and practically meaningful terms their own support for the right to an abortion separate and apart from abortion's now tenuous status as a constitutionally protected fundamental liberty. Through spring 1991, Mario Cuomo had nimbly refused to satisfy fully either one of these forces.

When *Webster* was handed down by the high court, Cuomo's immediate strategy was to defuse pressure from all sides by pointing out that the court's decision had not changed the law in New York, and that nothing in the decision had changed his opinion "about the right to abortion or the right of poor people to receive funding."[37] Speaking to the most relevant issue of continued abortion services in public hospitals, the governor said that "as a practical matter when I say I'm for Medicaid funding I'm saying I would reject a law that says you can't use public hospitals."[38]

Despite Cuomo's commitment to the legal status quo in New York, however, questions have persisted. Is the governor in favor of a woman's right to abortion as a matter of his own political conviction? Or is he only committed to protecting a right guaranteed by judicial doctrine and constitutional law? Some observers thought they heard Cuomo finally give a straight answer during a question and answer session that followed a speech he gave in Tucson, Arizona in September 1989. In an article titled "Cuomo Takes Abortion Stance Favoring Women's Right To Choose," the *New York Times* reported that Cuomo believed abortion "must be a matter of the woman's conscience." As a man, Cuomo said, he felt "presumptuous" making legal decisions concerning abortion. "I feel absurd," he said, "like I don't know why the judgment is mine or an all male court, except for one woman, or a mostly male Congress."[39]

Pro-choice activists welcomed Cuomo's apparently deepened commitment to abortion rights. Marilyn Fulton Fitterman, for example, president of New York's chapter of the National Organization for Women, declared herself "very happy to see the Governor taking a leadership position. . . . Many people," she recalled in an understatement, "weren't really satisfied with the Governor's position."[40] But Cuomo denied that his statement at Tucson represented a change in his position. In a letter to the editors of *Commonweal,* a lay Catholic journal of opinion, Cuomo claimed that everything he said in Tucson was "perfectly consistent with [his] position as stated at Notre Dame," and he restated the argument he had made so many times before *Webster* was handed down. "Here in America," he wrote, "where the law permits women to have abortions and preserves their right not to have abortions the terrible, hard judgment which that freedom permits must be a matter of the woman's conscience."[41]

Of course, this statement is true as a declaration of current legal fact. But would Cuomo still believe that abortion must be a matter for a woman's conscience if "the law," that is to say, the Supreme Court, no longer guaranteed this right of conscience? Does he personally believe the U.S. Constitution holds within it a fundamental right to abortion? He did not directly answer these politically charged questions in Tucson or in his letter to *Commonweal.* But to many observers the implication of Cuomo's remarks was that he believed a woman *should* have the right to an abortion. And to some Catholic bishops such a position, particularly when held by a Catholic politician, was cause for outrage.

Bishop Austin Vaughan, Cardinal O'Connor's vicar for Orange County, expressed this outrage in a uniquely provocative way. On January 22, 1990, the seventeenth anniversary of the Supreme Court's decision in *Roe v. Wade,* Bishop Vaughan spoke to reporters from jail, where he was serving a ten-day sentence for blocking entry to an abortion clinic. In that interview, the bishop warned that Mario Cuomo was running a "serious risk of going to hell" for his support of abortion in New York state. [42] Cuomo, Vaughan said, could not be a "good and faithful Catholic" and continue to hold his current position on abortion. During the media flap that predictably followed Vaughan's remarks, Cardinal O'Connor defended his fellow bishop. "Would anyone deny," the cardinal asked, "that the bishop has the right and even the *obligation* to warn *any* Catholic that his soul is at risk if he should die while deliberately pursuing any gravely evil course of action, and that such would certainly include advocating publicly, as the Bishop puts it, 'the right of a woman to kill a child?'"[43]

Just as the *legal* context shapes the content and tenor of the abortion debate between politicians and bishops, so the *political* context shapes the particular meaning of that debate at any given time. In this regard, it is important to point out that Vaughan's and O'Connor's actions in 1990 took place at a time when the political status of abortion was undergoing fundamental change.

Since 1976, when their platform first expressed opposition to legal abortion, national Republican candidates have used abortion to their political advantage. Republicans have placed abortion at the center of the so-called social issues agenda, and they have skillfully used that agenda as a wedge with which to divide the Democratic party. In the late 1970s and early 1980s social conservatives grew progressively disillusioned with the national Democratic party. Republican opposition to abortion appealed both substantively and symbolically to these voters and allowed political alliances to be formed across historical chasms like that separating Southern Evangelicals and Northern Catholics. These alliances, along of course with economic stagnation, flagging influence abroad, and intractable racial divisions within the Democratic party, destroyed the New Deal coalition at the presidential level, inaugurated a shift to the right in national electoral politics, and sent Republicans to the White House in 1980, 1984, and 1988.

Abortion's role in the largely symbolic but highly successful politics of the social agenda accounted for the drift toward the pro-life camp on the part of George Bush and other ambitious Republicans. But in 1989 and 1990, the political calculations associated with abortion grew a good deal more complicated. When the Supreme Court retreated from *Roe v. Wade,* and the pro-life movement demonstrated underappreciated skill at political mobilization, Republicans learned that abortion could cut across their own national coalition as well. It was one thing to hold antiabortion activists and free market capitalists in the same coalition when the right to abortion was firmly protected by the Constitution. It was quite another thing to hold that coalition together once the right to abortion was seen as a matter for legislative action and individual political judgment. Would the upwardly mobile young voters of Ronald Reagan's coalition, attracted to the Republican party by tax cuts and deregulation rather than by opposition to abortion or respect for "traditional" moral values, support a party that was really serious about criminalizing abortion? Lee Atwater, the chairman of the Republican National Committee in 1990, feared they would not, and so he moved to limit the damage *Webster* could cause for George Bush and the Republican party.

Just days before Bishop Vaughan offered his musings on Mario Cuomo's prospects for salvation, Atwater averred that "there is no litmus test on any issue which would be grounds for repudiating a Republican who believes in our overall philosophy and who supports this President and this party." Republicans are an "umbrella party," Atwater announced ". . . big enough to accommodate different views on plenty of issues."[44]

This notion of an umbrella under which pro-life and pro-choice activists can peacefully coexist is a controversial one sure to remain a subject of great dispute within the Republican party. But among Republican leaders in New York State it was readily accepted and even taken an important step further. In a move that evoked the legacy of Nelson A. Rockefeller and New York's liberalization of abortion law in the early 1970s, the New York Republican platform of 1990 reaffirmed the party's "historic commitment to the right of privacy and reproductive rights."[45]

In part, the plank was adopted to accommodate the views of Pierre Rinfret, the party's pro-choice gubernatorial candidate, and just about the only New York Republican willing to stand in the way of Governor Cuomo's presumed, but as it turned out overrated, juggernaut. But the plank was also written in an effort to neutralize abortion as an issue in the 1990 campaign, a campaign in which New York's chapter of the National Abortion Rights Action League and other pro-choice groups were poised to strengthen the pro-choice majority in the State Assembly and turn the narrowly divided State Senate against any prospective restrictions on the right to abortion.[46]

In short, the Catholic hierarchy of New York faced in 1990 a rather dismal set of political circumstances. Both parties supported the right to abortion, though Democratic support was presumed rather than formal since the party did not release a platform. Pro-choice activists, already well represented in state government, were mobilized to derail any move to restrict access to abortion in New York. And both gubernatorial candidates, incumbent Mario Cuomo and his challenger Pierre Rinfret, were by the definitions relevant to the law in New York, pro-choice.

It was within this context, in light of these particularly grim political circumstances, that Cardinal O'Connor raised in June 1990 the specter of pro-choice Catholics being excommunicated for their views.

Where Catholics are perceived not only as treating church teaching on abortion with contempt, but helping to multiply abortions by advocating legislation supporting abortion or by making public funds available for abortions, bishops may decide that for the common good such Catholics must be warned that they are at risk of excommunication. If such actions persist, bishops may consider excommunication the only option.[47]

In 1986, when Assemblyman Dearie accused Cardinal O'Connor of acting in "anticipation of [an] election" O'Connor rejected the charge as "untrue . . . insulting and . . . libelous." I am not claiming the cardinal's threat of excommunication, if that is what it was, was necessarily in anticipation of the election or was a direct attempt to sway the campaign in any particular way. Rather, I am arguing that O'Connor's whole approach in 1990 to Catholic politicians and their special responsibilities concerning the legal status of abortion was shaped to a significant degree by the political status of abortion, both in New York and in the United States as a whole. As the right to abortion gained political momentum, Catholic bishops redoubled their efforts to resist that momentum. But as the Republican party temporized, either with talk of an umbrella at the national level or of a "historic commitment to . . . reproductive rights" in New York, Cardinal O'Connor and other bishops turned their attention to Catholic politicians.

What they found was a number of Catholic politicians, led by Governor Cuomo, who argued they could be good Catholics while remaining effectively pro-choice on abortion. We accept the church's moral teaching, many claimed, but we do not accept the church's right to impose that teaching on the society as a whole. In light of *Webster* and the new opportunities for restricting abortion it presented, this "personally opposed but . . ." position was even less acceptable than ever to New York's Catholic hierarchy. And they said so, in no uncertain terms.

Conclusion

The law governing abortion in New York is not likely to change in the near future, regardless of what actions the United States Supreme Court takes. As Kathleen Gallagher of the New York State Catholic Conference deadpanned, "the climate is not good" for such a change. Parental notification and elimination of public funding of abortion will continue to be introduced each year, but they will most probably continue to be defeated in the solidly pro-choice State Assembly. More germane to our purposes, however, is the relationship between Catholic bishops and pro-choice Catholic politicians. And that relationship promises to be more dynamic and uncertain than the fate of restrictive law in the state legislature.

As I stated earlier, neither side in this relationship is likely to change its view. Yet it seems to me that the logic of the dispute over abortion, when viewed in its proper political context, calls for movement by both the bishops and the politicians. First the bishops. New York's Catholic hierarchy will continue to view abortion in their state in terms of an acute moral, legal, and political crisis. Abortion, or as some of them would prefer, "women killing babies," continues in New York, and they want it stopped. More to the point, they want Catholics, especially the incumbent governor, to do all in their power to have it stopped. But when do threats and veiled condemnations end and real punitive actions begin? Will Mario Cuomo or any other prominent New York Catholics be formally excommunicated for their views on abortion? I doubt it. But I do think it is likely that Cardinal O'Connor and others will continue to condemn the "personally opposed but . . ." position and call those who hold it to task for refusing to carry out what the cardinal deems a central responsibility of authentic Catholicism. In light of *Webster* and the new politics of abortion, this challenge to Catholic officeholders is all the more central to the bishops' antiabortion commitment. Cardinal O'Connor and his supporters in the hierarchy, therefore, will continue to define support for legal abortion, no matter how qualified, as a fundamentally non-Catholic position. How long before those who express that support are accused by bishops of defining *themselves* as fundamentally non-Catholic as well?

As for Governor Mario Cuomo, circumstances will determine whether or not his position, so eloquently expounded in 1984 at Notre Dame, can endure. In response to Bishop Vaughan's attack in January 1990, Cuomo said that "women have a constitutional right to abortion whether the bishop likes it or I like it."[48] The governor's spokesman, when pressed on whether Cuomo himself believed the constitution afforded a woman that right, said the governor's views on *Roe* were not "relevant."[49] In light of *Webster* and the increasingly tenuous constitutional status of abortion, that claim of irrelevance is no longer tenable. *Roe* is teetering, and with it the federal shield behind which state officials have hid for almost two decades.

But as one constitutional protection of abortion erodes, another may move smoothly into its place. New York's *state* constitution may well serve as a guarantor of a woman's right to abortion, and therefore also serve to grant new practical meaning to Cuomo's position. In April 1991 Justice Carmen Ciparick of State Supreme Court in Manhattan overturned the state's provision of prenatal care, excluding abortion services, to women with incomes between 100 percent and 185 percent of the official poverty line.[50] Justice Ciparick declared that the exclusion of abortion services from this care, given the fact that publicly funded abortions are provided for women whose incomes fall below the poverty line, was a violation of state constitutional rights to due process, privacy, and equal protection.

Does this mean that the New York state constitution guarantees the right to an abortion? Not quite, not yet anyway. What it means is that if some state health programs include abortion services then all state health programs must do so. Of course, it also means that at least some members of New York's judiciary are willing to move towards the position that abortion is a fundamental right for New Yorkers even if it is no longer one for all Americans. At this writing, the state is deciding whether to move forward with an appeal. Should the state appeal, and should the courts find a state constitutional right to abortion, then Mario Cuomo can be expected to reiterate his claim that women have a right to abortions whether he thinks they should or not. Under these circumstances, of course, Cuomo would be pressured by bishops and others to appoint pro-life judges to state courts. But I have no doubt the governor would be able to withstand that pressure as deftly as he has withstood other pressures in the past. The point is that a state constitutional right to abortion would allow state officials, Catholic and otherwise, to escape the spotlight shone by *Webster;* it would allow Governor Cuomo to continue to deflect inquiries into his personal convictions on abortion by referring his questioners to his speech at Notre Dame.

I began this chapter by pointing out that the politics of abortion have not been as dramatic in New York as they have been in other states. That may be so, but after *Webster,* as it was before, New York is the center of a national discussion over the so-called "special responsibilities" of Catholic politicians. In light of the Supreme Court's retreat from *Roe,* state officials, state electorates, and in New York at least state courts have all responded to new challenges and opportunities. In New York these responses have resulted in a renewed debate between the governor and the cardinal, in a crisis for the "personally opposed but . . ." position on abortion, and in a very real possibility that *Roe v. Wade, Webster v. Reproductive Services, Inc.,* and indeed any future Supreme Court decisions on abortion will be rendered irrelevant by state court guarantees. The story is not nearly finished in New York. But as it unfolds, this story deserves the very close attention of anyone interested in the role of the Catholic Church in the new and very uncertain politics of abortion.

Notes

1. The poll was commissioned by Planned Parenthood of New York City and conducted in December 1989 by Penn & Shoen Associates, Inc., an independent polling firm. I was given a copy of the poll by Rebecca Saybolt of NYS NARAL.

2. Ibid.

3. J. Alan Davitt, Executive Director, New York State Catholic Conference, interview with author, 19 March 1991.

4. Raymond Tatalovich and Byron W. Daynes, *The Politics of Abortion: A Study of Community Conflict in Public Policy Making* (New York: Praeger, 1981) pp. 71, 75.

5. *New York Times,* 23 January 1973, p. 20.

6. *New York Times,* 4 July 1989, p. 31.

7. Press Release, New York State Catholic Conference, 3 July 1989.

8. This agenda is taken from a Conference Update, New York State Catholic Conference, Vol. 3, No. 1, 1989.

9. Kathleen M. Gallagher, Associate Director for Pro-Life Activities, New York State Catholic Conference, interview with author, 19 March 1991.

10. *New York Times,* 18 January 1990, p. B4.

11. "Pastoral Plan for Pro-Life Activities," in Hugh J. Nolan, ed., *Pastoral Letters of the United States Catholic Bishops, Volume IV, 1975–1983* (Washington, D.C.: United States Catholic Conference, 1983), p. 83.

12. Ibid., pp. 84–85.

13. Ibid., pp. 86–87.

14. Kathleen M. Gallagher, interview with author, 19 March 1991.

15. *New York Times,* 9 September 1984, p. A1.
16. The text of the letter was reproduced in the *New York Times,* 11 September 1984, p. A26.
17. *New York Times,* 11 September 1984, p. A1.
18. *New York Times,* 12 September 1984, p. B9.
19. *New York Times,* 4 September 1986, p. B2.
20. *New York Times,* 8 September 1986, p. B3.
21. *New York Times,* 9 September 1986, p. B1
22. *New York Times,* 12 September 1986, p. B4.
23. *New York Times,* 6 September 1986, p. A1.
24. *New York Times,* 9 September 1986, p. B4.
25. *New York Times,* 25 June 1984, p. D13.
26. *New York Times,* 3 August 1984, p. B2.
27. *New York Times,* 4 August 1984, p. A1.
28. Ibid.
29. Cuomo's speech was reproduced as "Religious Belief and Public Morality: A Catholic Governor's Perspective," in Patricia Beattie Jung and Thomas A. Shannon, eds., *Abortion & Catholicism: The American Debate* (New York: Crossroads, 1988), pp. 202–216.
30. Ibid., p. 202.
31. Ibid., p. 212
32. Ibid., p. 213.
33. This characterization is from "Abortion: Questions and Answers," first published in *Catholic New York* and reproduced in *Origins,* 28 June 1990, p. 105
34. Ibid.
35. *New York Times,* 6 September 1986, p. A1.
36. "Religious Belief and Public Morality," p. 212.
37. *New York Times,* 6 July 1989, p. A1.
38. Ibid.
39. *New York Times,* 11 September 1989, P. B1.
40. Ibid.
41. *Commonweal,* 23 March 1990, p. 196.
42. *New York Times,* 24 January 1990, B1.
43. *New York Times,* 1 February 1990, P. A1, emphasis in original.
44. *New York Times,* 20 January 1990, p. A10.
45. *New York Times,* 30 May 1990, p. A1.
46. In the event, the results of the election were mixed. In the State Assembly, pro-choice forces picked up eight seats. But in the State Senate, where NARAL and other activists concentrated their efforts, the pro-choice cause actually lost one seat.
47. "Abortion: Questions and Answers," p. 105.
48. *New York Times,* 24 January 1990, p. B1.
49. Ibid.
50. *New York Times,* 16 April 1991, p. B3.

9

Learning and Teaching Consistency: Catholics and the Right-to-Life Movement

James R. Kelly

As late as ten years before the Supreme Court ruled that abortion was a constitutional right very few Americans, even among those favoring it, expected that abortion would become legal. As late as five years before *Roe* few legal abortion activists themselves anticipated that all legal restrictions on abortion would be effectively removed. In 1967 Robert Hall, the president of the Association for the Study of Abortion, described the movement's goal as bringing the law into greater harmony with the fact that many doctors performed abortions for reasons of health. A co-founder of the National Association for the Repeal of Abortion Laws[1] recalled that until the late 1960s their movement was a "lonely" one consisting of "only a few clusters in a few states." Until *Roe,* no one publicly advocated elective abortion throughout pregnancy. On the back of the front cover of his *Abortion II* (1973) Lawrence Lader acknowledged, "It *[Roe]* came like a thunderbolt. . . . It was even more conclusive than any of us had dared to hope."

Although held on the very threshold of the interminable controversies about abortion, the Second Vatican Council (1962–1965), called to reform and update the Church, took practically no notice of abortion. The term "abortion" is not even mentioned in the forty-five page index of the American edition of the documents issued by the Council. The Council's failure to anticipate what was soon to become the most enduring divisive issue in many different societies can not be called singular. Even the distinguished gathering of Protestant and Catholic scholars participating in the 1963 Harvard sponsored Roman Catholic Colloquium failed to include a discussion of abortion in the sessions dealing with morality and pluralism. While it will be many decades before the full significance of abortion for conceptions of justice and equality is known with any confidence, this essay sketches the still evolving connection of the American Roman Catholic Church to the movement sparked by the legalization of abortion. Caught utterly by surprise, it took some time before Catholicism grasped what was implied by the desire to make abortion legal and the scope of an adequate response. Even the first parts of this still unfolding story can only be partially captured here.

Catalyst but Not Container:
Roman Catholicism and the Counter-Movement
to Oppose Legal Abortion

It was and is the common practice of reporters to specify the religious affiliation of abortion opponents who are Catholic while leaving unspecified the affiliations or non-affiliation of all others. Nathanson,[2] a co-founder of the National Association for the Repeal of Abortion Laws, acknowledges that the description of opposition to abortion as financed by the American Catholic bishops was a movement strategy consciously adopted to "personalize" and discredit abortion opposition. While the Catholic Church played the central role in the initial opposition to legal abortion, it was far from solitary or controlling. Scholarly observers[3] commonly found that the first abortion opponents, while disproportionately Catholic, were broadly based, ecumenical, largely self-recruited and self-financed. They used Catholic parishes as resources for recruitment and meeting spaces, but often complained about lack of clergy support. Until the Supreme Court decision in 1973 striking down all state restrictions on abortion, the right-to-life movement was thoroughly fragmented and—almost—completely decentralized. Even groups within the same state often had no knowledge of each other and first met during legislative hearings. It is in this context of a fragmented, decentralized counter-movement reacting to abortion reformers that the role of institutional Catholicism should first be viewed.

Soon after *Roe,* the movement opposing abortion became national and took on a distinct life of its own. As I will describe, the evolution of Catholicism's approach to legal abortion has not completely overlapped with the larger movement. While the most noticed sectors of the movement have come to focus narrowly on politics and law, the Catholic Church has increasingly emphasized a comprehensive analysis of abortion largely resisted by dominant movement leaders. The 1989 Supreme Court *Webster* decision which returned some measure of state authority to restrict abortion will increasingly make evident long-standing cleavages in the movement which, although obscured, is comprised by sectors which can be described as "antiabortion," "right-to-life," and "pro-life" (or "consistent ethic") wings. The authoritative centers of American Roman Catholic life are now unambiguously connected only with the movement's "pro-life" wing, presently its weakest and least noticed component. The evolution of this part of the movement offers perhaps the best long-range hope for any satisfactory social and cultural resolution of the deep and divisive conflict about abortion.

A Brief History of Institutional Catholicism's
Relationship with the Antiabortion Movement

Among all major American institutions it was the Catholic Church which first noticed in any systematic fashion the incipient movement to make abortion legal. In 1966 Rev. (now Bishop) James McHugh of the Catholic Family Life Bureau began to monitor abortion law activities in all the states. That year he invited a small number of already active abortion opponents to serve as his advisors. He called these advisors the National Right-to-Life Committee (NRLC), and it was only after the 1973 *Roe* decision that the NRLC became an actual organization with an independent leadership and a grass roots membership. Even from the start, there were some differences separating the approaches of grass roots abortion opponents and institutional Catholicism. The first grass roots opponents of abortion law were almost entirely reactive and limited to efforts to maintain the status quo, while even the early statements about abortion published by the National Conference of Catholic Bishops (NCCB)[4] explicitly acknowledged that a persuasive response to legal abortion must be more than reactive and had to include efforts to "provide to all women adequate education and material sustenance to choose motherhood responsibly and freely."[5] These early episcopal statements linked opposition to abortion with community assistance to women burdened with unwanted pregnancies, much like the grass roots assistance started in 1970 by Birthright and Alternatives to Abortion which now includes the Christian Action Council and countless other groups contributing many thousands of volunteers to the more than 3,000 emergency pregnancy centers in the "service" wing of the movement. The first unambiguous break by a Catholic bishop with a "social work" response to abortion that I can locate is a July 4, 1971 sermon entitled "A Call to a consistent Ethic of Life and the Law" given by the late Archbishop of Boston Cardinal Humberto S. Medeiros at a special mass for Catholic judges, lawyers and public officials at St. Patrick's Cathedral in New York City. Medeiros preached that "a strong stand on abortion demands a consistently strong stand on social issues. . . . If we support the right of every fetus to be born, consistency demands that we equally support every man's (sic) continuing right to a truly human existence." The theme that opposition to legal abortion must be combined with support for government assistance to women and children and with critiques of other threats to human life has become the authoritative approach of the NCCB.[6] But major parts of the movement opposing abortion have disagreed with the bishops' approach. Here it is necessary to grasp the complexity and the autonomy of the many different kinds of opposition found in the movement.

The Complexity of the Right-to-Life Movement

While the first voices to speak against efforts to make abortion legal were lawyers and doctors, the grass roots organizations that began forming in 1966 were filled with far more ordinary people. More than half were women, almost always mothers with small children still at home.[7] Few, men or women, had any experience in political life beyond voting. The first president of NRLC, Edward Golden, took a course in public speaking to overcome the discomfit he felt in lobbying and talking to reporters. Undoubtedly the majority of activists in each of the first groups were Catholic, and from the start they sought to make the movement ecumenical and interfaith and indeed had some immediate success. They convincingly describe their motivation as non-sectarian and their primary method of recruitment and debate was vivid pictures of dismembered aborted fetuses with unmistakably human features. Dr. Jack Willke, the president of the NRLC since the mid-1980s, attributes the movement's defeat of the 1972 Michigan and South Dakota referenda proposals for liberalizing state abortion laws to the hundreds of thousands of pictures of aborted fetuses distributed in each state by many thousands of movement activists. Scores of activists tell stories of abortion supporters refusing to debate them if they did not leave their "pictures" home. Appealing solely to biological data and sensory confirmation of the humanity of the fetus, no activist has described the movement as "religious" much less sectarian. The term "religious" probably fits the movement best in the sociological sense, indicating that matters of ultimate belief related to human purposes and limits are at stake in the controversy rather than simply denominational identity. But, nonetheless, Catholic moral teaching was an important part of the early mobilization of the movement.

While these activists were self-financed and often complained they received little help from the local clergy, a major ideological resource in their mobilization was the Catholic teaching that all directly intended abortions were immoral. Protestant theologies took more varied positions and the limited aims first publicly proclaimed by abortion law reformers did not clash with most Protestant moral reasoning about abortion. It was, for example, only on July 26, 1982, that the *New York Times* acknowledged as misleading its characteristic description of *Roe* as making abortion legal "in the first three months of pregnancy" and instructed its staff simply to write "the Court legalized abortion."

The initial limited aims of abortion reformers could be interpreted as continuous with a moral traditionalism, namely that abortion should be legal for "tragic" cases such as the preservation of maternal health and for pregnancies resulting from rape and incest and that these legal abortions would merely replace more dangerous "back alley" ones. Only after *Roe* were arguments publicly advanced promoting elective abortion justified solely by the choice of the women and described as birth control. Even today, very few prominent Protestant moralists can be found to justify elective abortion.

The contribution of Roman Catholic teaching about abortion was both a strength and a liability for the movement. On the one hand, its unambiguous condemnation of all abortions provided a principled objection to even those therapeutic abortions which the first activists anticipated would be used as the initial wedge to decriminalize all abortions. A common theme in all parts of the movement opposing abortion is the "slippery slope" argument that uncontested legal abortion, by eroding the taboo against deliberately terminating innocent human life, would lead in "slippery slope" fashion to infanticide and euthanasia. After all, fetuses have more "potential" life than the enfeebled old.

On the other hand, the absoluteness of the Catholic position discomfited many non-Catholics (as well as some Catholics) who shared a moral antipathy to abortion, but not in all cases. An even greater impediment to movement growth among non-Catholics was the fact that the strong Catholic influence in the early right-to-life groups precluded coupling an opposition to abortion with support for non-abortive birth control which would have kept open the possibility of coalitions with those who sought to reduce abortions by reducing unplanned pregnancies. Catholicism provided the absolute principle activists psychologically required to start a movement, but deprived social movement organizations of the adaptive flexibility required for even limited success. Indeed, these tensions caused the first major schism in the movement.

How the National Right-to-Life Committee Became a Single-Issue Organization

In 1970 Rev. James McHugh called a national meeting of prominent antiabortion activists. By this time there were thousands of independent right-to-life groups in almost all states. New York, for example, had almost seventy such groups. About seventy people—each paying their own way—attended this first meeting of the NRLC in Chicago. While many of the activists acknowledged that there was a need for a fully autonomous national organization independent of Catholic auspices, state groups lacked the finances to support a national entity and disagreed about who should direct it. But after the January 22, 1973 *Roe* decision itself "nationalized" abortion politics by declaring (until corrected by *Webster*) unconstitutional any effective state legislation protecting fetal life, movement activists temporarily suppressed their many differences and formed a fully autonomous, legally incorporated NRLC which, after innumerable setbacks and upheavals, remains the movement's dominant organization, with chapters in each state, yearly elections, a twice-monthly newspaper, an office in Washington, D.C. with a staff of about twenty and a membership that, estimated in various ways, might approach a half million. While the steady financial donors to NRLC are shy of 200,000 its leadership can produce many thousands more even for such formidable tasks as marching on Washington. Four Protestant women were among the first nine member board of directors, Caroline Gerster, MD, Marjorie Mecklenburg, Gloria Klein and Judith Fink. Gerster, a Methodist, and later Mildred Jefferson, MD, a Baptist, served terms as president of the NRLC.

But on the very day NRLC was legally incorporated, Joseph A. Lampe legally incorporated a second organization called American Citizens Concerned for Life (ACCL). ACCL existed only in its articles of incorporation until the next year when some key Protestant founders of NRLC judged that the organization would not become an effective answer to legal abortion. According to Lampe they sought a more pragmatic organization that would support efforts to make unwanted pregnancies less likely and which would accept laws that did not immediately ban all abortions. ACCL promoted social programs designed to help women, families, and children and which promised to reduce the economic and social pressures on women to solve problems by aborting. They lobbied locally and nationally for disability rights for pregnant employees, childcare benefits, family-planning funding, increased welfare benefits and employment-training programs. Fink recalled that whenever abortion opponents debated they were always asked about contraception, which NRLC took no position on. Lampe found that "Having no policy on family planning is not sufficient in the public policy arena. You can't walk in and say we haven't any position because that's not what the legislators want to hear. They want to know what you are going to do about this problem" (personal interview).

In 1987 the ACCL ended its lobbying efforts and restricted its operations to the provision of teaching materials. ACCL had run out of support. During its peak years its budget never reached $200,000, and its membership never exceeded 4,000. Lampe thought the lack of support of major liberal Protestant leaders was a major factor for its demise. He explained that liberal Protestants did not see that ACCL broke the standard liberal-conservative stereotypes: "You were introducing cognitive dissonance when you tried to break up the package that liberalism included legal elective abortion while conservatives opposed abortion and social programs. We separated them saying there was a different synthesis that you might try."

Political Success but Moral Narrowing

Still, throughout the movement's history, and even within the NRLC, there remained strong tendencies toward viewing abortion comprehensively in terms of root causes and the need for social equality and justice. Among the first books written by acknowledged leaders of the movement was *Abortion and Social Justice* by the founder of Americans United for Life and the founder of the Pro-Life Youth Committee. From the start, all abortion opponents described themselves as populists battling economic elites. In the September 1974 edition of the *National Right to Life News (NRL News)* its editor Janet Grant characterized legal abortion activists as upper class elites. "The rich," she editorialized, "want to 'share' abortion with the poor. But 'sharing' stops when it comes to wealth, clubs and neighborhoods." In the February 1973 *NRL News* Donna M. Sullivan asked, "Are social pressures now geared more to getting rid of poor babies than assisting their mothers with their economic problems?" She reported that "when pro-life people object to the use of tax money for abortions, we are really saying that even if it costs us more to help those who cannot help themselves, we are willing to spend more, if necessary, so long as it is spent to foster and sustain life." The March 1974 *NRL News* found it ironic that some congressmen were arguing that abortion lowered welfare costs when Congress had spent "billions to wage a war in Indochina." Among the first congressmen to support a reversal of *Roe* were two prominent critics of the Vietnam War, Senators Harold Hughes and Mark Hatfield. In other words, in the years immediately following *Roe* it was by no means obvious that important parts of the movement opposing legal abortion would come to align themselves with the fiscally conservative Republican party. Indeed, the movement's first political hopes were more with the Democrats which, in fact, a majority of the first activists claimed as their party. Ellen McCormick, the housewife leader of the Long Island, New York based Women for the Unborn, started the movement's first direct political effort when she sought to influence the Democratic convention to support a candidate favoring a Human Life Amendment by quixotically seeking the Democratic nomination for president in 1975 and again in 1979. While McCormick's 1975 tactic was applauded by the entire movement, her 1979 bid was almost universally criticized. The shift in appraisal was due to Ronald Reagan's successful courting of grass roots opponents of abortion, promising them that he would seek a Human Life Amendment reversing *Roe*. The story of the Republican Party and the right-to-life alliance is complicated, but the outlines are clear.

Fundamentalist and Evangelical Protestants
Enter Abortion Politics

While more theologically conservative Protestant denominations, such as the Missouri-Synod Lutherans and the Southern Baptist Convention, expressed disapproval of *Roe,* they became politically active only in the mid and late 1970s. In 1975 the first Evangelical Christian right-to-life organization, the Christian Action Council (CAC), was founded by Rev. Billy Graham, Dr. Harold Lindsell, Mrs. Edith Schaeffer, Elisabeth Gren and the now controversial Dr. C. Everett Koop (whose January 1989 "Koop" Report—concluding that scientific studies neither proved nor disproved the movement's contention that abortion did psychological harm to women—disappointed activists who, almost alone, had supported his Reagan appointment as Surgeon General). By 1987, CAC claimed 120 local affiliates and 400 emergency pregnancy centers. A decade later the antiabortion group receiving the most public notoriety was Operation Rescue started by Randall Terry, a fundamentalist preacher. While court fines have driven Operation Rescue into bankruptcy and limited its operations, by 1988 approximately 10,000 of its members had been arrested (with many thousands more participating) for blocking the entrances to abortion clinics in dozens of cities. While the active participation of so many fundamentalist Christians energized the movement, because they largely distrusted an activist government in spheres other than national defense, they also contributed towards the movement's alliance with the Republican Party, whose platform during the Reagan and Bush eras (so far) supported a Human Life Amendment unlinked to questions of social justice and women's equality.

An important preparation for Reagan's incorporation of dominant sectors of the movement into the Republican Party was Dr. Mildred Jefferson's ascendancy to the NRLC presidency (1975–1977). Jefferson, a black Baptist physician educated at Harvard, was herself a political conservative who defined issues of poverty and equality largely in terms of a voluntarism congruent with

Republican ideology. During Jefferson's NRLC tenure, a Mrs. Judy Brown rose from secretary to executive secretary in charge of daily operations. Brown accepted invitations to attend Republican strategy meetings about the need to expand the party's membership to include those from ethnic and religious traditions historically attached to the Democratic Party. When Jefferson lost her bid for a third term, Brown's authority was greatly diminished and she resigned and began her own group called the American Life Lobby (ALL) and immediately challenged NRLC for movement leadership. Her group best fits the movement stereotype of antiabortionists coopted by the ideological conservative wing of the Republican Party. ALL received financial help and advice from right-wing strategists such as Paul Weyrich. ALL calls other movement organizations "heretical" and claims that it alone embodies the "pure" right-to-life position because it rejects any abortion law that does not prohibit all legal abortion. Since the NRLC and the American Catholic Bishops supported measures such as the defeated (1983) Hatch Amendment which, like *Webster,* does not itself ban any, much less all, abortions but simply permits states to vote on restrictions, ALL accuses NRLC and the bishops of betraying the movement. ALL shuns all coalitions that require even an apparent compromise with the principle that all abortion is murder.

ALL vigorously dissents (as does the CAC and several groups led by one or only a few activists with very limited membership, such as the Ad Hoc Committee for Life, the National Pro-Life Action League, the U.S. Coalition for Life as well as the National March on Washington Committee) from a "consistent ethic approach," charging that with this approach the American Catholic Bishops dilute opposition to abortion by linking it to issues such as poverty, capital punishment and the arms race. ALL, however, has its own form of "linkage" and supports prayer in the schools, opposes public school sex education, and routinely accuses "secular humanism" for the moral decline of America. Unlike NRLC, ALL holds no elections, no annual convention and has no formal state offices.

Webster Exposes the Fragmentation of the Movement

Ideological cleavages have always been present in the movement, stemming from disagreements about the causes of abortion, the relationship between law and morality, and the role of government regarding equality and justice. But before *Webster* it was at least possible to evade these cleavages, for the Court had consistently ruled against any abortion limits. *Webster* undid the possibility of politicians declaring opposition to legal abortion without specifying what laws they would seek and what policies for women and children they would promote. The immediate effect of *Webster* was a loosening of support among some antiabortion officeholders and seekers. Within six months of the *Webster* decision James McFadden's *Lifeletter* (January, 1990) described fifteen democrats and six republicans as "turncoats," officeholders once counted as abortion opponents but who now described themselves as "pro-choice."

In other words, the largely tactical alliance between major segments of the movement and the Republican Party began to unravel immediately after *Webster.* Soon after the 1989 elections, Lee Atwater, then Chairman of the National Republican Committee, announced that the "Republican umbrella" now extended to Republicans who rejected the party platform's support for a Human Life Amendment and its restrictions on government medicaid funding for abortion. Three new Republican political action committees formed specifically to raise funds for pro-choice candidates. When *Webster* moved the question of abortion restrictions from the Court to the state legislatures the Republican Party simply followed the worldwide pattern noted earlier by Francome[8] that fiscal conservatives quickly come to support abortion as a way of controlling the births of what they take to be the "unproductive" classes.

Indeed, even before *Webster* it was clear that in addition to the affluent, the cultural and professional elite of America had come to view legal abortion favorably and to contest even modest *Webster*-like restrictions.

A breakdown of *amici curiae* briefs filed in *Webster* quickly shows the enormous institutional and cultural support for elective legal abortion. These briefs dramatically show how little parity there is in the organizational and cultural strength in each side of the controversy. Signing anti-*Webster* briefs were seventy-seven distinct women's groups, the National Association of Public Hospitals, the American Medical Association, the American Psychological Association, the Association of Reproductive Health Professionals, the American Nurses Association, American Law Professionals, the American Academy of Child and Adolescent Psychiatry, the American Academy of Pediatricians, the American Fertility Society, the Pathfinder Fund, the Population Council, Planned Parenthood Federation of America, the Sierra Club, Worldwatch, Population-Environment Balance, the National Urban League and many more.

It is instructive to contrast this massive professional support for elective abortion with those groups supporting Webster. They include far fewer professional groups, no women-studies academics or ad hoc women's groups, and except for the legal scholarship represented by such groups as the Southern Center for Law and Ethics and the Association for Public Justice, no coalitions of scientists, law and medical school deans, or academicians. Moreover, those professional groups signing pro-*Webster* briefs were more likely to have formed in opposition to legal abortion and to have few general goals apart from opposing abortion. For example, the American Academy of Medical Ethics, the American Association of Pro-Life Pediatricians and Gynecologists, and the American Association of Pro-Life Pediatricians all exist to dissent from the pro-choice positions of larger professional organizations. Even the women's service groups signing pro-*Webster* briefs (Birthright, Feminists for Life of America, Women Exploited by Abortion, the National Association of Pro-Life Nurses and Let Me Live) owe their existence to the abortion controversy.

The briefs show that opposition to abortion is by no means limited to Roman Catholicism. Pro-*Webster* briefs were signed by Agudath Israel, the National Organization of Episcopalians for Life, Presbyterian Pro-Life, American Baptist Friends of Life, Southern Baptists for Life, Moravians for Life,

United Church of Christ Friends for Life, the Task Force of United Methodists on Abortion and Sexuality, and the Christian Action Council. But in terms of an ongoing cultural presence, it is the Catholic Church that stands out from all other groups and organizations opposing legal elective abortion. The Roman Catholic post-*Webster* role is as likely to affect decisively the movement in the next century as it did in the early 1960s.

The Post-*Webster* Movement
Opposing Abortion

The editors of the 1989 edition of the *Encyclopedia of Associations* were able to obtain information from sixty-one distinct antiabortion groups. While the complexity of any social movement defies simple typologies, there are solid historical and philosophical reasons for distinguishing three dominant sectors: an antiabortion wing, a right-to-life wing, and a pro-life or consistent ethic wing. *Webster* has (1) begun the dismantling of the antiabortion wing, (2) made possible some limited achievements of the right-to-life wing, and, in the long run, (3) highlighted the cultural significance of the pro-life wing.

Webster has begun to show how tactical the alliance was between the fiscal conservatives of the Republican Party and the movement's moral conservatives. Arguments based on equality have never been appealing to economic conservatives and the central philosophical argument of the movement has been that each human life has intrinsic worth and substantial claims on the community. It has become obvious that opposing legal abortion is too costly for fiscal conservatives. For example, at the end of 1989 New York State Health officials predicted that the cost of the medical intensive care alone (excluding long-term welfare costs) for babies born in New York State to crack-addicted mothers (10 percent of all non-white births in 1987) would exceed $1 billion by 1995. Henshaw and Silverman[9] report that while 14 percent of all American women fall below the poverty line, one-third of all abortion patients do. Torres and Forrest[10] found that second among the dozen reasons women give for aborting was she "couldn't afford the child." Before *Webster* fiscal conservatives could court grass roots antiabortion sentiment without much fear that very costly abortion restrictions were likely. Indeed, in the past decade, much of the movement's congressional strength has been among fiscal conservatives. In 1986 Justlife—a consistent ethic PAC formed in 1986 with a membership close to 5,000—was able to identify only eighty congresspersons (less than 15 percent of the Congress) as "consistently pro-life." *Webster* made plain that with regard to abortion, moral and fiscal conservatism will become in the long run incompatible.

The "right-to-life" sector of the movement opposing abortion is best represented by the National Right-to-Life Committee. During its second decade, NRLC made tactical alliances with the Republican Party but remained true to its founding spirit and steadfastly stuck to its "single-issue" approach to abortion (which includes opposition to infanticide and euthanasia) and gave strong support to Democrats opposing elective abortion. Its basic premise is that the right to life underlies all other rights and NRLC can be described as maintaining that the authentic liberal conception of rights continues to include even early unborn life. Since its 1983 support of the Hatch Amendment, NRLC has practiced an organizational flexibility, supporting abortion laws that restrict some abortions while permitting others. NRLC's gradualist strategy—such as, seeking parental notification laws, the prohibition of abortions performed for gender-selection, and measures making more likely informed consent—will probably lead to difficult but continued success of these partial kinds. Polls show great support for restrictions that restrain abortion without removing its legality. Less certain but still quite possible are efforts to restrict abortions after viability to those that are medically indicated or the results of rape and incest. But these right-to-life successes would simply make American abortion law more similar to the laws of most other Western nations, which typically describe fetal life as human and limit late term abortions.[11] Nor would they lead to any great lessening of the abortion rate, presently averaging more than 1.5 million annually. Finally, these limited goals did not give rise to the movement nor would their achievement exhaust its dynamism.

The pro-life or consistent ethic sector of the movement is likely, in the long run, to achieve the most lasting cultural presence. This sector has already pushed beyond a "human rights" critique of abortion characteristic of liberal philosophy to a more comprehensive analysis congruent with religiously influenced socialisms. This sector has always been present in the movement, but much obscured by the political alliances which seemed to the majority of activists the most promising way to restore communal protection to the unborn. Indeed, a decade before (August 14, 1975) Operation Rescue there were abortion sit-ins by groups such as Women Against Massacre and Brutality and whose membership was drawn from antiwar and civil rights activists. Four years before Cardinal Bernardin's "Consistent Ethic of Life" address, Judy Loesch formed Prolifers for Survival whose 2,000 plus membership thought their opposition to military spending, capital punishment and abortion stemmed from the same root values. The most respected religious groups on the left— such as Pax Christi, Sojourners, Evangelicals for Social Action—include opposition to abortion within their general opposition to violence and their radical notions of equality. Prolifers for Survival disbanded at its March 1987 Convention and became part of a larger interreligious network called The Seamless Garment Network which promotes a consistent ethic of life. The Network's June 1990 publication *Consistent Ethic Resources* (San Francisco: Harmony) listed fifty-five member organizations, eleven pages of available speakers, and the titles of five consistent ethic journals/newsletters (*Sisterlife, Harmony, Justlife, Sojourners* and *Salt*). The pro-life sector of the movement has steadily grown since the end of the 1970s and, if the analysis is correct, will show the movement's most persistent post-*Webster* cultural presence.

The religious left's attempt to frame support for laws protecting fetal life as a social justice issue connected to the foundations of equality have so far evoked little sympathy from the more diffuse American "left" of center. Undoubtedly part of this neglect results from ignorance and the common perception that there exists *only* an antiabortion movement. Shaw[12] found that major print and television media almost always report abortion in terms favoring pro-choice arguments. Ethan Bronner of the *Boston Globe* told Shaw that "opposing abortion, in the eyes of most journalists, is not a legitimate, civilized position in our society." *Media Monitor* (October 1989) reported that major television networks and newspapers are almost twice as likely to cite pro-choice advocates than abortion opponents and rarely present any in-depth discussion of abortion, much less the complexity of the movement against it. Few Americans have an unbiased view of any part of the movement opposing abortion at all, much less a part that inverts the stereotypes.

But it is not likely that the left of center can continue to ignore the social class factors apparent in support for elective abortion. Almost unknown is the fact that while black women are far more likely than whites to have abortions, they are also far more likely than all other Americans to oppose legal abortion. Hall and Ferree[13] report that even after numerous statistical controls for education, gender, income, religion, etc., blacks have been and still are more opposed to legal abortion than any other classification of Americans. On almost any other issue, this and other indications of a class cleavage—affluent whites, especially males, support elective abortion while the less affluent, especially minority women, oppose it—would engage critical minds. In terms of a "center versus periphery" approach to abortion it is worth noting that the largely elite anti-*Webster* briefs were not distinguished by any confidence that ordinary men and women might decide wisely about their states' abortion laws. The Planned Parenthood brief cautioned that "there is no promise and there should be no expectation that leaving abortion to the states will result in some acceptable 'compromise' of the conflict."

As the tactical alliances between abortion opponents and the fiscal conservatism of the Republican Party erodes, it is likely that the pro-life sector of the movement will become more visible. It is firmly supported by the institutional resources of the Catholic Church and interreligiously secure in many autonomous groups. Some prominent lay Catholics who direct their own small centers of abortion opposition (Judy Brown of American Life Lobby, Joe Scheidler of the Pro-Life Action League, Nellie Grey of the March on Washington, and Jim McFadden of the Ad Hoc Committee for the Defense of Life) will continue to criticize a "consistent ethic" approach. But it is significant that neither they nor any other acknowledged movement leader has ever formally advocated social welfare cuts, increased military spending, or capital punishment. Surveys of Catholics show they are similar to Protestants in that they neither accept elective abortion nor favor banning all abortions,[14] that they are far more likely to say their faith is strengthened than weakened by the Church's teaching on abortion,[15] and that they are likely to agree that opposition to abortion ought to be consistent.[16] Indeed, there is surprisingly little evidence linking abortion opponents with inegalitarian notions of gender or class. Cleghorn[17] found that educated Catholics largely affirmed a consistent ethic approach and found no evidence that abortion opponents generally fit "new right" stereotypes. Wilcox and Gomez[18] found few abortion opponents supported the "Moral Majority" and that "a sizeable block of pro-life support adopted fairly liberal positions on . . . equality values, including gender equality." Granberg and Denny[19] found that NRLC leaders were far more likely than Americans generally to support an expanded public role for women. They and Kelly[20] found that abortion opponents were far more likely than the general public *and* supporters of elective abortion to oppose capital punishment.

More Consistent and More Differentiated

Although it is not widely noticed, the approach to legal abortion gradually adopted by the NCCB not only stresses the linkage between opposition to abortion and the requirement of social justice for women and children but it contains differentiations between law and morality which make possible a wide range of legitimate responses to the many complex issues raised by legal abortion. A succinct summary of the more than twenty episcopal pastoral letters written by American Catholic Bishops immediately after the 1989 *Webster* decision (between October 1989 and June 1990) reads like this:

> Abortion is a human rights issue. But besides protecting the 'right to life' of the unborn, abortion opponents should be consistent and promote social justice for women and their families. Consistency involves not only the other 'life' issues of euthanasia, infanticide and capital punishment, but also issues of poverty, employment and medical care. No return to the pre-*Roe* era when only medically necessary abortions were legal can be expected. Good laws require social consensus and thus laws prohibiting all non-medically necessary abortions are highly unlikely. Any realistic hope for lowering the abortion rate and restoring some legal protection for the unborn rests on the application of a consistent ethic of life. A single-issue approach to abortion is not advisable and there is no single approach to achieving better abortion laws in contemporary secular societies. Catholics themselves will legitimately disagree about which laws might best achieve a lower rate of abortion and garner the most public support. The only clearly proscribed approach for Catholic office holders and seekers is a self-description as personally opposed to abortion but publicly pro-choice. Such a sharp dichotomy between morality and politics undermines both personal and political integrity.

The powerful role that the "consistent ethic of life" now plays in the Catholic Church's approach to abortion, and the increasing prominence bishops give to the differentiation between law and morality and the importance of consensus, will continue to evolve. In their 1986 pastoral letter "Economic Justice for All," the Bishops criticized the social and gender discrimination that is "one of the causes for high rates of joblessness and low pay among racial minorities and women." They critically observed that women who work full time and year round earn only 61 percent of what men earn. They noted that more than one-third of all female-headed families are poor and that the poverty rate among female-headed minority families is 50 percent. They reported that most divorced or separated mothers do not get child-support payments. Increasingly the Church's social thought will criticize the largely privatizing and inegalitarian aspects of America's "democratic-capitalism," using the democratic component to critique the capitalist component. Needless to say, this explicit linkage of the rights of women and the unborn in public policy and economic life raises questions about justice toward women in the church. Deeper reflection into the equality of women will affect church life and practice, straining any authority that seems to incorporate gender views that subordinate women.[21]

Conclusion

The argument here is that the eroding tactical alliance of the movement opposing abortion with ideological fiscal conservatives makes likely only those abortion restrictions congruent with the actual ruling of *Roe* (protection after viability) and congruent with public sentiment (regulations ensuring informed consent, parental notification) and raises to greater cultural prominence the pro-life sector of the movement. The "consistent ethic" component of the movement defines itself as publicly guarding the foundational principle of all authentic humanisms, namely that each human life, with no regard to its achievements, real or potential, has intrinsic worth and moral claims on the community. This moral insight, dramatically and energetically present in the movement, resists all conceptions of a social order based on meritocracy or economic efficiency, the final justification for capitalism. The protection of even fetal life against the claims of personal autonomy and the efficient ordering of economic life is so profoundly premodern that only the naive would predict any significant political victories. Among other things, the collapse of state commanded economies in Russia and elsewhere and the ascendancy of economic liberalism have further weakened socialism's egalitarian aspirations. Once again, liberty and equality seem to be contrary moral values. Principled defense of a moral equality deeper than the formal equality of an equal opportunity for the meritorious to achieve (and others to lose) now resides with any focused grass roots vitality mostly in segments of the movement opposing legal abortion, and there in largely underdeveloped ways. The mainstream movement so far has represented mostly a "liberalism" applied to fetuses, and even this has not been fully grasped by the media and elite opinion. The consistent ethic of life significantly broadens the moral conviction that the right to life is foundational and carries its political dimensions to a more organicist conception of society animated by an egalitarianism that collides with the premises of both economic and political liberalism.

Webster will in time expose the weakness of the movement's political power, but it will strengthen its cultural presence as liberals and the secular left, less fearful of losing legal abortion, begin to question the relationship between poverty and abortion and whether abortion is often voluntary. Increasingly there is concern in the feminist left that the promotion of "abortion rights" abstracted from critiques of poverty will in practice lead to coercive pressures to abort. Hartman[22] notes the class basis for construing population problems as "management problems" and the willingness to use force or coercive incentives to control births that destabilize existing wealth and power distributions. She notes[23] the historical tendency in eugenics and the population control movement to view poverty in Social Darwinian terms with no principled objection to compulsory sterilization. Back[24] notes the achievement of "establishment status" of almost all family planning and population groups and traces the "transformation of the movement beyond its original goals of removing social barriers to contraception and providing freedom of choice to seeking enforceable norms of birth control."

Not only the poor confront severe social pressures to abort. Lower middle income women have experienced similar coercion. The New York City Department of Investigation acknowledged that their supervisors urged pregnant female correction officers to obtain abortions[25]. Shaw[26] explicitly includes family income as a factor in computing whether doctors should perform surgery on handicapped children that would be performed on "normal" children. Almost immediately after the announcement of the availability of a five year effective contraceptive in which small tubes releasing a pregnancy preventing hormone are implanted under a woman's skin, an editorial (December 12, 1990) appeared in the *Philadelphia Inquirer* entitled, "Poverty and Norplant—Can Contraception Reduce the Underclass?"

In short, *Webster* has weakened the political power of the movement opposing abortion by slowly disengaging it from its alliance with fiscal conservatives. Its long term fate now resides in the willingness of others to take note of the movement's pro-life sector and its significance for the elusive ideal of equality and the pursuit of dignity rooted simply in the fact of a shared humanity. In 1984, movement leaders became allies of major disability rights groups (such as the Association for Retarded Citizens, the National Down's Syndrome Congress, the American Coalition of Citizens with Disabilities, etc.) and co-sponsored "Principles of Treatment of Disabled Infants" which (as part of the Child Abuse Amendments of 1984) now legally protects the rights of handicapped neonates to receive the same medical benefits as normal babies.

Although they still seem unlikely, future coalitions with at least those on the left gradually alert to the coercive and to the Malthusian dimensions of abortion are plausible. In retrospect, the *Webster* decision might be seen as a particularly decisive challenge to the movement sparked by legal abortion to grasp better the moral intuition which from the beginning prompted almost all of its activists to describe their activities as pro-life rather than antiabortion. It will be a long time still before the complete significance of legal abortion is clear, both to those who in the spirit of liberty seek to expand it and to those who in the spirit of the sanctity of human life seek to restrict it. Because of its accepted prominence in the on-going conflict over legal abortion, the Catholic Church will be especially challenged to learn more and teach better the still evolving meanings of a consistent ethic of life.

Notes

1. Lawrence Lader, *Abortion II: Making the Revolution* (Boston: Beacon Press, 1973), p. vii.

2. Bernard N. Nathanson, *The Abortion Papers* (New York: Frederick Fell, 1983), p. 177ff.

3. See Peter J. Leahy, "The Anti-Abortion Movement," Ann Arbor, Mi.: University Microfilms International, 1975; Kristin Luker, *Abortion and the Politics of Motherhood* (Berkeley, Ca.: University of California Press, 1984); Colin Francome, *Abortion Freedom: A Worldwide Movement* (London: George Allen and Unwin, 1984); James R. Kelly, "Beyond the Stereotypes: Interviews with the Right-to-Life Pioneers," *Commonweal*, November 1981; Kurt W. Back, *Family Planning and Population Control* (Boston: Twayne, 1989); Michael W. Cuneo, *Catholics Against the Church: Anti-Abortion Protest in Toronto, 1969-1985* (Toronto: University of Toronto Press, 1989).

4. National Conference of Catholic Bishops, "Human Life in Our Day," November 15, 1968; "Statement on Abortion," April 17, 1969; April 22, 1970; "Declaration of Abortion," November 18, 1979.

5. National Conference of Catholic Bishops, "Human Life in Our Day," November 15, 1968.

6. National Conference of Catholic Bishops, "Respect Life Program," November 20, 1975; United States Catholic Conference, "Political Responsibility: Reflections on an Election Year," 1976, 1979; Cardinal Joseph Bernardin, "A Consistent Ethic of Life: An American Catholic Dialogue," presented at Fordham University Gannon Lecture, Bronx, NY, December 6, 1983.

7. James R. Kelly, "Beyond the Stereotypes: Interviews with Right-to-Life Pioneers," *Commonweal*, November 1981, p. 655; Peter James Leahy, "The Anti-Abortion Movement,"(Ann Arbor Mi.: University Microfilms International, 1975); Kristin Luker, *Abortion and the Politics of Motherhood* (Berkeley, Ca.: University of California Press, 1984), p. 138.

8. Colin Francome, *Abortion Freedom: A Worldwide Movement* (London: George Allen and Unwin, 1984), p. 210.

9. Stanley K. Henshaw and Jane Silverman, "The Characteristics and Prior Contraceptive Use of U.S. Abortion Patients," *Family Planning Perspectives* July/August 1988, pp. 158–60.

10. Ada Torres and Jacqueline Darroch Forrest, "Why Do Women Have Abortions?" *Family Planning Perspectives* July/August 1988.

11. Mary Ann Glendon, *Divorce and Abortion in Western Law* (Cambridge: Harvard University Press, 1988).

12. David Shaw, Three-part series on abortion reportage, *Los Angeles Times*, July 1–4, 1990.

13. Elaine J. Hall and Myra Marx Ferree, "Race Differentials in Abortion Attitudes," *Public Opinion Quarterly* 50 (1986).

14. Joseph Gremillion and Jim Castelli, *The Emerging Parish: The Notre Dame Study of Catholic Life* (San Francisco: Harper & Row, 1987) pp. 42–3.

15. William D'Antonio, James Davidson, Dean Hoge and Ruth Wallace, *American Catholic Laity* (Kansas City, Mo.: Sheed & Ward, 1989), p. 135.

16. George Gallup and Jim Castelli, "The Seamless Garment," in *The American Catholic People* (Garden City, NY: Doubleday, 1987).

17. J. Stephen Cleghorn, "Respect for Life: Research Notes on Cardinal Bernardin's Seamless Garment," *Review of Religious Research*, December 1986.

18. Clyde Wilcox and Lepoldo Gomez, "The Christian Right and the Pro-Life Movement," *Review of Religious Research*, June 1990.

19. Donald Granberg and Donald Denny, "The Coathanger and the Rose: Comparison of Pro-Choice and Pro-Life Activists in the U.S.," *Transaction/Society*, May 1982.

20. James R. Kelly, "Aids and the Death Penalty as Consistency Tests for the Pro-Life Movement," *America,* September 1987.

21. Archbishop Rembert Weakland, "Listening Sessions with Women on Abortion," *Origins,* May 1990.

22. Betsy Hartmann, *Reproductive Rights and Wrongs* (New York: Harper & Row, 1987), p. 120.

23. Ibid., p. 97.

24. Kurt W. Back, *Family Planning and Population Control* (Boston: Twayne, 1989), p. 127.

25. Douglas Martin, "Women Given Uncruelist Choice Now Fight Back," *New York Times,* October 21, 1989.

26. A. Shaw, "Defining the Quality of Life," *Hastings Report* 7 (1977).

10

The Loyal Opposition:
Catholics for a Free Choice

Mary C. Segers

Dissent from church teaching on abortion is not unusual within the American Catholic community. Although Catholic teaching holds that direct abortion is morally impermissible, a substantial number of American Catholics believe that abortion can be a moral option. Moreover, a large majority of American Catholics disagree with their bishops' position that abortion should be illegal in all circumstances. Gallup polls indicate that large percentages of Catholics support legal abortion in instances—cases of rape, incest, fetal deformity, and threat to woman's life or health—which are condemned by their church.[1] To be sure, Gallup and Castelli maintain that American Catholics are sensitive to the abortion issue and have a concern for the well-being of the unborn child which translates into a general rejection of abortion on demand. However, they also contend that Catholics "are less than certain of their position and are reasonably tolerant of those who disagree with them and of legal abortion itself."[2]

This uncertainty is reflected in Catholic practice, which is widely at variance with official church teaching. Figures from a 1988 study by the Alan Guttmacher Institute, an organization that researches and analyzes family planning and population issues, indicate that even though they constitute 22–23 percent of the U.S. population, Catholics have 30 percent of the abortions in the United States. Moreover, according to a 1987 AGI survey of 9,480 women who had abortions, Catholics have 30 percent more abortions than Protestants and Jews (among those women who reported a religious affiliation).[3]

These data about Catholic belief and practice suggest the existence of a loyal opposition within the American church on the morality and legality of abortion. Indeed, a variety of loosely-styled Catholic "pro-choice" groups have appeared from time to time among American Catholics.[4] The most famous of these is a public interest organization, Catholics for a Free Choice (CFFC), which has attracted considerable popular support, foundation funding, and media attention throughout the 1980s and early 1990s. Indeed, from rudimentary beginnings in 1973, CFFC has grown to achieve legitimacy as a public interest organization articulating a thoughtful dissent from the official Catholic position on abortion.

This essay examines the history and activities of Catholics for a Free Choice and analyzes the role it plays in the secular world of pro-choice politics. I focus especially on the evolution of ideas within CFFC, on the rationale the organization has developed in its eighteen-year existence, and on the ways in which it brings a distinctively Catholic perspective to deliberations within the pro-choice community. Some attention will also be given to the varied criticism accorded to CFFC over the years and to the response CFFC officials make to such critiques.

A Brief History of CFFC

In the early 1970s, a small group of Catholic laity founded CFFC to oppose Catholic church efforts to reinstate restrictive abortion laws in New York.[5] Founding members included Patricia McQuillan Fogarty, Joan Harriman, and Meta Mulcahy, three Catholic feminists who were members of the local New York chapter of the National Organization for Women (NOW). As feminists they sought to apply the tenets of the women's movement and the struggle for gender equality within the church. Since New York had repealed its antiabortion law in 1970, the state had been the scene of major protests by pro-life forces led by Cardinal Terence Cooke and the New York Catholic archdiocese. Because abortion was the most prominent issue of women's rights at the time, CFFC began to defend New York's policy of legalized abortion. This broadened into a defense of legal abortion nationally in the wake of the 1973 Supreme Court decision in *Roe v. Wade.* In response to *Roe,* CFFC was officially chartered as a corporation in New York in 1973.

In keeping with the colorful, flamboyant tactics of the women's movement in the early 1970s, CFFC organized several events designed to draw attention to the existence of pro-choice sentiment within the Catholic community. On January 22, 1974, the first anniversary of *Roe,* they crowned Patricia McQuillan Fogarty as pope in a mock ceremony on the steps of St. Patrick's Cathedral in New York City. A second major event occurred in the summer of 1974, when Boston's Bishop Humberto Medeiros instructed parish priests in Marblehead, Massachusetts, to deny baptism to an infant whose mother had said she was pro-choice at a rally supporting legal abortion. Medeiros said the woman was unfit to raise her child. In response, a Jesuit priest, Father Joseph O'Rourke, offered to baptize the infant on the steps outside the Marblehead church (since church authorities would not permit baptism within the church). CFFC alerted the press to this event and afterwards held a press conference in New York City at which O'Rourke defended the baptism. CFFC also arranged an appearance by O'Rourke on a local WABC-TV morning talk show in order to answer questions about the possibility of pro-choice Catholics dissenting from the official church position on the legality of abortion.[6]

In these ways the organization sought to provide an alternative voice in the early days of the abortion controversy and to serve as a balance to the bishops on the issue. CFFC's role was largely reactive, that is, it reacted primarily to initiatives the bishops took. Frances Kissling, President of CFFC, has described the role CFFC played in those initial years:

> From the beginning, it was always important that there was a thing called Catholics for a Free Choice. The simple existence of the organization, even though it did almost nothing, was extremely valuable. It gave people the sense that there wasn't just this one viewpoint, [that] there were people who disagreed. It could be pointed to: "Well, there are Catholics who disagree." Other people made more use of us than we were able to make of ourselves at that time. And in a positive way. It wasn't as if we were manipulated or anything like that. But our success depended upon other people pointing to us.[7]

From 1973 to 1976, CFFC remained a small group housed in New York City, having no money, no staff, and no ongoing programs. The group had intermittent contacts with other pro-choice organizations such as Planned Parenthood, N.O.W., and the National Abortion Rights Action League (NARAL). It was also an affiliate of the Religious Coalition for Abortion Rights (RCAR), an association of over twenty-five national religious organizations joined together to protect the option of legal abortion. A June 1975 position statement illustrates how CFFC defined itself at this time.

> Catholics For a Free Choice is a national organization of Catholics dedicated to the principle that women have the right and the duty to follow their conscience regarding decisions on contraception and termination of pregnancy; and that the law has a corresponding right and duty to make it possible for them to implement those choices under medically safe conditions. We affirm the religious liberty of Catholic women and men and those of other religions to make decisions regarding their own fertility free from church or governmental interventions in accordance with their own individual conscience.[8]

This position statement was repeated frequently in various RCAR publications and enabled RCAR to define itself in the 1974 to 1979 period as a coalition of national religious organizations drawn from Protestant, *Catholic* and Jewish denominations. The fact is that CFFC was the only Catholic organization in RCAR and the only formally-organized Catholic group then challenging the American church's policy position on abortion. Predictably, its allies were pro-choice groups such as NARAL, RCAR, and Planned Parenthood. Only later—in the early 1980s—did CFFC develop ties with Catholic women's groups such as the National Coalition of American Nuns (NCAN), the Women's Ordination Conference (WOC), the National Assembly of Religious Women (NARW), and others.

In 1976, a decision was made to move CFFC to Washington in order to facilitate its lobbying. Joan Harriman and Meta Mulcahy remained in New York to direct "Catholic Alternatives," a counseling center for pregnant teenagers and women in crisis. In Washington, CFFC hired Ginny Andary as a part-time lobbyist. From 1976 to 1979, Andary, who had no office, worked through the pro-choice coalition and visited members of Congress to make them aware of the existence of pro-choice Catholic opinion. The organization operated with a small budget ($15,000 to $20,000) provided mostly by grants from a Unitarian Universalist Church in New York.[9]

In 1979, Patricia MacMahon became director of CFFC, and under her leadership, this small organization began to change in significant ways. Realizing the need for a firm theoretical foundation underlying CFFC's position, MacMahon secured a large educational grant ($75,000) from the Sunnen Foundation in Missouri and initiated CFFC's publications program. The "Abortion in Good Faith" series, a popular collection of pamphlets on the history of Catholic thinking about abortion and on the church's role in a pluralist democracy, was MacMahon's idea. Her CFFC Board also decided there was no reason the organization should continue as a lobby, since its strength was not in numbers, but in the power of ideas and in the articulation of an alternative Catholic perspective on abortion policy. She therefore shifted the organization's status from a 501(c)(4) lobby to a 501(c)(3) tax-exempt, educational organization.[10] This made CFFC eligible for foundation grants and placed the organization on a more secure financial footing. Finally, she expanded the CFFC Board of Directors and invited Frances Kissling, who was then executive director of the National Abortion Federation (NAF), to join the Board.[11] By 1982, MacMahon had retired and Kissling had become the new executive director of CFFC.

The period 1979 to 1984 saw additional changes at CFFC. As feminist consciousness spread to more Catholic women's organizations, CFFC won gradual acceptance by groups such as NCAN, WOC, NARW, Chicago Catholic Women, Boston Catholic Women, and Women-Church Convergence. This led to a reevaluation of CFFC's membership in RCAR. The organization withdrew from RCAR in order to avoid duplication of effort. As Kissling put it:

> We're not an institutional body like the United Methodist Church, and we really didn't belong in RCAR. As doors opened to us within the Catholic community, we began to put more of our limited resources there instead of in the Protestant community or the interfaith community. We didn't think it was necessary to be at that table, and indeed [we thought] RCAR would be stronger with more official denominational representation than with dissident groups from within a particular faith.[12]

Secondly, CFFC began to define its relationship with the secular pro-choice coalition more concretely. CFFC continued to work with the coalition while at the same time refusing to be identified as simply the Catholic extension of the pro-choice movement. "We don't see ourselves as another Planned Parenthood or NARAL," Kissling says. "Our role is to keep the secular pro-choice movement sensitized to dealing with Catholic issues in a way that is fair, balanced, and honest."[13] Through the 1980s, CFFC sought to combat the occasional, latent anti-Catholicism of the movement and to insist upon the necessity of a moral and ethical framework in deliberations about abortion. While CFFC is obviously committed to keeping abortion legal, Kissling insists that CFFC's positions are not the same as the rest of the movement's and that "the way in which we come to those positions is different." She notes that the organization sells far more of its literature to Protestants and Jews than to Catholics and that within the pro-choice movement CFFC is distinctive in addressing moral and ethical aspects of abortion.[14] In this fashion, the organization has gradually differentiated itself from the world of secular pro-choice politics.

With a new director, increased funding, and a new headquarters in the nation's capital, CFFC became increasingly prominent through the 1980s. In 1981, the National Conference of Catholic Bishops took notice of the organization for the first time after CFFC held a press conference at the U.S. Senate to protest the bishops' testimony supporting the Hatch Human Life Amendment. At this press conference on November 5, 1981, CFFC officials claimed the bishops' position was unrepresentative of Catholic opinion and behavior. When the *New York Times* ran a front-page story covering the CFFC press conference, the NCCB felt called upon to respond. On November 25, 1981, Rev. Edward Bryce issued a statement on behalf of the Bishops' Pro-Life Committee saying that CFFC "carries no official status within this Catholic Church" and that CFFC's position on abortion is in direct contradiction with the tradition and teachings of the church.[15] To date, this is the only time the NCCB has formally and officially taken note of CFFC.

In September 1982, CFFC held a briefing for Catholic members of the House of Representatives, sponsored by Congresswoman Geraldine Ferraro, Democrat of New York. The purpose of the briefing was to provide assistance to Catholic lawmakers in coping with the abortion issue in electoral and legislative politics. The speakers at this breakfast meeting included Washington journalist Jim Castelli, media consultant Ken Swope, pollster Greg Martire, and theologian Daniel Maguire. Their presentations were later assembled in a monograph entitled "The Abortion Issue in the Political Process: A Briefing for Catholic Legislators." In her brief introduction to this booklet, Congresswoman Ferraro wrote that the presentations "show us that the Catholic position on abortion is not monolithic and that there can be a range of personal and political responses to the issue."

It was this statement that embroiled Ferraro in controversy with the church hierarchy when she became the Democratic Vice-Presidential candidate two years later. In 1982, no bishop paid any attention to Ferraro's claim. But in the 1984 presidential campaign, then-Archbishop John O'Connor of New York and several other prelates seized upon this statement to criticize Ferraro for misrepresenting Catholic teaching on abortion.[16]

The ensuing controversy over Ferraro's pro-choice policy position provided the background and context for what is arguably CFFC's most controversial media intervention, a full-page advertisement in the *New York Times* on October 7, 1984.[17] The statement printed in this ad, "A Catholic Statement on Pluralism and Abortion," was written in 1983 by Daniel Maguire, Marjorie Reilly Maguire, and Frances Kissling; it was then circulated among professional theological societies within the Catholic community for supporting signatures. As church officials' attacks on Ferraro accelerated in the fall of 1984, many

Catholics became concerned that the hierarchy was treating Ferraro unfairly and taking partisan sides in the presidential campaign. These concerns prompted an ad hoc Catholic Committee on Pluralism and Abortion to enter this full-page ad, with 97 supporters' signatures, in the *Times*. The ad was paid for by CFFC.

The *Times* ad described a diversity of opinion on abortion within the church and the theological community, decried clerical attacks on political candidates over the issue, and called for dialogue on the issue. This public statement drew an immediate reaction from the Vatican and triggered a series of repressive actions by church-related agencies against the ad's signers, particularly those signers who were members of religious communities. Twenty-four women religious resisted the Vatican's demand that they publicly retract the statement or face dismissal from their congregations. From 1984 through 1988, the Vatican Congregation for Secular and Religious Institutes (CRIS) negotiated individual settlements with most of the sisters.[18]

The *New York Times* ad and the subsequent controversy kept CFFC in the media spotlight for a considerable period of time. The organization was accused of using the controversy to aggrandize itself at the expense of considerable anguish suffered by the ad's signers. The *National Catholic Reporter,* a liberal Catholic weekly, accused CFFC of taking the abortion issue "from the level of serious religious commitment and theological discussion to that of a mere political sign-up campaign."[19] A more serious, systematic analysis of the controversy, written by feminist theologian Mary Hunt (who has served on the CFFC board of directors) and by Frances Kissling, appeared in the *Journal of Feminist Studies in Religion* in the spring of 1987. Despite the serious, negative consequences for individual signers of the ad, Hunt and Kissling claimed that the controversy had some positive results.

> First, the ad and the resulting dispute effectively and finally put to rest the myth that Catholics, especially professional Catholics (i.e., those whose identity is tied to church position, or whose lives and/or social support is founded on the institutional church) share the belief of the Vatican and the U.S. bishops that abortion is to be absolutely prohibited both legally and morally. Second, the *New York Times* ad ended the hegemony of both bishops and male clerics as the public interpreters of Catholic teaching, belief, values, and practice. This is true not only in the abortion arena, but in all areas of public interest. In the [then] two years since the ad appeared, it has become common practice for electronic and print media to seek the views of Catholic feminists on all major news events concerning Roman Catholicism.[20]

Hunt and Kissling also claimed that signers of the *Times* ad created new links between religious and secular feminists, and aroused new interest and respect for religious feminism among leading secular feminists. Moreover, the signers of the *Times* ad were a source of hope and inspiration for women whose religious feminism was just beginning to take root. Finally, the controversy forced members of religious communities to which signers belonged to study the question of abortion, some for the first time.

Perhaps an historian's distance and perspective are necessary in order to reach a balanced, judicious evaluation of the positive and negative consequences of the 1984 *New York Times* ad. But one result seems clear: the controversy over the ad forced the church and the secular media to take CFFC very seriously. By the late 1980s, CFFC had achieved legitimacy within the Washington world of public interest educational groups. The organization had also acquired stature within the Catholic community, as evident in the frequent media and public speaking appearances of its officers. In April 1991, Boston College invited CFFC President Kissling to debate the abortion issue with Helen Alvare, spokeswoman for the United States Catholic Conference's Secretariat for Pro-Life Activities. And in February 1991, the same *National Catholic Reporter,* which had tended to dismiss the organization in 1985, published a lengthy, thoughtful interview with Kissling about the positions and perspectives of CFFC.

The Organization of CFFC:
Its Structure and Functions

CFFC is a national educational organization with a board of directors, an operational staff of approximately ten people, and a headquarters in Washington, D.C. It is a non-profit, tax-exempt organization which is primarily foundation-financed. Its 1991 budget was $750,000 (compared with a budget of $232,000 in 1982 and $15,000 in 1979).[21]

Much of CFFC's growth and success may be attributed to strong leadership. Frances Kissling, CFFC's President, is a lifelong Catholic and a feminist who has been active in the women's health movement since 1970. An articulate, one-time Sisters of St. Joseph candidate (she stayed six months), Kissling became involved in the pro-choice movement in 1971 when she took a job running a Pelham, N.Y., abortion clinic. She came to CFFC in 1982 after two years as executive director of the National Abortion Federation, an association of abortion clinic directors which she founded. As an articulate and thoughtful commentator on the issues of women's rights, reproductive health, and the efforts of Catholics to bring substantive change to their church, Kissling makes frequent public speeches and is often interviewed by national media. She has appeared on "CBS Morning News," ABC's "Nightline," and NBC's "Today Show" and was the subject of a *Washington Post* Sunday Magazine cover piece in 1986. Asked to explain her commitment to CFFC, Kissling commented:

> It combines interests for me in a very profound way. I'm a thoughtful person with a real interest in philosophy, religion, and ideas. Obviously, I was born and raised a Catholic. I had some experience running an abortion clinic, and my interest in religion and politics and my interest in women's rights are long-standing, so it's all very connected for me. And I'm very good at it, I know I'm good at it, so it's very rewarding to have something you think you can really make a contribution with.

CFFC's Director of Public Affairs is Mary Jean Collins, formerly the Vice-President-Action for the National Organization for Women. She directed the

Illinois ERA ratification campaign in 1982 and serves on the board of directors for Project VOTE! Collins brings to CFFC an expert knowledge of state and national politics, and she is frequently invited to speak on feminist issues and reproductive health. Finally, CFFC's Director of Communications is Denise Shannon, an editorial consultant and journalist with considerable experience covering Washington politics. Shannon handles all press relations and directs major publications projects. A variety of program specialists, project coordinators, and public affairs associates completes the CFFC staff.

The organization's Board of Directors is a small board of approximately ten members drawn from law, business, academia, and the world of Washington governmental analysts. The board formulates policy, deliberates about funding, and oversees the activities of the organization. Scholars and theologians who have served on the board include John Giles Milhaven, professor of religious studies at Brown University; Rosemary Radford Ruether, professor of applied theology at Garret-Evangelical Seminary in Evanston, Illinois; Mary Hunt, feminist theologian and co-director of Women's Alliance for Theology, Ethics, and Ritual (WATER); the novelist and writer, Mary Gordon; Sylvia Marcos, anthropologist and director of the Center for Psychoethnological Research in Cuernavaca, Mexico; Patricia Hennessey, a New York lawyer who is a cooperating attorney with the ACLU Reproductive Freedom Project; and Eileen Moran, a professor of labor studies at Brooklyn College.

What does CFFC do with its sizable ($750,000) budget? As a national educational organization, CFFC's efforts are directed primarily towards ordinary citizens, Catholic and non-Catholic, who contact the organization seeking information and assistance in thinking about abortion. The organization spends a good deal of its time trying to persuade anyone who will listen that "pro-choice Catholic" is not a contradiction in terms. Concretely, this means that a significant portion of its budget is allocated to its publications program and to communications and public relations. Kissling and Collins are in demand as public speakers to articulate a pro-choice perspective. CFFC publishes *Conscience*, a bimonthly "newsjournal of pro-choice Catholic opinion"; the mailing list of subscribers to *Conscience* had grown to 10,000 by 1987.[22] CFFC also publishes and distributes upon request pamphlets from its "Abortion in Good Faith" series. In addition, the organization has developed a line of publications such as *Abortion: A Guide to Making Ethical Decisions* (written in 1983 by Daniel and Marjorie Maguire), and *Reflections of a Catholic Theologian on Visiting an Abortion Clinic* (by Daniel Maguire) which are designed to assist women callers seeking information.

CFFC also provides educational materials to more specialized audiences. It runs a press clipping service focusing on the Catholic Church and abortion-related issues, and serves as a media clearinghouse for Catholic and non-Catholic activists. The organization holds Congressional briefings periodically and has developed materials advising politicians how to approach the abortion topic. In 1990, in the wake of the Supreme Court's decision in *Webster*, CFFC published its *Guide for Prochoice Catholics*, a compendium of articles and essays designed to assist pro-choice Catholic politicians and candidates whose right to make independent policy judgments about abortion was being challenged by the bishops. Six thousand copies of this publication were mailed to state legislators across the United States. The *Guide* was also translated into Spanish and sent to Mexican lawmakers in the state of Chiapas who were under similar attack from their clergy.

CFFC also conducts more specialized projects directed at particular audiences. In the mid-1980s, as part of its commitment to religious feminism, it inaugurated "Bishops Watch," a program surveying the extent to which dioceses incorporated women into their ministries and offices. CFFC's Hispanic Project does educational outreach among Hispanic Catholics in the United States. Selected articles in its bimonthly *Conscience* appear in Spanish as part of this effort. Indeed, CFFC has developed an international focus through the work of Dr. Cristina Grela, a Uruguayan physician and coordinator of *Catolicas por el Derecho a Decidir* in South America.

On the domestic front, in the wake of the *Webster* decision returning some abortion regulation to the states, CFFC has sponsored a Grassroots Organizing Project to assist pro-choice Catholic activists in the development of a network of state affiliate organizations. To date, representatives from twenty-seven states have attended training conferences held in 1990 and 1991. CFFC's Washington headquarters acts as a resource center for these state affiliates.

The organization also does occasional research: in 1981 it conducted a poll of Catholic women who had had abortions, and in 1990, staff at Sawyer-Miller, a New York–based public relations and issues campaign firm, conducted a poll for CFFC which showed that an overwhelming majority of American Catholics strongly oppose the bishops' use of punitive sanctions, including excommunication, against pro-choice Catholics.[23] The organization has also held two national conferences in 1986 and 1989 on ethics and reproductive health.

Finally, CFFC has filed *amicus* briefs in several abortion cases which have reached the Supreme Court. It first filed a brief with other members of RCAR in *City of Akron v. Akron Center for Reproductive Health* (1983). In the *Webster* case, CFFC filed its own brief, written by Board member and attorney Patricia Hennessey; material from this brief was quoted directly by Justice John Paul Stevens in his dissenting opinion in *Webster.*[24]

Who pays the bills for all these projects and efforts? As mentioned earlier, CFFC is primarily foundation-financed. In its eighteen-year existence, the organization has received grants from a variety of foundations including the Ford Foundation, the George Gund Foundation, the Ms. Foundation, the Packard Foundation, the Sunnen Foundation, the Alida Rockefeller Dayton Foundation, the Brush Foundation, and the Veatch Program of the North Shore Unitarian Church. Other foundations supporting CFFC in the early 1980s included *Playboy* (which gave $10,000 in both 1982 and 1983), Scherman, Educational Foundation of America, and Mary Reynolds Babcock.[25] Since some of these foundations have also funded population control groups and litigation groups fighting for abortion rights, CFFC has been held guilty by association—guilty of being anti-Catholic and pro-abortion. Kissling responds to criticism about CFFC funding sources in this way:

We have been criticized by pro-lifers for getting money from three sources: Sunnen, Veatch, and *Playboy*. Sunnen has always been a very big funder: we get from $50,000 to $100,000 a year from the Sunnen Foundation. The money for the Sunnen Foundation comes from a tool and die company in St. Louis, Missouri. But Mr. Sunnen was also a very creative and prolific inventor; and one of the things he invented was EMKO foam. So pro-life critics always say, "Well, these people who invented contraceptive foam give them money." In addition, Mr. Sunnen was a very ardent, feisty Midwestern St. Louis-type who believed in religious freedom and church-state separation, who thought the Catholic church was always interfering. As a result, we were accused of taking money from "those anti-Catholics" associated with the Sunnen Foundation. We have also been criticized for getting money from the Veatch Program of the North Shore Unitarian Church. This small Unitarian church in Plandome, Long Island, has an income from North Sea oil leases, donated by Mr. Veatch, a church-member, in excess of three million dollars a year. They give this money away to a variety of causes: community organizations, peace and justice work, anti-capital punishment, ACLU-type work, and separation of church and state, religious freedom, and abortion rights. So we received early money from them as well, mostly smaller grants. About this pro-lifers say, "Oh, you see, they're not really Catholics, they get money from the Unitarians."

Finally, Kissling responds to those who criticized CFFC for taking money from the *Playboy* Foundation.

The *Playboy* situation is very complicated. . . . There are legitimate arguments to be made that people should take their money, that at least some good should come of that money. It's reparations to women. I think that is a legitimate argument. And I also think it's legitimate to say we shouldn't touch their money and we shouldn't give them credibility. A lot of other groups, anti-Klan groups, Sister Margaret Traxler's Institute of Women Today, take money from *Playboy*. We don't take it now.

Kissling is frank about CFFC financing and states that she has never had strings attached to grants received. She does approach foundations for money for specific programs that she has designed. But she insists that CFFC has "never been controlled or driven by the kind of money that's available in the foundation community. For example, there was a period of time when teenage pregnancy was the big thing for which one could get funding. But that wasn't what we wanted to do, so we didn't go running around trying to figure out a teenage pregnancy program so we could get foundation dollars. That's not what we're about."

CFFC's Perspective on the Morality and Legality of Abortion

CFFC's first position statement of June 1975 (printed above) was firmly pro-choice with respect to law and public policy, a position which the organization derived from a principled commitment to freedom of conscience in reproductive health matters. The organization, in conjunction with other

RCAR members, also stressed the religious freedom of Catholics and non-Catholics in a pluralist society. However, in the 1980s, CFFC's rationale shifted towards a more feminist emphasis, a shift which accompanied the organization's role as part of a strong, vital network of religious feminists. This is reflected in the more recent position statement of the organization; CFFC now defines itself as "a national educational organization that supports the right to legal reproductive healthcare, especially family planning and abortion. CFFC also works to reduce the incidence of abortion and to increase women's choices in childbearing and childrearing through advocacy of social and economic programs for women, families, and children." What is new in this more recent statement is the emphasis on reducing the number of abortions, which suggests that the organization is not pro-abortion yet remains firmly pro-choice.

How is it possible for a group of Catholics to maintain such a position in view of the the church's traditional opposition to abortion? CFFC's answer to this question is two-fold. First, CFFC firmly defends the right of American Catholic citizens, including Catholic bishops, to contribute to the public debate on abortion and to attempt to influence abortion policy—within the legitimate constraints of the institutional church's tax-exempt status.[26] These pro-choice Catholics firmly resist any suggestion that the bishops' participation in the political process of abortion policymaking violates constitutional norms of church-state separation and religious freedom. At the same time, CFFC contends that the manner in which church authorities have pressured and coerced politicians and voters is wrong. In a pluralist democracy, bishops have no right to issue voting instructions to citizens and lawmakers on a policy matter of such complexity. Citizens and public officials must weigh several competing factors—rights of privacy, the religious and conscience rights of non-Catholic citizens, and considerations of sound public policy—in arriving at judgments concerning proper public policy on abortion.

Obviously, CFFC differs from the official church on the policy question. Concerning the legality of abortion, Kissling states flatly, "We don't want to see abortion recriminalized or prohibited. Our position is: no restrictions and no parental consent or notification." However, the reasoning behind this stance is complex. As Kissling notes:

We have different starting points in the sense that we see the social dimension to the question of abortion—for example, the position of women, the lack of support for them, the teenagers with special needs. We do not start with "No" to everything, we start from "What assists women? How can society assist women in making good decisions?" In that sense, we don't think that parental consent or parental notification contributes to good decisionmaking. But that doesn't mean we don't think parents should be involved, and it doesn't mean we do not think the society or the state have a responsibility to protect teenagers from everybody, including their parents. We see a role for the society in making sure that teenagers are not coerced into having abortions and that they are not coerced into childbearing. But the route for that is not through parental consent. Our position is strongly a freedom position, with a recognition of social responsibility to women, and that includes teenagers.

Thus CFFC strongly affirms the reproductive freedom of individual women to make the decision which they in conscience believe to be correct. This strong feminist emphasis upon a woman's right to decide in matters so intimately affecting her body and soul is one reason pro-choice Catholics question the church's moral teaching on abortion. CFFC is not unmindful of the fact that, through the centuries, women have been excluded from theological deliberations regarding sexuality and childbearing. Because of this, one must approach church teaching with what feminist theologians have called "a hermeneutics of suspicion." Kissling also argues that, in other questions concerning justifiable killing (e.g., just war or capital punishment), church teaching is complex and nuanced—in contrast to the church's absolute prohibition of direct abortion. Finally, Kissling points to the uncertainty in Catholic moral theology about the status of fetal life; she concludes that since there is doubt in the church on whether the fetus is a person, that doubt should lead us to follow a direction of liberty and respect for the rights of individuals to make decisions of conscience. All these considerations lead CFFC to question the church's moral teaching on abortion. As Kissling states:

> We think the moral teaching is uncertain. We believe that abortion has to be dealt with in the context of the general moral principles of the Church and the general policies and principles that guide human behavior. . . . We're more interested in the concept that in doubtful circumstances or doubtful teachings, conscience rules. In that sense we would say that we don't acknowledge the Church as able to make a definitive, infallible teaching on the subject of abortion [because of doubt and uncertainty regarding the status of fetal life]. In the context of the church's own rules for teaching, the conditions do not exist [for the church] to take a definitive, infallibly binding position on the morality of abortion. There has to be a lot more room to allow individual conscience to operate in sifting through the theological, scientific, and philosophical data that is available on this issue.

At the same time, Kissling does not dismiss church teaching. As she states, "I am not putting forward the position that Catholics have a right to disregard the teaching of the church on the subject of abortion and its opposition to abortion. We have a responsibility to take those teachings quite seriously and examine them in any decision about abortion."[27] Moreover, CFFC accepts the idea that abortion is negative, it is not something to be welcomed or celebrated or viewed as positive. This point was very clear in the interview with CFFC officials:

> We do not think abortion is a moral good. We think the capacity to make choices is a moral good. We would agree that there is always tragedy connected with having to make the choice not to continue a pregnancy. Would that we lived in a world where every pregnancy, no matter what its circumstances could be nurtured. But we don't live in that world, and we don't think you can condemn women for having to bear the burden of this. What the bishops are seeking and what so-called communitarians are seeking to do is to socialize decisionmaking around reproduction while continuing in a state in which the burdens are individualized.

You can't have a dichotomized system in which burdens are individualized and decisions are socialized. If the burden is socialized, there is some credence to the notion that we as a community will make decisions in such matters. Even then, it's difficult.

What emerges from all this is a position that is subtle and nuanced, and that actually retains much of the almost instinctive Catholic antipathy for abortion. Given these views, it is not accurate to describe CFFC as pro-abortion; the organization views abortion as a negative rather than a positive event, and indeed seeks to reduce the incidence of abortion. CFFC insists, as do the U.S. Catholic bishops, that one cannot ignore the ethical questions in discussions of abortion. Finally, in accordance with its Catholic feminist principles, CFFC insists upon respect for women's moral agency in matters of reproductive decisionmaking, and endorses policies of social assistance to women and children that will create conditions of genuine reproductive freedom.

What does Kissling see as the future of the abortion controversy in the United States? She and other CFFC officials think the focus of the controversy will shift towards greater efforts to reduce the incidence of abortion by reducing the incidence of unintended pregnancy. Kissling predicts that over the next twenty years, there will be a second contraceptive revolution in this country, and she is encouraged to hear her colleagues in NARAL and Planned Parenthood (Kate Michelman and Faye Wattleton) emphasizing the need to reduce the number of involuntary pregnancies through better contraception and better sex education. However, CFFC officials are discouraged by the fact that once again the Catholic bishops will be left out of this part of the solution because of church opposition to artificial birth control.

On the other hand, the church can be, and already is, part of the effort to enact public policies to assist women. Kissling notes that the most ardent advocates in the Coalition on Family Medical Leave in 1990-1991 were the NCCB and various women's organizations (the National Women's Law Center, the Women's Legal Defense Fund, and NOW). These organizations worked beautifully together on that issue, and the women's groups acknowledged how good the bishops were. In her NCR interview in February 1991, Kissling commented that "the lobby program of the NCCB on women's issues, on poor people's issues, is a very, very strong program and should be supported. If I were designing a policy program for the church, my policy agenda would be focused on prevention of pregnancy and making available every possible resource to those who wished to carry their pregnancies to term."

One final point should round out the description of CFFC's perspective on abortion. The organization's conviction that abortion is negative opens the group to a logical objection—namely, that one cannot create the ideal society by using means which are incompatible with that end. However, CFFC has no quarrel with this means/ends correlation. They agree that abortion is not designed to create the ideal society.

None of us have ever said abortion is the solution to the bankruptcy of our society. Abortion is a symptom of the bankruptcy of our society, of the lack of hope that exists in all of us, of the lack of social resources that exist. It is a sign of the failure of the society. It is sometimes a sign of personal failure, but it is almost always a sign of social failure. But denying it is not an answer to the social failure either.

Kissling tends to dismiss arguments of feminists for life that, if abortion were not available, society would start providing benefits for children and/or men would take better care of their children. She maintains that abortion is not the solution in either direction.

Making it available or making it unavailable has very little to do with our social problems. It is intended, in my opinion, to redress, on a temporary basis, the profound social imbalance that exists in society in terms of our failure. But it's only temporary. If it solves anything, it solves only a very immediate need that an individual woman may have. It doesn't solve social problems. Nobody I know who is pro-choice ever said that abortion solves the problems of child-abuse, the problem of poverty, or the problem of men not supporting their wives.

In its short, eighteen-year history, CFFC has made a contribution to the abortion debate in the United States. It has played a dual role within the church—as a balance to the NCCB and as a spur to the bishops to be more truly feminist in supporting programs of assistance to women and in respecting women's capacity for moral decisionmaking. At the same time, CFFC acts as a moderating influence, within the secular pro-choice community, to mute occasional displays of anti-Catholic prejudice. Above all, CFFC insists that the moral dimensions of the abortion issue cannot be ignored. Because they view abortion as a negative, undesirable event, these pro-choice Catholics work to eliminate the need for—and thereby reduce the incidence of—abortion in the United States.

Notes

1. George Gallup,Jr., and Jim Castelli, *The American Catholic People: Their Beliefs, Practices, and Values* (Garden City, NY: Doubleday & Co, 1987), p. 101. These results are supported by other surveys: According to a CBS/*New York Times* September 1989 poll, only 15 percent of Catholics agree with the bishops that abortion should not be permitted under any circumstances. See Denise Shannon, "Outside the Chancery: Catholics Take Issue," in CFFC, *Guide for Prochoice Catholics* (Washington, D.C., 1990), pp. 24–28.

2. Gallup and Castelli, p. 101.

3. Stanley K. Henshaw and Jane Silverman, "The Characteristics and Prior Contraceptive Use of U.S. Abortion Patients," *Family Planning Perspectives,* Vol. 20., No. 4 (July/August 1988), pp. 158–168.

4. In a letter to the editor of *Commonweal* in 1983, Christine Niebrzydowski, president of a Pittsburgh-based group, Catholics for Choice, criticized the church's application of the canon law penalty of automatic excommunication to abortion; see *Commonweal,* April 8, 1983, p. 223. A group entitled St. Louis Catholics for Choice signed an *amicus* brief prepared by Professor Martha Minow of Harvard Law School on behalf of thirty-five religious organizations in the *Webster* case. In addition, several other

Catholic organizations have officially adopted a pro-choice position: the National Coalition of American Nuns (NCAN), the National Assembly of Religious Women (NARW), Loretto Women's Network, Chicago Catholic Women, and the Feminist Action Coalition.

5. Sources for this account are an interview with CFFC officials, Frances Kissling (President), Mary Jean Collins (Director of Public Affairs), and Denise Shannon (Director of Communications), January 25, 1991; an address by Frances Kissling at a conference of the CFFC Grassroots Organizing Project, June 2, 1990; and Richard Doerflinger, "Who Are Catholic for a Free Choice?" *America*, November 16, 1985, pp. 312–317.

6. For his actions at this time, Father O'Rourke was expelled from the Jesuits.

7. Interview with Frances Kissling, January 25, 1991.

8. Religious Coalition for Abortion Rights (RCAR), *How We Stand: The Positions on Abortion of 27 National Religious Organizations*, (Washington, D.C., 1979), p. 9.

9. Doerflinger, p. 313.

10. For a discussion of these types of organizations, see Ronald G. Shaiko, "More Bang for the Buck: The New Era of Full-Service Public Interest Organizations," in Allan J. Cigler and Burdett A. Loomis, eds., *Interest Group Politics*, 3rd ed. (Washington,D.C.: CQ Press, 1991), pp. 109–130.

11. See below for a brief biography of Kissling.

12. Interview with Kissling, January 25, 1991.

13. Interview with Kissling, January 25, 1991.

14. Address by Kissling at Conference of CFFC Grassroots Organizing Project, June 2, 1990.

15. Statement by Reverend Edward M. Bryce on behalf of the Bishops' Committee for Pro-Life Activities, November 25, 1981 (copy supplied to me by Denise Shannon, Director of Communications, Catholics for a Free Choice).

16. See CFFC, "The Abortion Issue in the Political Process: A Briefing for Catholic Legislators" (Washington, D.C., 1982). See also Geraldine A. Ferraro, *Ferraro: My Story* (New York: Bantam Books, 1985) and Mary C. Segers, "Ferraro, The Bishops, and the 1984 Election," In Clarissa W. Atkinson, Constance H. Buchanan, and Margaret R. Miles, eds., *Shaping New Vision: Gender and Values in American Culture* (Ann Arbor: UMI Research Press, 1987), pp. 143–168.

17. See Barbara Ferraro and Patricia Hussey, *No Turning Back: Two Nuns' Battle with the Vatican over Women's Right to Choose* (New York: Poseidon Press, 1990); also Maureen E. Fiedler, "Dissent Within the U.S. Church: The Case of the Vatican "24", in Mary C. Segers, ed., *Church Polity and American Politics: Issues in Contemporary American Catholicism* (New York: Garland Publishing, 1990), pp. 313-333; also Mary E. Hunt and Frances Kissling, "The *New York Times* Ad: A Case Study in Religious Feminism," *Journal of Feminist Studies in Religion*, Vol. 3, No. 1 (Spring 1987), pp. 115-127.

18. Two women, Sisters of Notre Dame Barbara Ferraro and Patricia Hussey, refused to compromise with Vatican authorities, were not dismissed by their community, but decided to resign from their community in July 1988. See Ferraro and Hussey, *No Turning Back*, p. 270.

19. Editorial, *National Catholic Reporter*, September 27, 1985.

20. Hunt and Kissling, "The *New York Times* Ad: A Case Study in Religious Feminism," *Journal of Feminist Studies in Religion*, pp. 124-125.

21. Interview with Frances Kissling, January 25, 1991.

22. Ruth A. Wallace, "Catholic Women and the Creation of a New Social Reality," *Gender & Society*, Vol. 2, No. 1 (March 1988), p. 34.

23. Several Sawyer-Miller staff formerly worked at Hill and Knowlton, the public relations firm hired by the NCCB; they were so disturbed by Hill and Knowlton's decision to publicize the bishops' antiabortion campaign that they offered pro bono services to CFFC. See KRC Research & Consulting, Inc., "National Poll on the Catholic Church and Abortion: Summary of Findings," prepared for Catholics For a Free Choice (New York, October 25, 1990). Copy supplied by Denise Shannon, CFFC Director of Communications.

24. *Webster v. Reproductive Health Services, Inc.* (1989).

25. Doerflinger, p. 313.

26. See Joe Feuerherd, "Kissling's Crusade for Catholics' Free Choice," *National Catholic Reporter,* February 8, 1991.

27. This and subsequent quotations are taken from an interview with Kissling and other CFFC officials, January 25, 1991; from an October 10, 1989 address on "Catholics for a Free Choice"; from the *NCR* interview of February 8, 1991, and from Kissling's essay, "If War Is 'Just,' So Is Abortion," which appeared as an op-ed column in the *Los Angeles Times* in spring 1991.

About the Editors and Contributors

Timothy A. Byrnes is assistant professor of political science at the City College and Graduate Center of the City University of New York. He is the author of *Catholic Bishops in American Politics* (1991) and a number of published articles on the political activities of the American Catholic hierarchy.

Mary C. Segers is associate professor and graduate director of political science at Rutgers University, Newark. She is coauthor, with James C. Foster, of *Elusive Equality: Liberalism, Affirmative Action, and Social Change in America* (1983) and has written many articles on abortion and on the Catholic bishops and public policy. She is editor of *Church Polity and American Politics: Issues in Contemporary Catholicism* (1990).

MaryAnne Borrelli holds a Ph.D. in government from Harvard University. She is assistant professor of political science at Knox College in Galesburg, Illinois, where she teaches courses in bureaucratic politics and American government.

Spencer McCoy Clapp is an attorney in Hartford, Connecticut. In addition to his legal work, he writes fiction and non-fiction and is active in local Catholic assistance to the homeless.

Christine Day is assistant professor of political science at the University of New Orleans. She is the author of *What Older Americans Think: Interest Groups and Aging Policy* (1990).

James R. Kelly is professor and chair of the Department of Sociology at Fordham University. His articles on the prolife movement have appeared in *Commonweal, America, The Christian Century,* and *Review of Religious Research.* He is a contributor to *Research in the Social Scientific Study of Religion* (1989).

Thomas J. O'Hara, C.S.C., is assistant professor of political science at Kings College in Wilkes-Barre, Pennsylvania. He is author of "The Multifaceted Catholic Lobby," in Charles Dunn, ed., *Religion in American Politics* (1989). He has also written "The Catholic Lobby in Washington: Pluralism and Diversity Among U.S. Catholics," in *Church Polity and American Politics* (1990).

Rebecca M. Salokar is assistant professor of political science at Florida International University in Miami, where she teaches judicial politics and American government. She is the author of *The Solicitors General: The Politics of Law* (1991).

Index